blossoms & blood

BY JASON SPERB

blossoms & blood

POSTMODERN MEDIA CULTURE AND
THE FILMS OF PAUL THOMAS ANDERSON

University of Texas Press
Austin

Requests for permission to reproduce material from this work should be sent to:
Permissions
University of Texas Press
P.O. Box 7819
Austin, TX 78713-7819
http://utpress.utexas.edu/index.php/rp-form

♾ The paper used in this book meets the minimum requirements
of ANSI/NISO Z39.48-1992 (R1997) (Permanence of Paper).

LIBRARY OF CONGRESS CATALOGING-IN-PUBLICATION DATA
Sperb, Jason, 1978–
Blossoms and blood : postmodern media culture and
the films of Paul Thomas Anderson / Jason Sperb.
    pages   cm
Includes bibliographical references and index.
ISBN 978-0-292-75289-4 (hardback)
ISBN 978-1-4773-0221-7 (paper)
1. Anderson, Paul Thomas—Criticism and interpretation.   I. Title.
PN1998.3.A5255S64   2012
791.4302'33092—dc23   2013008528

doi:10.7560/752894

To the Castleton Arts Theatre

contents

acknowledgments

$\mathfrak{I}$ stumbled quite by accident into a screening of *Hard Eight* during its initial theatrical run in early 1997. The film just happened to be playing at the Indianapolis art cinema I frequented during my formative teen years. It's very rare to go into a movie with no sense of what it is—but I had that privilege fifteen years ago. I'm probably one of the few people alive who can honestly claim to have seen every single one of Paul Thomas Anderson's films during its original theatrical release. As such, I suppose I've always had a certain investment in this body of work, having been unexpectedly thrilled by his debut effort—an advocate in that small window *before Boogie Nights*—and watching his career develop—unevenly—in the years since. Of course, as I noted, I didn't go to see *Hard Eight* because I thought it was the start of anything meaningful. But then what are Anderson's narratives if not meditations on the aftereffects of random chance and fate?

And, like Anderson, I didn't get here on my own. I'm deeply indebted to those who supported me and this book over the last several years. First, I wish to thank my friend James Naremore. In addition to blazing the definitive auteurist trail with his own work, Professor Naremore was the one who first planted the idea for this book over a casual cup of coffee in the late summer of 2007. He suggested that, after finishing my dissertation, I consider writing a book on a contemporary auteur. One doesn't ignore such inspiring confidence. At that moment, I remembered a long-gestating idea on various aspects of Anderson's films, an interest that only intensified a few months later with the debut of *There Will Be Blood*.

At the time, I was knee-deep in my project on Disney's *Song of the South*, but such a hiatus proved to be just what I needed as I developed into a more focused thinker and writer. The opportunity to begin drafting a study on Anderson's films emerged in 2010 in the form of the Department of Radio/Television/Film at Northwestern University. The good folks at RTVF hired me out of grad school to teach 300-level courses on authorship and genre studies. During the first quarter, they let me design a course around Anderson's films—the perfect chance to build both my scholarship and teaching experience. I'm deeply grateful to the support of the faculty there—in particular, David Tolchinsky, Lynn Spigel, Max Dawson, Jeffrey Sconce, Jacob Smith, Mimi White, Kyle Henry, and Scott Curtis. I'm also indebted to my RTVF-321 students from that fall—Emma Carlin, Daniel DeSalva, George Elkind, Spenser Gabin, Daniel Johnson, Eric Kirchner, Travis Labella, Ryan Luong, Evan Morehouse, Daniel Ochwat, and Milta Ortiz-Pinate. In addition to fostering a supportive learning environment and teaching experience, their classroom contributions and insightful writing helped me better work through my own understanding of Anderson's films at a crucial moment in the process.

As this research began to get more attention, I was invited by Scott Dunham to give a talk at the University of Chicago's legendary Doc Films Series in February 2012. There, I introduced a screening of *Punch-Drunk Love* as part of their Paul Thomas Anderson series. It was exciting to have a chance to share my research on his films with an audience, and to see *Punch-Drunk Love* on 35mm for the first (and last?) time since its initial theatrical run a decade earlier. I'd like to thank Scott and the rest of the Doc Films group for their generosity.

The book itself came together relatively quickly but would not have done so without the confidence of others. I'm once again most grateful for the support of the University of Texas Press and for the unwavering belief and guidance of my editor, Jim Burr, who continues to be my biggest benefactor. I'm also especially appreciative of the feedback from R. Barton Palmer and Robert Kolker, both of whom believed in me and in the work itself.

As always, I'm appreciative of friends and colleagues always there in ways large and small (even the ones who thought I was crazy for writing this): Tim Anderson, Scott Balcerzak, Mark Benedetti, John Berra, Corey Creekmur, Sarah Delahousse, Seth Friedman, Michael B. Gillespie, Catherine Grant, Mack Hagood, Eric Harvey, Selmin Kara, Michael Lahey, Leonard Leff, Meredith Levine, Drew Morton, Michael Newman, James Paasche, Carole Lyn Piechota, Mike Rennett, Jeremy Richey, Matthew Rodrigues, Sean Stangland, and Greg Waller. I must also give a special shout-out to an old friend, Tim Davis, whose obsession with *Boogie Nights* continues to inspire and confound me.

A special thanks is also due to the Woodstock Public Library in Woodstock, Illinois. I don't know—in all that time he had to kill—if Phil Connors ever got over there. But if he did, he'd have found it was the perfect place to cure writer's block. Over and over again.

Summer 2012

blossoms & blood

this is the face. there's no great mystery.

"Facing the past is an important way in not making progress," that's
something I tell my men over and over . . . and I try and teach the
students to ask: "What is it in aid of?" . . . "The most useless thing
in the world is that which is behind me"—Chapter Three.

FRANK T. J. MACKEY (TOM CRUISE)

Introduction

WHITE-NOISE MEDIA CULTURE AND

THE FILMS OF PAUL THOMAS ANDERSON

One of several iconic moments in the brief career of American filmmaker Paul Thomas Anderson comes early in his flawed but deeply illuminating final-cut opus, *Magnolia* (1999). With Richard Strauss's *Also sprach Zarathustra* playing in the background, celebrity salesman Frank T. J. Mackey (Tom Cruise) emerges from the harsh glare of a lone spotlight on an empty stage. As he announces his larger-than-life presence, the lonely, pathetic men packed into the room wildly cheer his dramatic introduction. Mackey is there to sell his lucrative how-to guide for "seducing and destroying" women, a self-help program that he's carefully cultivated through numerous ballroom seminars and countless late-night infomercials. He's also selling the carefully crafted idea of "Mackey" himself—the *hypermediated* persona of an aggressive, confident masculine sexuality who doesn't want for female attention. And that identity is inseparable from the intertextual connotations of Cruise, the movie star. This vignette from *Magnolia* is usefully problematic and extremely enlightening as an introduction to Anderson's films.

This book is a critical history of Anderson's complicated journey from the sprawling suburbs of Los Angeles to the 1990s independent film scene and of his rise, fall, and rise again to industry and

0.1. Mackey's infomercial for "Seduce and Destroy." In *Magnolia*, self-reflexive images of salesmen, commodities, celebrities, and masculinity often overlap.

cinephiliac prominence. Finished just after *The Master* (2012) debuted, this project remains attentive to the larger historical narrative of authorship implied, yet I approach Anderson's films as neither self-contained nor *ahistorical* products of an imagined singular authorial vision that exists outside space and time. Instead, I seek to put informed film readings in dialogue with the contexts in which the films were made. Anderson's persistent thematic and stylistic investment in the white-noise culture of celebrity, media, commodities, salesmen, patriarchy, and pop-leftist historicity reveals a consistently ambivalent history of postmodern America at the dawn of the twenty-first century.

BIG, BRIGHT, SHINING STARS

Mackey's introduction is an acute instance of the affective indulgence and self-promoting flair that often marks the director's films, but we can dig deeper to find themes and histories worth closer scrutiny. Mackey's introduction illustrates a number of prominent themes at work throughout Anderson's films. First are self-reflexive instances of intertextuality and hypermediation. Mackey's presence is inseparable from the crafted televisual image of him within the film's diegetic space—his character is first introduced in a commer-

0.2. At the end of *Boogie Nights*, the son (Dirk Diggler) returns to the symbolic father (Jack Horner)—a common trope in Anderson's films.

cial on television. Part of Mackey's status as a purely mediated image echoes the character's own disavowal of his biographical past. Dirk Diggler (Mark Wahlberg) in *Boogie Nights* (1997), Daniel Plainview (Daniel Day-Lewis) in *There Will Be Blood* (2007), Sydney (Philip Baker Hall) in *Hard Eight* (1996)—these characters continually attempt to reinvent themselves as they outrun their pasts.

Mackey is also outrunning his father, just as Anderson's characters time and again negotiate complicated relationships with their biological or surrogate fathers. Cruise's character, originally named Jack Partridge, is abandoned by his celebrity parent. "Mackey" is thus reborn—new name, new persona—on and beyond TV. As scholars such as Susan Jeffords have argued,[1] Hollywood's collective depiction of dominant masculinity during the 1980s age of Reagan was one centered repeatedly on broken homes and the desire for a strong father figure. As a cinephiliac child of this era, Anderson reveals in his work a similar conservative impulse—love between a father and son is often more important than that between a man and woman. Like Mackey's return to his dying father, most every film ends with a son's return to his elder—though this makes the final, unexpected rejection at the end of *There Will Be Blood* all the more devastating. Even the notably father-less *Punch-Drunk Love* (2002) is defined—Timothy Stanley[2] and Julian Murphet[3] have argued respectively—by a family's *absent* father figure, a void filled by overbearing sisters.

Growing up within a postmodern media culture of the late 1970s and 1980s, Anderson was inundated with a range of father-figure

0.3. Anderson's geographical obsession with the American West
is reflected by a map in Barry Egan's office in *Punch-Drunk Love*,
which shows the western states circled in red ink.

films: from the *Star Wars* trilogy (1977–1983), to *Back to the Future* (1985), to *Field of Dreams* (1989), and to every other Steven Spielberg film. Each one repeatedly dramatized the need for a dominant father figure. "Every time I eat mashed potatoes," Anderson said, "I still think of [Spielberg's] *Close Encounters* [*of the Third Kind*, 1977],"[4] referencing a key scene in one of many Hollywood films from Anderson's childhood that dramatized the disintegration and subsequent reconstitution of the white suburban nuclear family. Similarly, notes Sharon Waxman, after Anderson first "saw [Spielberg's] *E.T.*, he began dressing up as the Henry Thomas character—another towheaded boy from the Valley—and tried to ride his bike into the clouds."[5] Another film about unmoored suburban families in the San Fernando Valley, *E.T.* echoed a larger trend of films in the Reagan era featuring a fatherless son searching for a larger purpose to life.

A story of troubled fathers and white-noise celebrities in Southern California, *Magnolia* is perhaps Anderson's most transparently autobiographical—the one film to deal directly with the television industry. All of Anderson's films are set in the American West—California, Utah, and Nevada (and a brief excursion to Hawaii in *Punch-Drunk Love*). Anderson was born in Studio City, California, the symbolic heart of Hollywood, on June 26, 1970. Los Angeles's postwar, postmodern celebrity culture appropriately thus figures as a central concern. His father was Ernie Anderson, cult host of the 1960s Cleveland-based late-night TV program *Ghoulardi*, which recycled bad horror movies (Anderson's production company is named Ghoulardi). While he worshipped his often-distant father, Anderson was less close to his mother, who influenced Eddie Adams's (Wahlberg) angry, unsupportive mom (Joanna Gleason) in *Boogie Nights*. Meanwhile, he grew up in a household as the youngest sibling to three sisters (along with several children from Ernie's first marriage), anticipating Barry's (Adam Sandler) large, sister-dominated family in *Punch-Drunk Love*.

Ernie's modest celebrity throughout his life no doubt shaped the ambivalent preoccupation with stardom in Anderson's body of work. Ernie moved out to California to take a lucrative gig as the voice of a major national network, ABC (American Broadcasting Company), where he did everything from *Love Boat* promos to the original introduction of *America's Funniest Home Videos*. His voice is instantly recognizable to a whole generation of American TV audiences. Neither the elder Anderson nor his Hollywood buddies (such as Tim Conway) were ever major stars on par with Cruise, Sandler, or Burt Reynolds—big names that have anchored Anderson's films. Yet they were exactly the sort of marginal celebrities who reflected the white-noise media culture that Anderson's films consistently interrogate—typified by the televisual presence in *Magnolia* of Mackey, TV host Jimmy Gator (Philip Baker Hall), and the two Quiz Kids.

The narrative interest in celebrities reflects a deeper intertextual fascination with stardom. In most of Anderson's films, the bona fide star in the cast (Cruise, Sandler, Wahlberg, Day-Lewis) plays a character who invariably becomes a grotesque exaggeration of the actor's own existing persona. Mackey in *Magnolia* is no exception. His overhyped seduction skills are predicated on the illusion of a "cool" hypermasculinity that straddles the fine line between flippant indifference and calculated manipulation. In other words, Mackey is not selling just any masculine persona—he's selling a "Tom Cruise" persona. Mackey's carefully presented image of control for sexual advantage is barely one or two steps removed from the Cruise-persona seductions of Kelly McGillis's character in *Top Gun* (1986) or Nicole Kidman's in *Days of Thunder* (1990). But in *Magnolia*, Anderson pushes that persona to a grotesque extreme, and the character becomes a crass misogynist manipulating women for sexual gratification, laying bare the misogyny of Cruise's early persona.

Meanwhile, Mackey's boisterous use of sexist language transparently announces the filmmaker's often-complicated negotiation of misogyny and offers no easy solution. Anderson's emphasis on sons and fathers leaves open the troubling question of women's reduc-

0.4. Clementine: the first prominent, and hardly unproblematic,
female character in Anderson's body of work.

tion to one-dimensional supporting roles. The female family members in *Boogie Nights* and *Punch-Drunk Love* are seen as the primary source of tension, while the men are either nonexistent or ineffectual in such matriarchal environments. If *There Will Be Blood* is the least problematic, it's only because there are almost no female characters at all. In *Hard Eight*, the only woman, Clementine (Gwyneth Paltrow), is a prostitute whose bad professional decisions initiate the film's narrative trouble. Meanwhile, she is "saved" from herself in the end by marrying John (John C. Reilly). Women in *Punch-Drunk Love*, *Boogie Nights*, and *Magnolia* are more complicated characters still often defined through their sexual use-value for men. In addition to the porn stars (Rollergirl [Heather Graham] and Amber Waves [Julianne Moore]) who use their bodies as commodities in *Boogie Nights*, Claudia's (Melora Walters) first scene in *Magnolia* involves swapping sexual favors with a stranger for a new supply of cocaine. Claudia and Clementine have both lowered themselves to prostitution and must be redeemed narratively through a stable relationship with the character played by Reilly.

MY CELEBRITY, MY NAME

This idea that there is often a *transaction* involved in Anderson's films is as important a theme as any highlighted above (stardom, masculinity, self-reflexivity). In *Magnolia*, the scene of Mackey's adoring diegetic crowd lays bare the relationship between idealized images of sexuality (movie stardom) and the pathetic, sexually unhappy audiences who buy into the promise of that lifestyle. Mackey is a diegetic celebrity, a narrativized televisual image, and an abandoned son (played by a movie star). He is, in the end, also a *salesman*, and what to make of all the salesmen throughout Anderson's films (Mackey, Barry Egan, Daniel Plainview, Quiz Kid Donnie Smith [William H. Macy], Buck Swope [Don Cheadle], "mattress man" Dean Trumbell [Philip Seymour Hoffman])? There's an appropriate level of irony when these characters sell a commodity—whether oil or "fungers"—given that stardom itself attempts to sell products through affiliation with an established brand. As Richard Dyer wrote in *Heavenly Bodies*:

Stars are made for profit. In terms of market, stars are part of the way films are sold. The star's presence in a film is the promise of a certain kind of thing that you would see if you went to see the film. Equally, stars sell newspapers and magazines . . . toiletries, fashions, cars and almost anything else.[6]

Mackey and Diggler are less people than brand names—"Frank T. J. Mackey" and "Dirk Diggler" are not even these characters' real names. This is a particularly acute instance of, as Dyer notes, "the fact that [a star's] labour and what it produces seem so divorced from each other."[7] In a world of increasingly free-floating commodities, many Anderson characters ambivalently engage in endless cycles of consumption while the physical act of labor—of actually producing a material good with use-value—seems nonexistent. Barry, Mackey, and Plainview spend much of their respective introductions immersed in a sales pitch: Barry sells toilet plungers; Mackey sells self-help programs; Plainview sells the tools, skills, and manpower for oil drilling. Meanwhile, in *Boogie Nights*, producer Jack Horner (Reynolds) sells the cinematic spectacle of sex to consumers, while also selling Eddie Adams (Diggler's given name) on the lifestyle of being a pornographic star. Diggler, Horner, Mackey, and phone-sex pimp Trumbell all sell sexual gratification. Barry, on the other hand, has to pay for it through a phone-sex service that, as with the indulgences of *Boogie Nights*, comes with a price. (One can easily imagine Barry sitting in the front row of one of Mackey's seminars.)

As the former Quiz Kid, Donnie in *Magnolia* is defined by the cultural ambivalences of celebrity and the financial intersection of that status with its exchange-value. Whether trying to get braces or crashing his car into the front of a convenience store, people still identify him as the Quiz Kid from thirty years earlier. At his sales job, Donnie's greatest use to Solomon & Solomon Electronics

0.5. Egan in *Punch-Drunk Love*: characters are often lost—
literally and figuratively—in a generic consumer world.

is through the attention his former success brings to the business. "I put your name up on a fucking billboard," says his disappointed boss (Alfred Molina) while firing him. "I put you in my store. My salesman. My fucking representation of Solomon & Solomon Electronics. The Quiz Kid Donnie Smith from the game show." Donnie desperately replies, "I lent you my celebrity, my name!" Like "Diggler" and "Mackey," Donnie is little more than a free-floating celebrity name commodified for its faded market value.

The narrative investment in salesmen intensifies a thematic investment in the *cost* of abstract commodities such as stardom. In *Boogie Nights*, Horner repeatedly references the financial side of filmmaking. "What I'm trying to tell you, Eddie," he says during his own sales pitch, "is it takes a whole lot of the good old American green stuff to make [a movie]." Then, when Eddie's mother kicks him out of the house, she reminds him that "none of this stuff is yours because you didn't pay for it." Later, Horner introduces Eddie to the Colonel, noting that the Colonel "puts up all the money for our films. It's an important part of the process." Horner humorously understates what is so often key to Anderson's films—the access to material wealth in all aspects of everyday life.

This "important part of the [filmmaking] process," finally, moves us toward the heart of the matter. Thematic continuity is crucial to holding together Anderson's body of work, and yet it is important for us to move beyond the self-referential surface of textual analysis. Any serious such study must also deal directly with the complicated economic and cultural histories grounding each film's production and reception. Thus, Cruise's dramatic introduction in

Magnolia also reflects deeper histories informing the making of the film. Most immediately, the ambitious three-hour epic was easier for Anderson to get greenlit with final-cut authority precisely because Cruise—the biggest box-office star in the world—agreed to be in it. There might never have been a *Magnolia* as we know it without Cruise's direct involvement.

Magnolia's dramatic use of the *Zarathustra* tone poem and the shot preceding Mackey's introduction (of the old man on his deathbed being towered over by another presence in the room) draw direct parallels to Stanley Kubrick's *2001: A Space Odyssey* (1968). Aside from a clever self-conscious moment of intertextuality (Anderson's films are hardly modest or unique in this regard), the allusion pays homage to the creative origins of Mackey's character. The *2001* references in Mackey's introduction allude to Cruise and Anderson's first encounter in 1998 on the set of Kubrick's final film, *Eyes Wide Shut* (1999). Impressed by *Boogie Nights*, Cruise committed to doing a film with Anderson before the young filmmaker had even written a page. Cruise told him that "anything you do I would love to take a look and be involved."[8] Like Egan and Plainview would be, Mackey was written from the ground up with the star in mind.

As Cruise's unconditional commitment to *Magnolia* highlights, the star here is also Anderson's emergent reputation as an American filmmaker whose small but impressive number of films reveal a considerable depth and complexity. Yet the anecdote about Cruise's involvement in *Magnolia* is also a cautionary tale to overzealous auteurists. Would Anderson have gotten final cut from a generally cautious New Line Studios on the basis of sheer determination and *Boogie Nights* alone? The director's second film was critically well received but not a huge box-office success. Meanwhile, he was still haunted by industry whispers of his being a "difficult" director during the making of his first film, the little-seen neo-noir *Hard Eight*. His reputation for indulgence was not assuaged by the bloated and uneven *Magnolia*. Thus, Anderson's films, their production histories, and his critical reputation as a filmmaker worthy of analysis must be understood within the contradictions and ambiguities of their varying historical contexts.

POSTMODERN MEDIA CULTURE

Blossoms and Blood posits Anderson's body of work as the product of U.S. postmodern culture at the turn of the millennium. Commonly applied to the post-Sundance moment of American independent cinema in which Anderson participated, the term "postmodern" is frequently misunderstood in film criticism. Most often, the word articulates a distinctive set of stylistic and narrative conventions within a wide range of texts. It evokes images of films that in some way reflect back on their own style, genre, or history—*movies about movies*. More precisely, they're about the aesthetic, cultural, and economic practice of *mediation* (film, TV, radio, phones), which in some way casts doubt on notions of origins and absolute truth. When we look at this period of American cinema, "postmodern" can refer to the cinematic intertextuality of Quentin Tarantino, the ironic tone of the Coen brothers, the loss of objective truth in Christopher Nolan's work, or the pastiche mise-en-scène of Wes Anderson. This is what Michael Newman has aptly dubbed "pop pomo," or "trickle-down postmodernism": what began "as a top-down theory that looks for instances of culture to illustrate its claims . . . is appropriated in a more bottom-up fashion, opportunistically (when it works) to explain the appeal of specific texts, genres, styles, or oeuvres."[9] Although effective as aesthetic categories, terms like *self-reflexivity*, *pastiche*, *intertextuality*, and so forth obscure the idea of the postmodern more than they clarify.

Postmodernism is also a *history*. A paradoxical history, to be sure—what began as an articulation of the "crisis in historicity,"[10] the loss of historical consciousness, over time developed ironically into a historical moment of its own. Postmodernism is one way to understand the cultural and economic transition in U.S. culture since the Second World War—a shift based on the increasing centrality of media and mediation to our everyday lives. As film and television became the dominant modes of communication in the twentieth century, we developed into a culture whose relationship to the world, each other, and "reality" was mediated by images in an unprecedented fashion. If this sounds unremarkable now, it's only because of how ubiquitous postmodern culture has become today—indeed, what exists "outside" mediation? This isn't to say that reality ceases to exist, but that reality and media are irresolvably intertwined. Although we could trace it back to Guy Debord's notion of a "society of the spectacle," the term "postmodern" didn't seep into widespread usage until the late 1970s and 1980s, as cultural critics began to reflect seriously on the implications of a society whose cultural and economic relations were mediated by images with no necessary relationship to their referents.

But the dominance of media in everyday life is only half the is-

0.6. Re-created hand-cranked black-and-white footage to connote "pastness" in the opening montage of *Magnolia*—in postmodernism, history and history's mediation are inseparable.

sue if we take seriously what's at stake in articulating postmodern media culture. Thinking of the postmodern as connoting no reality outside mediation is to risk sliding back into using it as simply an aesthetic category to describe media texts that celebrate (or condemn) their own processes of mediation through various stylistic choices. For Fredric Jameson, the postmodern era reflected a larger moment of late capitalism—the shift from manufacturing to information-based economies. The aesthetic obsession with surface appearances was merely symptomatic of an economic transition from material commodities to immaterial ones in the long historical march to a digital age. The crisis in historicity, then, was not about whether films could represent a past lost to the proliferation of images. Jameson sees links to the general practice of pastiche and the "nostalgia film,"[11] which is more interested in the present romanticization of the past than in the past itself. The loss of historical consciousness was rooted in an emerging inattention to, and even ignorance of, the larger economic issues underlying the age of late capitalism, which the stylistic conventions of postmodernism both reflect and conceal from view.

On the surface of Anderson's films, we see many of the usual "trickle-down" postmodern attributes: the persistent self-reflexive emphasis on celebrity culture, media's history and function in negotiating social relations, and countless intertextual references to other films and filmmakers. Beneath that, there is also an admirably consistent exploration of the economic imperatives that ground those otherwise immaterial surfaces: the numerous characters who work as salesmen, the explicit centrality of commodities and transactions to everyday life, and the dissatisfaction with (yet dependence upon) material wealth. Finally, there's also a curious presentation of history in several of his films, a distinct manifestation of historical consciousness. *Boogie Nights*, *There Will Be Blood*, and *The Master* are postmodern period pieces ("nostalgia films") that forsake historical complexity for the ability of stylized presentations of the past to defamiliarize our relationship to the present. In all, Anderson's films reveal a uniquely ambivalent vision of postmodern media culture at the end of the twentieth century.

Why ambivalent? Anderson's collective body of work both critiques and reinforces a cultural logic driven by capitalism. His films explicitly posit characters' drive for financial success, as well as their conspicuous consumption, as an emotionally unsatisfying journey, filled with moments of excess, egomania, and greed. These same people are often situated as socially marginalized. Even before the appearance of *Punch-Drunk Love* and *There Will Be Blood*, Brian Goss noted with eerie prescience that "Anderson's films and their apparent embrace of marginalized subjectivities often embrace mainstream ideologies, particularly with respect to the patriarchal family and the market."[12] Anderson's early films—set in the media-saturated commodity culture of upper-middle-class Southern California—also suggest that no other meaningful options exist. They often end on a cautious note of reconciliation that implies patriarchal capitalism is the solution to the same problems it created.

So how to get beyond the self-referential surfaces of commodity culture? I seek to *historicize* Anderson's body of work as something beyond a self-contained collection of different motifs. To focus only on the dominant themes and stylistic continuities would be to commit the same offense that so often limits other examinations of trends in postmodern cinema. Reflecting its position in the era of postmodern media culture, the emergent claim to authorship underlying this project must be regarded as both a product of particular historical contexts and a history unto itself. There are four such interlocking frameworks that historicize these films: the most immediate is the filmmaker himself and his professional transition from a talented but arrogant product of the Sundance scene to a more reclusive, more deliberate veteran filmmaker; second, the detailed and often fascinating production history of each film, a source of valuable insight into the industry's mindset; third, the larger industrial trends that shaped the potential for each film to be made (developments in neo-noir, the ancillary value of movie soundtracks, the brief rise of the Hollywood maverick, etc.); and, finally, the broader political and cultural contexts that shaped each movie's reception—from the emergence of the Bill Clinton sex scandal and "porn chic" during *Boogie Nights*'s release in the late 1990s to the economic and geopolitical climate of Bush's America in *There Will Be Blood*.

INDIE CINEMA AT THE DAWN OF THE TWENTY-FIRST CENTURY

Understanding Anderson's emergence onto the Hollywood scene in the mid-1990s requires first appreciating the larger transition the industry was undergoing at the time. The 1980s had seen the return of the father figure and the continued rise of the Hollywood blockbuster. The blockbuster mentality had several negative repercussions for studio filmmaking—bigger and bigger budgets went to fewer and fewer films as companies went for the big payoff on one high-profile event film instead of investing smaller sums in a larger number of titles. The blockbuster era also saw the elevation of science fiction and fantasy films, long the purview of B-level filmmakers, to industry dominance. These "otherworldly" films provide a number of financial benefits: they translate better to the global audiences necessary to offset their production costs and are well suited to ancillary markets (toys, video games, etc.) that can be as lucrative as the box-office totals.

But the blockbuster also left a particular aesthetic and film-industry vacuum in its wake. Massive multiplexes and nascent home-video markets expanded to feed blockbuster demand; this had the unintended effect of creating more venues theatrically and at home for smaller films as well. The emergence of video and cable television in the 1980s also created more production companies looking for low-budget content to fill their distribution quotas. In turn, a generation of artists shut out from the blockbuster model found increased opportunities to create relatively low-risk films that found modest distribution but growing critical attention. The modern American independent film scene was born as much here—in the wake of *Star Wars* and *Jurassic Park* (1993)—as at the more celebrated site of the Sundance Film Festival. For example, few people today realize that Steven Soderbergh's trail-blazing *Sex, Lies, and Videotape* (1989) was made by a direct-to-video production company looking for another title to quickly market. (As I discuss in the first chapter, Anderson's debut film, *Hard Eight*, was produced under very similar circumstances by Rysher Entertainment a few years later.)

As its provocatively misleading title indicates, *Sex, Lies, and Videotape* was destined originally for the back row of rental chain stores and late-night Cinemax viewings. But Soderbergh aimed higher—hoping that critical buzz from a premiere at Sundance would catapult the film to a more desirable theatrical release. There, it caught the attention of an upstart company named Miramax, which began its business acquiring premade international and low-budget films on the cheap and then distributing them to domestic markets. More than producing, Harvey Weinstein's greatest gift was always the art of promotion. After Miramax's publicity machine helped make *Sex, Lies, and Videotape* into the cultural and critical phenomenon we know today, Sundance emerged as a site for young filmmakers looking to break into the studio system. But working on low-risk projects within the critical comforts of Sundance also planted the idea of creative independence, which made many of them ill-suited to work in the top-down industry. In the early 1990s, Sundance began a mutually uncomfortable power relationship with the major studios, serving as a pipeline of new talent to Southern California while benefitting from the attention and revenue that Hollywood generated for it back in Utah.

The emergence of the American independent scene was not the result of a collection of talented, determined artists like Soderbergh, Tarantino, Anderson, and so forth, who all just happened to arrive on the critical scene at the same time. This art film culture was a niche market of film distribution that catered to those audiences uninterested in the usual blockbuster and other formulaic fare. Jeffrey Sconce has provocatively termed this the "smart film" scene: a series of movies produced throughout the 1990s and 2000s that cover a wide range of styles, subject matter, and directors (from Todd Haynes to Paul Thomas Anderson). The smart film rested at "the symbolic and material intersection of 'Hollywood,' the 'indie' scene and the vestiges of what cinephiles used to call 'art' films."[13] Although the films were viewed as consistently dark, from playfully ironic to downright nihilistic, what really defined them collectively was their positioning in opposition to standard Hollywood fare. Yet they were still by and large studio films.

The smart film can be thus regarded as Hollywood's quick appropriation of the post-Sundance, quasi-independent American film culture. For example, Anderson's move after *Hard Eight* to a rather generous creative environment at New Line was facilitated by the studio's desire to attract those emerging auteurs in the mid-1990s. With Sundance filmmakers a hot commodity, young directors like Tarantino were becoming household names and box-office draws. Following Miramax's lead, New Line executives like Mike De Luca wanted to be the ones who "discovered" and supported the next young auteur on the "independent" film scene. Thus, De Luca jumped at the chance to produce the unproven Anderson's second film, *Boogie Nights*, and to provide greater creative freedom in post-production than Rysher had granted on *Hard Eight*. Then, with *Boogie Nights* a relative critical success, New Line gave Anderson full final-cut rights on *Magnolia*, hoping his developing *brand* of authorship would attract vocally supportive critics and particular cinephile audiences. Thus, Anderson's right to final cut was as much the result of a business decision—how to gain inroads into the niche market of the smart film—as it was the result of Anderson's creative output by 1998.

Boogie Nights and *Magnolia* were both representative, as Sconce argued, of larger narrative tendencies in the smart-film trend. One defining quality was the "fascination with 'synchronicity' as a principle of narrative organization [and] a related thematic interest in random fate."[14] The clearest example of this formal and thematic investment in serendipity was *Magnolia*, which "begins by explicitly meditating on the role of coincidence and synchronicity in modern life,"[15] and famously ends with frogs inexplicably falling from the sky. A similar dynamic plays out on a smaller scale in *Boogie Nights*, particularly during an elaborate sequence late in the film in which multiple characters each experience separate traumatic events in the same general geographical location. A verité porn shoot, *On the Lookout*, goes awry while Diggler is beaten by a crowd of homophobic thugs. Most dramatically, Buck Swope becomes the unwitting financial beneficiary of a violently botched donut shop robbery—

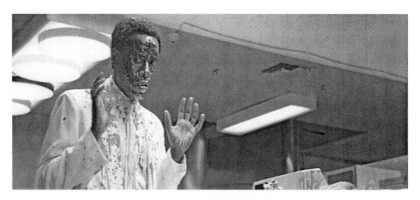

0.7. The common narrative of random chance comes into particular relief during a deadly botched robbery, which allows sole survivor Buck Swope to walk away with the money needed to start his own stereo store. Moments earlier, he'd been denied a business loan by the bank.

all occurring more or less simultaneously. In nearly every Anderson film, the logic of random chance plays a clear role.

André Crous has argued that Anderson's celebrated use of the roving, extended Steadicam shot reinforces this thematic notion of finding order in chaos. He adds that this shot is Anderson's defining auteurist image—for its thematic as well as stylistic implications.[16] Certainly, the celebrated opening of *Boogie Nights*—each character is introduced via the uninterrupted camera wandering through a nightclub—was intended as an auteurist statement at the very beginning of the movie Anderson retrospectively viewed as "his" first film. These Steadicam shots are distinctive for their *lack* of any particular character's point of view, attempting the perspective of an order always just out of reach. While stylistically influenced by the Steadicam work of Kubrick, the long take of Robert Altman, and the tracking shots of Martin Scorsese, Anderson uses the wandering long take to create its own distinctive, ethereal effect in his films—a search for meaning within an essentially meaningless world.

Both camera and characters move aimlessly through Anderson's diegetic worlds—people wander out of and back into frame, losing and finding one another with regularity—Eli's flock in the desert of *There Will Be Blood*, the ensembles of *Boogie Nights* and *Magnolia*, or Sydney's meander through the endless slot machines and gambling tables of a Reno casino in *Hard Eight*. A. G. Harmon argues that Anderson's first three films foreground the value in realizing that chaos might coexist with harmony, that symmetry and misrule might, after all, be allies . . . Anderson's works tease out this conundrum, never losing the opportunity to show human beings—mistaken, befuddled, foolish—thrashing through the mysteries of dishonored existences in hope of finding higher things.[17]

The intersection of disorder and harmony is most explicit in *Magnolia*'s ambiguous appeal to "matters of chance" as a way to organize the meandering, ensemble narrative. However, it also appears in the form of *Punch-Drunk Love*'s harmonium, which arrives in a moment of chaos and guides Barry toward a sense of balance and purpose in a world overrun initially with a disharmony that is both visual (Jeremy Blake's stunning artwork) and aural (Jon Brion's amazingly anxiety-inducing sound design). Meanwhile, *There Will Be Blood* repeatedly invites its audience to views of a vast, barren wilderness that clashes with and eventually succumbs to Plainview's obsessive drive to control everything in sight.

The emphasis on negotiating chaos and control reaches back to the intersecting narrative of Anderson's early short *Cigarettes & Coffee* (1993) and to the primary subject matter of *Hard Eight*: Sydney's long-term success as a gambler is entirely based upon playing methodically to maximize profit and minimize loss within gaming's essential chaos. John Scanlan has read *Hard Eight*'s "spontaneous combustion" moment to meditate on gambling's nature as an "engagement with uncontrollable chance."[18] Anderson's body of work reveals a narratively rich and stylistically engaging cinematic view of an often chaotic and meaningless world, a filmic vision of the material frustration that people can feel in the ambivalent comforts of a certain sector of consumer society.

THE LUXURY OF TIME

So why the sudden interest in the whims of random fate in quasi-indie smart films such as Anderson's? For Sconce, the synchronic yet causally unrelated events that anchor the smart-film narrative reflected a larger postmodern preoccupation with being "fucked by fate"[19]—the idea that there's no deeper meaning to life. Yet this ideology reflects a distinct position of privilege. Anderson's films, like many Hollywood productions, foreground white masculinity as centered on characters who don't lack basic material needs. As evinced by Eddie Adams's crowded little bedroom in *Boogie Nights*, Anderson's characters often have too much stuff instead of too little. The

0.8. Anomaly as historical consciousness. *Magnolia* attempts to ground its elaborate tale of serendipity in the history of weird scientific phenomena, such as the research done by Charles Fort (1874–1932) on events that defied rational explanation.

themes of alienation running throughout his films are grounded in specific cultural, historical, and economic contexts, starting with Anderson's own autodidactic background as a young cinephile with a whole lot of time and technological resources at his disposal.

Growing up in the 1970s and 1980s, Anderson was privileged in the way that few such young cinephiles were. In a 2008 *Esquire* article, John Richardson posited that the filmmaker's well-documented youthful arrogance—dropping out of film school, butting heads over *Hard Eight*—was rooted in the overconfidence derived from his own extensive childhood experiences making amateur films with his friends.[20] This was the product of growing up in a household where his passions could be indulged. His father was the first in the neighborhood to own a Betamax camera, which Anderson and childhood friends utilized to great effect. His own bedroom, meanwhile, contained not one but two VCRs, a laser disc player, and a computer—back during a largely predigital era in American history when most families didn't own any of these home-media technologies. The most infamous of Anderson's early movies today is *The Dirk Diggler Story* (1988). Borne from Anderson's childhood obsession with his father's VHS porn collection, this mockumentary would inspire the more somber *Boogie Nights*. It was an amazingly sophisticated achievement given the circumstances of its production. Featuring his dad's legendary voice narrating a series of "interviews" and "cinema verité" footage, *The Dirk Diggler Story* showed the emergence of a talent supported by an assortment of technological resources and the free labor of friends.

With this context in mind, the most famous anecdote about the young Anderson makes more sense—that he dropped out of New York University's prestigious film school after only a few days. "I learned everything I needed to know," he told *Esquire* in 1997, "to bad-mouth film school."[21] That he could so easily afford to attend and quickly drop out of a program located on the opposite side of the United States is telling. Homesick for the simpler, less challenging creative environment back in his beloved California, Anderson believed upon arrival that the program had nothing to teach him. He proved it to himself by submitting a writing assignment plagiarized from David Mamet's script for *Hoffa* (1992), which received a C from the instructor. Anderson went back to California to pursue his dream independently. In an environment that offered the luxuries of excessive free time and unlimited resources, Anderson could indulge in constant film viewings and amateur filmmaking.

The existential dilemmas so often at play in these smart films reflected the privileged childhoods of this filmmaking generation. Anderson was born into wealth and comfort in the shadow of his TV legend dad. He, like many, spent his youth immersed in the ephemera of postmodern media culture and surrounded by an endless flood of commodities—only to later discover that perhaps such luxuries didn't lead to a fully satisfying life. In the absence of war (pre-9/11), economic disaster (2008), or some other material crisis in the generally prosperous 1990s, there was little to focus on besides abstract philosophical issues for which there were few profound or meaningful answers. In short, the theme threading through so many of his films—that life was all a big crapshoot—reflected a distinctly postmodern weakening of historical consciousness.

Thus, so many of Anderson's films locate the site of narrative tension within a distinctive domestic milieu common to the smart film. "Two themes seem particularly central to 1990s smart cinema," Sconce wrote, "interpersonal alienation within the white middle class (usually focused on the family) and alienation within contemporary consumer culture."[22] The disintegration of the white middle-class family as a source of meaning is key to both *Boogie Nights* and *Magnolia*, while the need for surrogate families motivates the action of *Hard Eight* and *Boogie Nights*. The ephemeral satisfaction of empty commodities and professional success, meanwhile, structures *Punch-Drunk Love*, *Magnolia*, and *There Will Be Blood*. Yet none of these films imagine a culture outside mediation

0.9. A classic "smart film" moment: the awkward white middle-class dining scene in *Boogie Nights*, where father and son make little conversation and even less eye contact.

or commodification. With the ambivalence toward consumption and material wealth, the lingering obsession with media as a central social force, and the failed search for deeper meanings amid the consumer culture of suburban Southern California, Anderson's films reflect a larger cultural frustration with the generally inconsequential, yet all-consuming, postmodern media environment his generation grew up in.

The seemingly unrelated thematic emphases on alienation, chance, technology, and so forth throughout his films take on particularly intriguing dimensions when one looks more closely at these cultural assumptions. Paternal and/or surrogate-father relationships form the backbone to each of Anderson's films to date. In some ways, his films are interesting for their unusual deviation from the standard love-story plot of many, if not most, Hollywood films. With the exception of *Punch-Drunk Love*, heterosexual romantic pursuit is not the primary structuring narrative of any Anderson film (and even *Love* problematizes, more than reassures, that cinematic tradition). Instead, most of his films are interested in existing families, with the plots of *Boogie Nights*, *Magnolia*, and *Punch-Drunk Love* in large measure set in motion by tensions within the biological family. These family narratives are often centered on finding, and/or returning to, a literal or symbolic father figure. The importance of surrogate families is central to the characters of *Hard Eight*, *Boogie Nights*, and *There Will Be Blood*. Finally, these surrogate families are explicitly structured around shared financial goals.

What, then, to make of a film like *There Will Be Blood*? Superficially, the movie rejects many attributes common to Anderson's films—it is not set in contemporary Southern California; the (surrogate) father ultimately rejects the son; and, interestingly, the film imagines a moment in American history before mediation. But deeper down, *There Will Be Blood* holds several themes in common with other Anderson films: the role of fate and random chance (Plainview is nearly killed in the film's opening moments and assumes the fatherly role of his dead partner), the disintegration of the biological family, the relationship between commodities and personal alienation, the shared financial interests that hold surrogate families together, and the ubiquity of salesmen in everyday life. More provocatively, *There Will Be Blood* can be said to imagine—in its own pastiche fashion—the historical origins of postmodern America.

There Will Be Blood is the story of the oil industry's rise in turn-of-the-century California. Oil money first supported the state during the arrival of the movie industry from the East. The film also comments on the emergence of mass communication in the twentieth century—oil spelled the beginnings of mass transit while automobiles replaced trains and suburbs replaced cities. "People always imagine that Los Angeles is founded on the film industry, but it's not," Daniel Day-Lewis said in 2008. "It's founded on muck, on oil. The early photographs of the city show a forest of oil derricks with tiny houses lined between them. All the thoroughfares would have been swamps, with crude oil and overspills running down the streets."[23] The one silent sequence in *There Will Be Blood*, after Plainview's son has lost his hearing, pays homage to Thomas Edison's Black Maria, one of the first movie soundstages. Later in the film, there is a reference to the infant movie industry as well as the emergent cultural power of radio (expanded upon in *The Master*). In its own populist way, *There Will Be Blood* is a critical allegory for the copresent economic origins of modernity's failure and the subsequent emergence of postmodern culture.

However, it would be a mistake to think of *There Will Be Blood* as a faithful representation of history, despite the meticulous preparation that went into the film's preproduction. Research consisted of drawing from countless photographs and even early films from the turn of the century. Anderson derived many visual and aural cues from Kubrick, while Day-Lewis drew inspiration for Plainview from filmmaker John Huston. Portions of *There Will Be Blood* were

0.10. Although known today as the symbolic birthplace of the postmodern entertainment industry, Los Angeles was founded on oil. The cinema came later. *There Will Be Blood* is a story not only of the oil industry but of its attendant cultural history, such as the replacement of the (public) train with the (private) automobile and the endless stretches of suburbia that it eventually engendered.

0.11. The silent "Black Maria" moment in *There Will Be Blood*, an homage to the first film soundstage (located in New Jersey). The Black Maria used a single beam of direct sunlight, cast against a black background, to adequately light actors for the camera. *There Will Be Blood* suggests that our familiarity with this period of time is intertwined with its cinematic archiving.

0.12. A literal instance of the film's connection to early cinema: this touching image of Plainview with his adopted orphan son H.W. was shot with lens components from an old 1910 Pathé camera, which was also used for the black-and-white images in *Magnolia*.

shot using lens components from a vintage 1910 Pathé camera[24] (also used for the turn-of-the-century sequence that opens *Magnolia*)—here, the historical past is inseparable from its mediation. In its own hauntingly sparse way, *There Will Be Blood* is as much pastiche as his flamboyant 1970s ode, *Boogie Nights*, or even, say, Tarantino's more contemporary *Inglourious Basterds* (2009)—a revenge fantasy set during World War II that gleefully flaunts its indifference to historical accuracy. All three movies are highly stylized historical epics, "nostalgia films," which draw on *cinematic images of history* to create historical reference points with audiences unmoored from the complexities of the past.

Yet, as a counterpoint, *Inglourious Basterds* differs from *There Will Be Blood* in at least one crucial way. In *Postmodernism*, Jameson makes a distinction between "historicism" and "historicity" as competing forms of historical consciousness in the postmodern era. They both involve the visual logic of the nostalgia film. Both draw on the visual histories of style to reconstruct a pastiche of history. Yet while historicism reuses media's past for the self-reflexive purpose of recycling styles, historicity is

neither a representation of the past nor a representation of the future (although its various forms *use* such representations): it can first and foremost be defined as *a perception of the present as history*.[25]

Historicity employs a pastiche of the past to defamiliarize the present. Thus, whereas *Inglourious Basterds* celebrates a postmodern un-

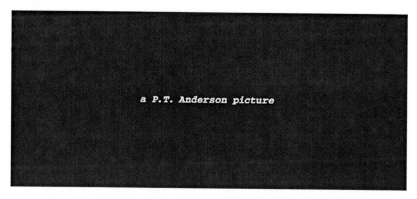

0.13. A title card from Anderson's first film, *Hard Eight*. Although he is still occasionally referred to as "P.T." by fans and the popular press, the filmmaker himself hasn't used the boyish moniker in credits since 2002's *Punch-Drunk Love*.

derstanding of history, one could posit that *There Will Be Blood* uses similar means to rethink the politics of the present—oil and religion as mutually affirming industries—in the wake of George Bush's presidency (2001–2009). We have a kind of *pop-leftist historicity* that uses signifiers of "pastness" to comment indirectly on the politics of the present. (One could regard *The Master*'s negotiation of Scientology in a similar fashion.)

POSTMODERN VISIONS OF EXCESS

Blossoms and Blood focuses on the ambivalent visions and histories of postmodern American media culture in and beyond Anderson's films. Each main chapter is devoted to one of his feature films: *Hard Eight, Boogie Nights, Magnolia, Punch-Drunk Love,* and *There Will Be Blood*. The afterword offers a shorter reflection on *The Master*. In addition to highlighting stylistic tendencies, these chapters expand upon the postmodern themes already previewed—representations of masculinity and patriarchy, random fate, consumer culture, social alienation, mechanisms of celebrity and stardom, cinephiliac love for the film medium, and a copresent anxiety over the cultural role of other media technologies. Each chapter also sustains a sense of historical consciousness—textual analysis is thus framed by various production anecdotes, notes on critical reception, and explorations of cultural shifts. Each of Anderson's films is its own set of complicated histories: chronologies that collectively add up to a larger body of work also worth exploring.

The first chapter concerns Anderson's debut film, *Hard Eight,*

0.14. An underappreciated debut, *Hard Eight* thematically foreshadows
many of Anderson's later films. Here, Jimmy (Samuel L. Jackson) walks
home with a prostitute (Melora Walters) past a casino advertising cheap,
late-night food. Anderson's consistent thematic connection between sex,
commodity, and excessive consumption comes nicely into focus.

which appeared in American theatres briefly in late 1996 and early
1997. Originally titled *Sydney*, the film is most famous today for Anderson's contentious battles with Rysher Production Company over
the final cut. The movie also signifies Anderson's only true link to
an "independent" film movement, beginning as it did with a series
of workshops at the Sundance filmmakers' lab in 1993. *Hard Eight* is
the neo-noir story of an old Nevada gambler (Hall) trying to outrun
his mysterious past. In spite of its fascinatingly troubled production, *Hard Eight* represents an audacious debut for the young American filmmaker—a thoroughly engaging character study of the aging
Sydney, an absorbing atmosphere of loneliness and anxiety, and a
tight narrative of fate and possible redemption amid an eclectic mix
of social outcasts, lost economic promise, and the glittering lights
of Reno.

Generally regarded as Anderson's breakout film, *Boogie Nights* hit
theatres with a much bigger splash less than a year later. The second
chapter explores the various historical and critical contexts for understanding his second film. Applauded for its formal energy, stylistic soundtrack, and sympathetic portrayal of the Los Angeles pornographic film culture during the 1970s and 1980s, *Boogie Nights* did
underwhelming box office but was well received in critical circles as
the arrival of a major talent. Some even went so far as to dub Anderson "the next Tarantino," an inaccurate but historically telling title. For all its deserved attention, Anderson's second film revealed

an uneven cinematic voice—more style than substance. Some, including Peter Lehman[26] and Robert Sickels,[27] scrutinized its problematic representation of gender politics, the porn industry, and home-video technologies. Others would question its relationship to a larger anachronistic trend of 1990s nostalgic representations of the 1970s as an idyllic pastiche of sex, drugs, and disco. At the very least, *Boogie Nights* was an interesting product of the Clinton 1990s, a moment when discussions about oral sex dominated the nightly news and porn was chic again—both in films (*The People vs. Larry Flynt*) and in culture (at the dawn of the Internet age).

Working with a Hollywood studio (New Line) that was anxious to enter the niche marketplace for edgy, auteur-driven films, Anderson was granted final-cut authority over his next production at the age of only 28. The third chapter focuses on the ambitious, sprawling, and flawed San Fernando Valley epic *Magnolia*, a near-apocalyptic story of people's inability to outrun their pasts, which seemed particularly timely at the end of the millennium. Many critics admired its scope, its nod to friend and mentor Altman, its themes of random chance, its particular performances, and its quirky creative ambitions (the controversial "raining frogs" sequence and the whole cast singing to Aimee Mann's "Wise Up"). However, its narrative excesses also smack of the indulgences expected from a talented filmmaker who achieved final-cut authority too early in his career. Nevertheless, critics and scholars, including Lucy Fischer and Joanne Dillman,[28] later found much of value in its complicated deconstruction of masculinity and its soap opera–like narrative structure. An interestingly complex text on its own, *Magnolia* was an important turning point in Anderson's overall career.

The young filmmaker next confronted the challenges of being a more disciplined storyteller and moving beyond the confines of epic, overlapping narratives set in twentieth-century Southern California. Released in late 2002 to mixed reactions, *Punch-Drunk Love* was a sharp departure from Anderson's earlier films. Although still set mostly in contemporary Los Angeles, the film was half the length of its predecessor and focused on the surreal experiences of a toilet-plunger salesman with anger management problems, Barry Egan (Sandler, in what is easily his best performance). But *Punch-Drunk Love* was a detour in other ways—there were suddenly no prominent father figures (real or symbolic), and Anderson's earlier downbeat tales of guilt and redemption were replaced by a sonically inventive, visually colorful, and richly affective style that playfully oscillated between dark humor and savage violence. Upon its release, some critics dismissed it as an inscrutable, minor oddity, little more than a quirky deviation from Sandler's usual frat-boy roles and a step back from Anderson's grandiose ambitions. Since then, scholars such as Stanley, Brian Price, and, most recently, James MacDowell[29] have offered provocative readings of the film's idiosyncrasies. Cubie King has argued that *Punch-Drunk Love* represents Anderson's true emergence into auteur status, that it breaks free from some of his most obvious visual and narrative influences (Scorsese, Altman) and presents a distinctive cinematic vision.[30] Not only visually stunning and aurally exquisite, Anderson's fourth film is a brilliant deconstruction of Sandler's persona and a heartbreaking vision of alienation in postmodern U.S. consumer culture. Building from King's argument, the fourth chapter polemically situates the alternately beautiful and horrifying, harmonious and disharmonious, stunningly colorful and hauntingly bare *Punch-Drunk Love* as Anderson's true auteurist emergence.

That said, the final chapter explores the themes and issues underlying the film generally regarded as Anderson's greatest success, *There Will Be Blood*. Released in late 2007, his fifth film earned near-universal critical praise and countless awards. Day-Lewis, as the unforgettably ruthless and hollow turn-of-the-century oilman Daniel Plainview, won the Oscar for Best Actor that year. The chapter begins with an extended look at the film's long production history, as well as a detour through Anderson's work as standby director on Altman's final film, *A Prairie Home Companion* (2006). Part of understanding *There Will Be Blood*'s success is based in Anderson's professional evolution as filmmaker during this time. *There Will Be Blood*'s critical success also stemmed from its timely examination of the mutually beneficial relationship of religion and oil in twentieth-century America—a historical presentation that came into particular relief during the conservative U.S. presidency of "faith-based" oilman Bush. Part of the film's visceral and dramatic power lies in the fact that Anderson's political film avoided sacrificing complex character development and aggressive storytelling in favor of reductive allegories or didacticism. To a point, *There Will Be Blood*'s straightforward representation of the past is consistent with Anderson's pastiche cinematic vision of history. Some scholars, such as Murphet, have criticized *There Will Be Blood*'s lack of a consistent political engagement or its sense of the history of labor. Yet *There Will Be Blood* remains an unforgettable vision of powerful, competing historicist iconographies. Showing *Hard Eight*'s atmospheric dread and methodical narrative drive, *Boogie Nights*'s historical ambition, *Magnolia*'s epic scope, and *Punch-Drunk Love*'s tight focus on a protagonist who is both intensely humorous and horrifying, *There Will Be Blood* brings many of Anderson's preoccupations to a thrilling crescendo.

Finally, *Blossoms and Blood* ends with a brief afterword on Anderson's latest film, *The Master* (2012), which was released theatrically around the time that the final draft of this book was otherwise completed. Given time constraints and a lack of critical hindsight, I do not focus on the film's production or reception, both of which provide much-needed historical context to the other chapters. Instead, the afterword limits itself to a brief textual discussion, highlighting the ways in which *The Master* presents a thematic continuation of the ambivalent vision of postmodern America that has been explored throughout this book. Anderson's most recent film, I argue, historicizes the now-familiar themes of serendipity, mindless consumption, and celebrity culture by situating them within the various existential crises that emerged in American culture after World War II. *The Master* is most similar to *Magnolia* in this regard; yet whereas *Magnolia* explores the idea of meaning(lessness) and American postmodern culture rather transparently, *The Master* engages similar questions with more satisfying subtlety and ambiguity. The characters of Lancaster Dodd (Philip Seymour Hoffman) and Freddie Quell (Joaquin Phoenix) reveal parallels to other Anderson characters (such as Mackey or Plainview), while *The Master* continues the increasing distrust of the surrogate family seen earlier in *There Will Be Blood*. In all, my goal is not to exhaust the film's possible meanings, but rather to use the occasion of *The Master* to reflect on the book's argument as a whole.

this is a very . . . fucked-up situation.

The effectiveness of [*Hard Eight*'s] narrative depends on the fascination Anderson finds in Philip Baker Hall's face. As Sydney, Hall makes the most of his face's scraggy lines, deep-set eyes with multiple bags under them, and distinguished, angular features. The audience studies Hall's face to try to get insight into Sydney's emotion.

MICHAEL NEWMAN, *CHARACTERIZATION IN AMERICAN INDEPENDENT CINEMA* (2006)[1]

CHAPTER 1

i remembered your face

INDIE CINEMA, NEO-NOIR, AND

NARRATIVE AMBIGUITY IN *HARD EIGHT* (1996)

When *Hard Eight* appeared briefly in a few art theaters throughout the United States in late 1996 and early 1997, few people outside the festival circuit knew anything about it. On the surface, the film looked like another low-key neo-noir, a genre common among independent films during the 1980s and 1990s. Most people recognized two of the actors: Samuel L. Jackson from his star turn in another neo-noir (Quentin Tarantino's 1994 *Pulp Fiction*) and Gwyneth Paltrow, who had already starred in such films as *Flesh and Bone* (1994) and David Fincher's *Se7en* (1995). But *Hard Eight*'s two key leads, Philip Baker Hall and John C. Reilly, were virtual unknowns. Even fewer, meanwhile, were talking about its upstart new writer-director, Paul Thomas Anderson. Those that did focused more on his notorious battles with the production company, Rysher, than on his talent. Those conflicts, moreover, helped spell *Hard Eight*'s theatrical doom, as Rysher refused to put much time or money into promoting the troubled project, which also had difficulty finding an independent distributor. Even those that liked the film wouldn't have believed then that *Hard Eight* was necessarily the start of anything worthwhile. It's important to remember that, in the very beginning, people didn't go to see *Hard Eight* with any

1.1. Sydney: the enigmatic figure at the heart of *Hard Eight*.

awareness that it was a "Paul Thomas Anderson film"—that would come later.

Yet those who had a chance to see the film in limited theatrical release were treated to a remarkably effective little story set in Reno, Nevada—with its glittering lights and seedy casinos—about the lonely life of aging career gambler Sydney (Hall). Moreover, those who expected a flashy, twisting crime story with femmes fatales, mob bosses, murder, and betrayal were instead treated to a quiet and moody character study. A lot happens in *Hard Eight*, but it takes place beneath the surface of the characters' stoic expressions and cynical observations. The film begins with Sydney mysteriously expressing sympathy for a drifter, John (Reilly), taking him under his care and teaching him how to be a professional gambler. But *Hard Eight* quietly veers off that path and turns into a character study of the enigmatic Sydney. Without family or ties of any kind, he is too carefully put together, too deliberate in his presentation, too much in control of the world around him, to be seen as weak, abandoned, or even necessarily sympathetic. Moreover, his mysterious past, his often-inexplicable actions, and his seeming ambivalence toward people prove a fruitful drive to *Hard Eight*'s narrative.

As Michael Newman noted in an excellent reading of the causally ambiguous narrative strategies of American indie films, the core of *Hard Eight* is in its fetishization of Hall's face in the role of Sydney. The actor offers a blank screen that, like the character, refuses to betray any specific details about motives. Looking like a vintage William Holden from his later *Wild Bunch* (1969) or *Network* (1976)[2] days, Hall was much less recognized by audiences than he would be a few years later, making his immersion into the character all the more uncanny. "In the end," Newman observed:

What is most fascinating about *Hard Eight* is Sydney, who is capable of acts of selfless love for John at the same time that he is capable of vicious cruelty to Jimmy, who is foolish enough to think that he can out-tough a tough guy. The contradiction in Sydney's emotional makeup is developed in a perfectly modulated performance, breaking through the internal norm of restrained stoicism with flashes of full emotion, and relying on modulations in narrative situation to further sketch out the character's psychological states. The clarity of other characters' emotional expressions makes Sydney's inexpressiveness all the more interesting.[3]

No shortage of historical irony rests in Newman's observations about the central importance of Hall's character to the film—an irony lost neither on Anderson nor on his later followers. *Hard Eight* was originally titled *Sydney* in deference to the film's most important character. Although no less ambiguous in its potential meanings than *Sydney*, the phrase *Hard Eight* evoked a noirish atmosphere of tough luck, hard-boiled criminals, and gambling with fate. It also pulled the story closer to the type of noir product Rysher wanted to sell. Years later, Anderson and some of his followers still defiantly refer to the film by its original title.

The battle over what to call *Hard Eight* was only the most visible aspect of this young director's head-butting with the production company. The emphasis on this clash over naming rights was somewhat misleading—in the end, the version of *Hard Eight* that hit theaters and DVD was largely the version that Anderson agreed to (though there are several distinct versions of the film, starting with his two-and-a-half-hour first cut). Thanks to Anderson's stubborn resourcefulness and the financial support of friends (including Reilly), a director's version was accepted at the 1996 Sundance and Cannes Film Festivals against Rysher's wishes, thus gaining the director decisive critical leverage in his battle over the film. As Anderson admitted in a *Rolling Stone* interview years later, *Hard Eight* "is my movie, with the exception that the credits [were legally required] at the beginning instead of the end."[4] Still, the mythology that surrounded Anderson's battle with Rysher played as central a role as the movie itself in establishing his credibility as an independent filmmaker with a distinctive personal vision. Yet, regardless of the circumstances under which it was made, in hindsight *Hard*

1.2. *Cigarettes & Coffee*: the title of Anderson's first professional short film, as well as a dominant motif in *Hard Eight*.

Eight strongly foreshadows thematic and narrative devices reoccurring throughout Anderson's later films.

Hard Eight begins quietly and ambiguously. Sydney's motivation for helping John remains unexplained throughout most of the film, as does his decision to help Clementine, a cocktail waitress and part-time prostitute they meet in Reno. The first third of the movie largely establishes the friendship between John and Sydney; the heart of the plot is set in motion later by the introductions of Clementine and Jimmy, a local "security consultant" who befriends John and who knows more about Sydney's past than he lets on. John and Clementine impulsively get married, which does not preclude Clementine from another act of prostitution with a man who refuses to pay. John then worsens the situation considerably by trying to kidnap and ransom the man for money.

A surrogate father figure, Sydney intervenes to help them, after which Jimmy reappears to blackmail Sydney with the dark secret at the film's heart: that Sydney is the one who killed John's father years ago, shooting him in the face at point-blank range. (Scenes from the longer version imply that John's father was a deadbeat loser.) Jimmy threatens to go to John with this information unless paid a hefty sum. In rare expressions of emotion, Sydney seems to panic over losing control of the situation, and then later confesses his fatherly love for John over the phone after the couple flees the crime scene for Niagara Falls. Sydney pays up but later ambushes Jimmy, executing him in cold blood and taking back his money. With everyone seemingly safe, Sydney returns to the roadside diner, has a cup of coffee, and uses his suit jacket to cover up a spot of blood on the sleeve of his white dress shirt—the first of several memorable final images in Anderson's films.

There's much more going on in *Hard Eight*, both on the screen and off. This chapter explores the film's troubled production history as well as those thematic and stylistic qualities that heralded the arrival of both a new cinematic talent and a rich cinematic text. The two methodological approaches to *Hard Eight*—historical and aesthetic—are not mutually exclusive but quite deeply intertwined in articulating the roots of Anderson's auteur mythology. Understanding the film's production context—not only the personal struggles between the director and the production company but also the result of several movements in 1990s neo-noir and independent cinema—helps us to better appreciate what *Hard Eight* does narratively. Meanwhile, the film's aesthetic merits point toward some of Anderson's initial interests and influences in the mid-1990s.

In its modest way, *Hard Eight* is as strong as the other uniformly noteworthy feature-length films that Anderson wrote and directed in the late 1990s. Its patient narrative, following characters without ever giving the audience too much or too little, its atmosphere of oppressive cool that owes equally to the barrenness of the Nevada desert and the suffocation of crowded casinos, and its memorable lead character: all these qualities suggest a true classic of the 1990s American indie scene. Although a more straightforward genre film than he would later make, *Hard Eight* fits thematically within Anderson's larger body of work. It is another vision of loneliness, of ephemeral moments for redemption and friendship, amid the endless postmodern consumerist clutter of the American West.

SYDNEY AND *CIGARETTES & COFFEE*

After leaving New York University film school, Anderson returned home determined to make his own career as a filmmaker. He used his contacts to land gigs as a production assistant on low-end Hollywood productions like PBS's *Campus Culture Wars* (where he met childhood idol Hall) and *The Quiz Kids Challenge* (a source of inspiration for *Magnolia*). He also leaned on childhood friends such as Shane Conrad, the son of television star Robert Conrad (*The Wild Wild West* and *Baa Baa Black Sheep*). The younger Conrad obtained tickets to premieres so that Anderson could network with established filmmakers like Alan Parker, while the senior Conrad secured Anderson another job as a production assistant on the made-for-TV movie *Sworn to Vengeance* (1993). The key, though, was his friendship with Hall—a relationship that would pay off over Anderson's next several films, starting with his first professional short movie, *Cigarettes & Coffee* (1993).

In both *Cigarettes & Coffee* and *Hard Eight*, Hall plays a character named Sydney. The name itself references a character named Sidney that Hall played in *Midnight Run* (1988), an action comedy starring Robert De Niro as a bounty hunter tasked with bringing a smarmy accountant (Charles Grodin) back to Los Angeles. It's unsurprising that the film, focusing prominently on Los Angeles and Nevada, appealed to the teenage Anderson. He had also been a fan of Hall's performance as Richard Nixon in Robert Altman's *Secret Honor* (1985). Hall's role in *Midnight Run* was very minor, but the appearance affected Anderson so deeply that he walked into his high school classroom the next day, according to John Richardson, and "handed [his teacher] a piece of paper. 'This will be my next film,' he told her. Scribbled on the paper was one word: Sydney."[5]

Finally meeting Hall on the set of *Campus Culture Wars* was the culmination of a childhood dream. Typical of the smaller roles that he was usually offered, Hall played a college professor accused of racial discrimination by his students. A former high school English teacher, Hall was a virtual unknown, aside from a memorable comedic turn as the relentless library detective on *Seinfeld* (1991). A productive but largely invisible character actor who never found a breakout role, Hall's appeal to the young Anderson was understandable. He was exactly the kind of everyday minor celebrity that Anderson grew up around and would focus on so affectionately in *Boogie Nights* and *Magnolia*: those hanging at the margins of stardom, half recognizable and half invisible, in and around Hollywood.

A common myth goes that Anderson took his otherwise-unused tuition money to fund the making of his twenty-eight-minute debut, *Cigarettes & Coffee*—the idea being that instead of paying for an education, one could just pay for a film production. In reality, the film, which even at its modest length cost $23,000,[6] was funded in large measure by a several-thousand-dollar loan from his father and from wealthy families connected to his childhood friends and industry contacts. Anderson was able to use these connections to get his hands on a Panaflex 35mm camera from the Panavision company for one weekend free of charge. (He proceeded to keep it for three weeks.) The cost was normally "a $6,000 rental to civilians."[7] With such immense resources at his disposal, Anderson was able to develop his skills into a promising filmmaking career.

Cigarettes & Coffee is a creative little film, one whose subtleties and intricacies foreshadow a promising career. The film was a deserving hit at Sundance and quickly earned Anderson a cult following, a slot at the institute's filmmaking program, and eventually a shot at a major feature-length movie. Although the film featured Hall as a character named Sydney and was set in an anonymous roadside dinner like *Hard Eight*'s opening scenes, *Cigarettes & Coffee* more closely resembles Anderson's later epic *Magnolia*. This early short features a remarkably complicated narrative and diverse cast of characters for such a brief running time. As in *Magnolia*, we are introduced to a variety of folks whose divergent stories at first seem unrelated but turn out to be clearly intertwined. Yet while the narrative is undeniably ambitious in its construction and plotting, the awkward dialogue reveals a certain kind of Mamet-esque stiffness in its repetitive presentation—a big difference from the more relaxed, even minimalist style of future films. In an interview years later, Anderson admitted to being heavily influenced by Mamet's intense but artificial style, only to realize that it's not how people really talk[8]—an especially ironic twist given the New York University anecdote about Mamet's *Hoffa* script.

With *Cigarettes & Coffee*, Anderson secured an invitation to the well-regarded Sundance Feature Film Program in Utah. He attended the institute in January and June of 1993, bringing both Hall and Reilly with him.[9] Reilly, an experienced film actor (1989's *Casualties of War*), saw in the young, unproven director a rare opportunity at bigger roles than those offered by more established filmmakers.[10] Anderson didn't forget Hall—quite the opposite; he revised and expanded the Sydney character, making him central to the script of his first feature-length film, at that point still titled *Sydney*. As he had for *Cigarettes*, Anderson began drafting a scene of two people—one young, one old—talking in a coffee shop, unsure of where they would go from there. He had finished a draft of *Sydney* three weeks later. Thus began Anderson's career-long insistence on working with his own tight-knit casts and crews.

At Sundance, Anderson directed several scenes on videotape—an ironic moment in his career, given that *Boogie Nights* would later dramatize the ruin of film art in the porn industry by the more inexpensive and logistically convenient medium of VHS. Scenes that were filmed and edited at the lab included versions of the first coffee scene between John and Sydney, the scene in the hotel room with Clementine and her client, the threatening scene between Jimmy and Sydney, and the final phone conversation between John and Sydney. Much of it was remarkably close in dialogue and shot composition to the scenes that appeared in the final version. The primary differences were the sparser settings (the coffee scene is not at a diner but a basic table while the two actors sat on folding chairs), the use of video instead of film, and Courtney B. Vance instead of Samuel L. Jackson playing Jimmy. Although the editing and sound mixing is understandably rough, each scene effectively conveys the intended dynamics between the different characters. They also nicely encapsulate Sydney's larger character arc from the mysterious but aggressive stranger who befriends John, to the seemingly frightened victim of Jimmy's bullying, to the loving father figure to both John and Clementine.

Workshopping scenes at Sundance certainly helped Anderson hone his craft; however, the experience involved more than intensive labor. At night, Anderson and friends would meet with a Sundance projectionist, stay up late, get drunk, and watch old reels from Robert Redford's personal collection, including a pornographic film that would plant the seed for *Boogie Nights*'s Rollergirl character. Anderson embraced the opportunity to network further with fellow filmmakers and other Sundance insiders. He benefitted from a diverse range of influences: legendary British director John Schlesinger (*Midnight Cowboy*, *The Day of the Locust*), actor/filmmaker Frank Oz (*What about Bob?*), actress/director Joan Darling (*Magnum, P.I.*), once-blacklisted screenwriter Walter Bernstein (*Fail Safe*), director Jeremy Kagan (*The Journey of Natty Gann*), Scott Frank (who wrote *Get Shorty* and *Out of Sight*), Richard LaGravenese (the screenwriter for *The Fisher King* and *The Horse Whisperer*), and actor/writer Todd Graff (*The Vanishing*). The connection that would prove most immediately helpful was with John Lyons, a casting director who would later become one of *Hard Eight*'s producers.

SUNDANCE AND THE INDIE SPIRIT

As his time at Sundance suggests, the independent film scene of the 1990s provides an important historical context for Anderson (as well as for directors like Tarantino and Steven Soderbergh). Started by Redford a decade earlier as a modest venue intended to support the production and showing of independent films outside Hollywood, Sundance quickly became another commodified hub for Hollywood power. Since the late 1980s Sundance has been seen as a place for young independent directors to showcase their work and break into

Hollywood moviemaking. While Anderson is not an independent filmmaker per se (most of his films have been backed by Hollywood studios), he acquired a certain critical cachet while there that gives the impression of creative, if not economic, independence.

In the mid-1990s, low-budget, quasi-independent films were the trend for marginal production and distribution companies. Rysher Entertainment was one such company looking to break into Hollywood on the cheap by gaining critical prominence. Rysher and plans for *Hard Eight* showed up on Anderson's radar around 1993. That year, Anderson met *Hard Eight's* primary producer, Robert Jones, "on the street at Sundance."[11] Hoping to capitalize on the buzz *Cigarettes & Coffee* had generated, Jones sold Anderson the idea of doing a feature-length film with Rysher. The largely unproven but promising Anderson offered Rysher the chance to break through critically with little up-front investment.

The king of the Sundance realm, Miramax, had built its "indie" empire by buying low-cost independent films from up-and-coming directors like Tarantino and Soderbergh and distributing them to critical acclaim and solid box-office returns. Anderson never worked with Miramax during its 1990s heyday. (Later, the company coproduced *There Will Be Blood*, and the Weinsteins collaborated on *The Master*.) Yet Miramax's huge critical and commercial success in the 1990s played a part in Anderson's early opportunities, creating an auteur-driven marketplace that allowed the unproven Anderson a chance to direct his own script and cast the unknown Hall in the title role. (His collaboration with New Line on *Boogie Nights* and *Magnolia* was also largely shaped by that company's attempt to mimic Miramax's success with Tarantino.) And Rysher was mostly a television company trying to break into feature-length films when Anderson made *Hard Eight*. Like Miramax and other production companies before it, Rysher was following the proven business model of using the Sundance scene as a way to obtain young, cheap (even desperate) talent, hoping that the prestige of the eventual product would catapult the production company to the status of major Hollywood player. If not for Rysher's Miramax-esque ambitions, one wonders what alternate directions Anderson's career might have taken in the mid-1990s.

Given the Sundance connections and the nature of Rysher's commitment, *Hard Eight* was explicitly a commercial product of the American independent film scene of its time. The movie was certainly intended by Anderson as a love letter to Sydney as character and to Hall as actor. Yet the main reason Rysher agreed to make the film had less to do with Anderson's talent than with how the script and its writer fit a preexisting business model. Anderson's script suggested a seductive little noir tale (common for the time) with the potential for an auteurist breakthrough in Hollywood that might carry the company. The final product, then, should be read within that context as one particular exemplar of the 1990s indie scene. This take is just as illuminating as reducing (or elevating) *Hard Eight* to the status of Anderson's first movie—to be either rejected as a compromised artistic text (due to Rysher's interference) or simply compared and contrasted with his later films, which were the product of very different historical circumstances. The film certainly foreshadows the style and themes seen in Anderson's other, more celebrated films. But that should not preclude an appreciation for how *Hard Eight* also reflected many other comparable films of its period.

Hard Eight is narratively and stylistically consistent with other American independent films from the 1990s. For example, Newman has argued that the ambiguity of *Hard Eight* is what makes the film typical of many American indie films during this period. Indeed, the seductive power of Anderson's first film is paradoxically located in its lack of clear character expressiveness to provide a strong point of audience identification. For so much of the film, we do not know how to read Sydney or the other characters. Many of the indie films' respective narrative strategies, such as *Hard Eight* and Todd Solondz's *Welcome to the Dollhouse* (1995), were structured around using expressionless, ambiguously motivated characters. *Hard Eight* is, Newman argued:

a film of shifting emotional tones, and of shifting narrative approaches. It begins by raising many more questions than it answers, in a rather mysterious fashion. It is not at all clear why the characters are behaving as they do. This is the case for large-scale narrative developments, such as Sydney taking John on as his protégé. It is also the case of smaller-scale details, such as Sydney's habit of passing many hours in a casino hotel cocktail lounge playing keno. It is typical of independent film narration to create enigmatic characters based on genre or social types; the work of spectatorship becomes the effort to decipher the clues leading to an interpretation of the character's identity.[12]

Part of the appeal of smart films is that the audience is supposed to be actively engaged in deciphering the film and its characters while watching rather than passively accepting them at face value, as with a typical Hollywood genre film playing at the local multiplex. For Newman, *Hard Eight*'s affective power is in the seductive blankness of Hall's face—yet blank faces were key, he argued, to the ambiguous narrative strategies of many well-known independent films. That Anderson was working within larger trends of the time does not make Hall's distinctive presence and performance or the memorably ambiguous character of Sydney any less powerful.

THE DEATH OF SYDNEY

It's too easy to look back and say that Rysher forced Anderson, in his pre–final cut days, to give the film a crisper running time and more box-office-friendly title. There are different ways of looking at *Hard Eight*'s troubled production history: one sees the boy-genius auteur versus the unsupportive and penny-pinching production company; another sees an arrogant, unproven screenwriter-turned-director who tried to hide the movie from producers for months and then cram his bloated first cut down Rysher's throat without studio input. These two versions of the story work together to bring us somewhat closer to the truth. The former narrative is a common one—then and now. For instance, James Mottram's *The Sundance Kids* (2006) comes back to this common story, which fits a larger cinephiliac pattern. Film critics and scholars almost always give the benefit of the doubt to the artist; no one wants to take the side of money when art is involved. Of all the young Hollywood directors during the mid-1990s, writes Mottram, "Anderson, in particular, suffered enormously. His battles with the production company Rysher Entertainment were protracted, spanning post-production, and would prove formative for the young director . . . Rysher treated [*Hard Eight*] with such disdain."[13] Certainly, Rysher's subsequent collapse and Anderson's success since *Hard Eight* would seem to validate the young director's demand for creative independence. But the latter narrative, as told by Sharon Waxman—the idea that Anderson's youthful arrogance perhaps got the best of him—is also worth revisiting. In no small way, it helps illuminate the evolution of Anderson historically from a struggling director to an established Hollywood auteur.

So what exactly happened in the history of *Hard Eight*'s production? Mottram's belief that Rysher treated the film with "such disdain" leaves quite a lot of gaps. For instance, *why* would a company, in Mottram's account, openly come to despise a project that it had at one point invested so much in? That question becomes especially complicated when taking into account that one of the film's producers, Lyons, was also one of Anderson's biggest allies from his Sundance days and the one who largely supported the young writer-director throughout all stages of production. There are more than two sides to the *Sydney/Hard Eight* story: Anderson's account of an intrusive company meddling in his work; Jones's exhaustion with handling an unprecedentedly arrogant and uncommunicative director (who told the editor not to show Jones any footage at all during the process); Lyons's more moderate opinion of Anderson as an incredibly talented director whose stubbornness and combative attitude worked against his creative potential and hampered logistical support among those who believed in him; and Keith Samples, Rysher's head executive, who tried to play peacemaker, but who ultimately got even more fed up with Anderson's obstinacy than the others had.

Each of these accounts begins at largely the same point—Rysher let Anderson go off to Nevada and shoot the script as written, largely without day-to-day interference. Anderson's refusal to communicate with Jones, the primary producer, during shooting and editing didn't help Anderson's cause when he finally did deliver the finished first cut. Nor did Anderson's decision, according to Waxman, to show the first cut to a crowded room full of his best friends before showing it to the producers.[14] That first cut was where the real problems began, even though the director had been pushing things for a while by shutting everyone else out. After principal photography and initial editing were completed, Anderson submitted his original cut of *Sydney* to Rysher, apparently expecting it to be accepted and proceed to distribution as is. In each account, company executives instead were upset with the film because they believed that Anderson's version didn't accurately reflect the script that they had purchased and signed off on. Anderson's defense was:

"Clearly they hadn't read the script," he says. "I delivered the movie and they were really confused. All I could do was point to the script and say, 'This is what I shot, this is what you paid for, this what you agreed to.' And this was the argument that would always come up—'Well, the script is not the movie and the movie's not the script.' I had the most horrendous, terrible time in the editing process."[15]

Yet, according to Waxman's more skeptical account, Anderson had somehow managed in the course of filming to turn a modest ninety-five page screenplay, which should have translated into a roughly one-and-a-half-hour film, into a lengthy cut that was at least an hour longer than that.[16] Certainly, Anderson's simple explanation that the original script was "what I shot" was probably not the full extent of the story. Rysher executives believed that the original script had too many drawn-out scenes when they bought it but thought that such issues would be resolved in the editing room later. For example, Lyons defended Anderson by stating, "I truly felt that Paul had an incredibly clear sense of what he wanted to do, did an amazing job shooting, and would find the film in post-production."[17] In either case, Anderson felt that his having written the shooting script also gave him final authority on what the finished product should look like. Understandably, Rysher felt differently: that such a long film with a largely unfocused narrative drive and a downer of an ending (Sydney was originally gunned down and left to bleed to death in the film's final scene) would be impossible to sell. The problems escalated when Rysher insisted on major cuts after the first screening.

Yet lest we simply chastise the narrow-minded company for thinking only about *Sydney*'s lack of commercial appeal, consider Rysher's larger perspective at this particular moment. Anderson was a twenty-five-year-old writer, with no feature-length directing experience at that point—little more than a production assistant with an interesting script for a crime drama (a dime a dozen in Hollywood). Rysher trusted him enough to guide a major project solely on the strength and buzz of *Cigarettes & Coffee*. It's deeply problematic to go back and argue in retrospect that Anderson's long-term success proves that he deserved greater creative freedom at the time. For one thing, Anderson had not yet become the artist he would be over a decade later when he made *There Will Be Blood*. It's foolish to assume that he was capable of such an accomplishment at that age. For another, when he did finally get final cut a mere three years later (*Magnolia*), the result raised as many questions as it answered about his undeniable but raw talent. Moreover, Anderson's decision to not show anyone, not even *Hard Eight*'s own producer, some of the daily footage, or to *communicate* with people from the company, created a standoffish environment. Anderson escalated the tension by engaging in heated verbal exchanges over cutting even a second of the film. When pushed further, Anderson proceeded to submit his cut to festivals behind executives' backs.

Economic considerations aside, many people within Rysher had every reason to be personally fed up with Anderson and thus unsupportive of him and the film.

Anderson also had as many supporters as critics involved with the film's production. Jones was sympathetic upon seeing the first cut, despite Anderson's persistent attempts to hide the footage from him: "There were great things in it, but it was obvious [Anderson] was so close to the film he couldn't see the woods for the trees."[18] Anderson was so in love with every single frame he had shot that he was unable to look at the overall project objectively or make even the most basic cuts necessary to producing a tighter film. Even Anderson's supporters were frustrated with his arrogance over *Sydney*: "This is my cut," he told producers after the first screening, "I'm not touching a frame."[19] As a result, he was fired, and Jones and others completed a very different cut of the film without him. Eventually, Anderson was brought back by Samples, who tried to make peace but quickly became frustrated by Anderson's tantrums and fired him again.

Undeterred by being locked out of the editing room, Anderson worked the mythology of the auteur to his advantage. Switching the game back to his home turf, Anderson submitted a copy of his version to the 1996 Sundance Film Festival, which was accepted over Rysher's version. Sundance, like most critical film institutions, was inclined to support the director's version, particularly since the director in question was one of its own. The Cannes Film Festival also agreed to show Anderson's cut rather than the production company's. "I would never not show the director's version," said Gilles Jacob, director of the Cannes Film Festival. In both cases, the festivals chose Anderson's cut because of the default cinephiliac assumption that the director is always right in a dispute with moneymen. That Anderson's version may be aesthetically superior to Rysher's is beside the point—what matters is that the young director was able to exploit indie art-film auteur culture to his advantage. By leaning on the proven critical commodity of the director's vision, Anderson was able to convince Rysher to go along with his version of *Sydney*.

However, the final theatrical version of *Hard Eight* had not yet been found. With Rysher agreeing to go with the festival version of *Sydney* (albeit with a title change), the young director won the battle over *Hard Eight*—only to eventually lose the war. After all that, his version of the film still failed to find a distributor. Thus, Anderson reluctantly agreed to more cuts anyway, trimming the film and changing the ending. One deleted scene, "The Kiss," was later included on the film's DVD release. This sequence is set near the end of the film (after the couple has left for Niagara Falls, but before Sydney kills Jimmy) and includes a phone conversation between John and Jimmy, followed by Clementine's asking John for forgiveness. The deletion was wise—aside from doing little to enhance the characters or the plot (specifically, it repeats a similar scene of forgiveness in the car), the scene between the young couple further draws out the uncomfortable misogyny that for the most part pervades the narrative. There were other scenes as well that did not lend themselves to the movement of the overall story, such as an extended anecdote told by Clementine about one man accidentally defecating on his lover and scenes that fleshed out Sydney's backstory more—a drunken phone call to his ex-wife, or a flashback to scenes with John's father. The last one, which makes Sydney's act of murder less reprehensible, might add to understanding his motivation. Yet one could also argue that moral clarity would make Sydney a less interesting character. His strength is the lack of clear empathy throughout most of the film—the notion that he shot John's father in the face, just as we are starting to like him, gives Sydney an unredeemed dark edge he maintains to the end. In all, the glimpses we have of the longer version suggest, as both Jones and Lyons believed, that Anderson's first cut wasn't necessarily without flaws.

The end result that finally hit theaters was a compromised version of *Hard Eight* that didn't quite reflect Anderson's original vision. Nor did it fit with others' suggestions for recutting. Yet, as I noted earlier, even Anderson conceded in 2000 that *Hard Eight* ultimately *was* his film. More precisely, Anderson's own later assessment—an appropriate metaphor given his films' thematic obsession with broken families—was that *Hard Eight* "was such a bastard child, the way it was released and the fights I had to go through."[20] The final version was distributed to theaters in limited release and with little promotional support from Rysher. It's hard to objectively argue that anyone *wanted* to see *Hard Eight* fail given the money that went into making it. But there's no question that, in the end, Rysher didn't throw its full weight behind supporting a film it didn't really believe in after all the hassle involved in making it and finding a distributor. It was destined to be one of those films that was rediscovered years later, with the revisionist perspective of its being an auteur's first, unappreciated achievement.

It's hard to feel sorry for Anderson when looking back at this moment—viewed retrospectively, the tumultuous story of *Hard Eight*'s production (regardless of who tells it) simply solidifies his mythology as an emergent auteur struggling to create an independent vision in a system overrun by the meddling interference of moneymen. Added to that, his nemesis Robert Jones got the worst of it in the long run. Anderson treated him with contempt throughout the whole experience, apparently for no greater transgression than having expected, as producer, to take part in the filmmaking process. More importantly, according to Waxman, his reputation among American filmmakers was ruined because of constant badmouthing from Anderson's agent, John Lesher.[21] As a result, the British native returned to Europe. Anderson may have felt slighted, but Jones also thought that "*Hard Eight* was pretty fucking traumatic . . . it took me a long time to get over the experience."[22] Rysher eventually went under, while Anderson went on to greater success and greater creative freedom. Anderson's biggest defender on the film, Lyons, summed up the experience by stating that "what people couldn't stand was that Paul was never humble. He would never acquiesce, and he just fought back."[23] Lyons highlights Anderson's personal conviction and persevering confidence and suggests that many of the problems and headaches he encountered early in his career were thoroughly of his own stubborn making.

THE RETURN OF NEO-NOIR

Rysher agreed to buy Anderson's script in the first place because it fit well within the proven low-budget, independent-friendly genre of neo-noir. These films dealt with crime, corruption, and double-crossing in the underbelly of American society, followed few upstanding or morally pure protagonists, and often led to fatalistic endings for one or more of the major characters, who had to pay for their crimes. As Mottram noted in *The Sundance Kids*, "the crime genre, in its broadest possible sense, has been broached by nearly all the directors [in his study of Sundance films]. Some, such as Quentin Tarantino, rarely dance to any other tune. Others, like Steven Soderbergh and David Fincher, return to it frequently. Even the likes of Wes Anderson, Paul Thomas Anderson, Robert Rodriguez, and Bryan Singer have dabbled."[24] In the 1990s, a strain of neo-noir emerged in films, both independent and Hollywood productions, pointing back for cinephiles to classic noirs of the old Hollywood studio system.

In the 1940s and 1950s, every major studio (as well as more than a few independent production companies) produced its share of classic noir titles—from *The Big Sleep* to *Out of the Past* to *Kiss Me Deadly*. "Noir" came to signify a wide range of mostly urban-set films that featured a bleak mise-en-scène (usually in stark black and white images), sympathetic but flawed antiheroes, intricate stories of criminality, and fatalistic endings. Historically, they were often seen as meditations on the alienation and disillusionment in modern life after the horrors and sacrifices of World War II. Many noirs were the products of European émigrés such as Billy Wilder and Otto Preminger, who had fled the Nazis, which also explains the dark worldview and stark stylistic influence of 1920s German Expressionism on film noir. Neo-noirs, meanwhile, were seen as an even broader category of films that debuted after this period (from the 1960s on) and that emulated many of the same character archetypes, plot twists and turns, and stylistic devices.

Hard Eight is not quite a typical noir—the incidental narrative only works at times toward the kind of narrative patterning and closure noirs often privilege, while the genuinely sympathetic affection for its characters seems at odds with the often hopeless cynicism of the genre. Indeed, noir expectations make the film even more engaging on a first viewing. Nevertheless, *Hard Eight* showcases some standard noir criteria: a mysterious antihero, a morally ambiguous world, several (unpunished) criminal acts, and enough twists and turns to suggest that everyone is capable of a (very) dark side. Like many neo-noirs, some of which were often outright remakes, *Hard Eight* was also an homage to an earlier film, Jean-Pierre Melville's classic, *Bob le Flambeur* (1956). Classic noir was largely, but not exclusively, a Hollywood trend, as French film critics and filmmakers were among the first to recognize (and emulate) the common narrative and stylistic tendencies that were coming out of the studio system. One such filmmaker was Melville, whose films often paid homage to American crime films such as the heist thriller and the gangster picture. Like *Hard Eight*, *Bob le Flambeur* is the story of an aging gambler, his compassionate relationship with a young part-time prostitute, and his friendship with a younger partner and protégé. However, *Bob* is also a more straightforward, intricately plotted crime narrative than Anderson's wandering character study. In Melville's film, the old gambler is desperate for cash and finds himself at the center of a plot to rob a casino safe in the early hours of the morning, all the while being pursued closely by the police. As with many noirs, things don't go as planned, nor do they end well for everyone involved. *Bob le Flambeur* features typical noirish devices like the doomed heist plot, femme fatale betrayals, and complicated antiheroes. It also anticipates *Hard Eight*'s sense of friendship and the way it can be threatened by poor choices and figurative ghosts who return from the past.

Starting with the Coen brothers' audacious debut, *Blood Simple* (1984), upstart independent filmmakers have chosen neo-noir for its reliably low-budget, audience-friendly story material that tapped into their own rabid cinephilia. Neo-noir, of course, is not restricted to low-budget indie films, but its established formulas proved fruitful for cost-conscious directors and producers, who could also pay homage to the influential directors who came before them. By the mid-1990s, John Dahl had written and directed several successful neo-noirs, including *Red Rock West* (1993) and *The Last Seduction* (1994). Singer burst on to the Hollywood scene with the twists and turns of *The Usual Suspects* (1995), while Christopher Nolan made a name for himself with the mind games of *Memento* (2000). Soderbergh later followed *Sex, Lies and Videotape* with *The Underneath* (1995), *Out of Sight* (1998), and *The Limey* (1999). Even the botched criminal plans and disrupted chronologies of Tarantino's debut, *Reservoir Dogs* (1992), and his even more prominent follow-up, *Pulp Fiction* (1994), owed much to noir influences in general and Stanley Kubrick's *The Killing* (1956) in particular.

Indeed, one of *Hard Eight*'s most fascinating aspects involves its thematic connections to the morality and ethical dilemmas inherent to noir. In "'Saint' Sydney: Atonement and Moral Inversion in *Hard Eight*," Donald R. D'Aries and Foster Hirsch argue that *Hard Eight* fits within the tradition of crime films centered on people who must make amends for illegal and immoral acts they've committed, while it also inverts the expectations of the genre. Namely, Clementine is not quite the traditional femme fatale, and Sydney is not a man who is apparently beyond redemption but is instead "the ethical compass of the film and its solitary guiding light."[25] While the typical noir would focus on the fatalistic inevitability that Sydney pay dearly for his crimes, *Hard Eight* is really about, they argue, Sydney's "quest to regain his humanity through selfless loving acts and, thereby, to placate his guilty conscience."[26] Rather than have Hall's character be a one-dimensional antihero protagonist with no hope of salvation, Anderson's "challenge to [noir] genre tradition, however, [is that] Sydney is tempted to perform a series of benevolent acts in order to unburden his conscience."[27] The main character, however, is hardly a "good" man by the end, as the film is still focused on showing Sydney haunted by his actions rather than ultimately redeemed. "The film's existential punishment for its protagonist—unmasking the character's self-loathing," they argue, "is morally more provocative than any expected form of [legal or karmic] admonition."[28] Thus Sydney emerges as the classic noir antihero—one sympathetic enough to follow, but also one who will be forever immersed in amorality.

"YOU LOOK LIKE YOU COULD USE A FRIEND"

When examined closely, *Hard Eight*'s narrative structure is a mix of moods and styles, containing three separate and only loosely related acts. This may be the result of excessively cutting footage and scenes from the longer version, but it may also result (as seen later in *Magnolia*) from Anderson's commitment as screenwriter to the characters more than the plot. The first twenty-plus minutes, humorous and playful, establish the origins of John and Sydney's friendship. The second act, which resembles an intense family drama, focuses on Clementine's relationships with the two men and how her choices threaten to disrupt their friendship. Finally, the third act focuses primarily on Sydney and Jimmy, a character who to that point has been nearly nonexistent but whose significance to the themes and story of *Hard Eight* becomes explicit by the end. Each part has a decidedly distinct storyline and feel—but upon a first viewing of *Hard Eight*, the inconsistencies are less noticeable because of the emphasis on Sydney's ambiguity throughout.

Many of the thematic concerns that stretch across *Hard Eight*—isolation in the American West, ephemeral friendships, the coming and going of father figures—are immediately revealed in the film. The opening features John in long shot as he sits, crouched, by the entrance to Jack's Coffee Shop. The theme of loneliness, the theme of needing a friend (and/or a father), is established by the image of the young drifter barely visible in a crowded but depopulated frame (John's isolation in the opening shot anticipates early shots in *Punch-Drunk Love* and *There Will Be Blood*). A semi pulling a large trailer passes in front of him—a seemingly random event, but another one that anticipates a similar moment in *Punch-Drunk Love*. Trucks wander occasionally through Anderson's frames—evoking the feeling of the open highway, of transition, but also of placelessness, searching for where one belongs. As the truck exits

1.3. The first shot of *Hard Eight*, which announces one of Anderson's key preoccupations: loneliness amid the generic consumer and leisure culture of the American West.

the frame right, we see John again for a moment until Sydney enters the frame.

Although initially focused on John, this shot visually establishes *Hard Eight* as Sydney's story. We see John from Sydney's point of view, and the camera only moves closer once Sydney starts walking. It keeps pace with the older gentleman as he approaches his destination. Later in the film, when we flash back to this moment, Sydney looks at John first in his rearview mirror—a bit of symbolic foreshadowing that hints John is someone from his past. The power that Sydney holds in this first scene is reinforced by the physical positioning of both men when they meet—Sydney is standing tall, engaging, and assertive, while John is sitting with his head down, passive. John at first ignores him when Sydney offers a cup of coffee and a cigarette. The asymmetry here is stark—Sydney is hidden, a black shadow on the right half of the screen, while John is exposed, looking up against a white wall on the left side. Curiously, we never see Sydney's face during this conversation; his head remains just out of the top portion of the frame. It adds to the character's mysterious presence, building up his aura, while also speaking to the baggage he carries with him.

We only finally see Sydney's face as he lights a cigarette when the film cuts inside the diner. Once there, we are invited to a series of shot/reverse shots between the two characters as we find out more about them, particularly John. Sydney remains the more forceful presence—the character driving the conversation, the one mak-

1.4. The opening shot follows Sydney and tracks up to John, hunched by the diner door. John's passivity and weakness are brought into sharp contrast with Sydney's assertiveness and (offscreen) ambiguity in the frame.

ing repeated eye contact with the frame (even at times when John is talking), while John looks down or out the window ("hey, John, look at me"). Sydney interrogates John intensely—asking him questions about his past, how much money he has, why he went to Vegas (to win money for his mom's burial), and so forth. The scene comes to a conclusion when Sydney stands up from the booth and towers over John again. He asks the young drifter if he'd like to go back to Vegas and try his hand again at gambling. It is here that we see an uncomfortable moment of homophobia play out. John insists he is not gay or willing to perform sexual favors in return. John's confusion as to the stranger's intentions is understandable, though the moment is played to excess.

Throughout this scene, Sydney is almost too insistent, forcing the story to move on to the next plot point. The scene's rushed feel may be the result of conflicts in the editing room over final cut, but it may also result from the opening's own narrative hesitation. The writing of *Hard Eight* began, like that of *Cigarettes & Coffee*, with a conversation between Sydney and one other person—without necessarily knowing where the story would go from there. The next sequence in the car, meanwhile, serves a similar function—the two characters continue to chat while the story finds itself (this is also an homage to the opening sequence of two people driving outside Vegas in *Melvin and Howard* [1980]). Once the characters were talking, Anderson believed, the audience would be willing to follow them in any narrative direction.

In some ways, the first twenty minutes of the film feel more uneven than the rest of *Hard Eight*—for one, there are the random narrative inconsistencies: "I lied when I said $50," Sydney tells John for no apparent reason, "You're gonna need $150," or the dead mother storyline that initiates the plot but is ultimately inconsequential, as Sydney uses the deus ex machina of a "friend in Los Angeles" to help John out. There is also a different tone up front. John provides a consistent source of goofy comic relief (misspeaking, telling the story of the combustible matchbox, bragging about pay-per-view, his Velcro strap shoes). The casino montage is straight out of a Scorsese movie with its quick camera movement and matching cuts, and then the film cuts jarringly to two years later, when John and Sydney are suddenly "old" friends. On the other side of this cut, we are invited to a very different story. Anderson himself wrote four different possibilities to follow up the scene before the jump, including flashbacks, but decided on the jump as the most interesting.

At the heart of the earlier car scene in the desert is an appropriately symbolic discussion about unpredictable matches—John tells the story of a box of matches that spontaneously ignited while sitting in his pocket. Hence, John no longer uses matches, only lighters. This memory leads to a humorous visual flashback when John's pants start on fire while in line for *The Outlaw Queen* (1957). Anderson's father Ernie played one of the other patrons in line. For A. G. Harmon, this seemingly insignificant moment is symbolic of Anderson's interest in notions of chance and "shocking coincidence": "Sydney does not scoff at such a preposterous story, even though it is a tale of wild coincidence not unlike the countless stories we have all heard and disbelieved."[29] The randomness here anticipates scenes

1.5. During the opening diner scene, Sydney asserts himself by constantly addressing the camera while John routinely avoids eye contact by staring down or out the window.

1.6. The flashback to when a box of matches exploded in John's pocket.
Note Anderson's dad, Ernie, standing in line directly in front of Reilly.

late in *Boogie Nights*, as well as the larger thematic structure of *Magnolia* and *The Master*. Likewise, in "Combustion: an Essay on the Value of Gambling," John Scanlan uses this scene from *Hard Eight* to demonstrate how the act of gambling is structured around "the potential impact of unpredictable phenomena on reasonable expectations."[30] Scanlan's interesting observation draws out the ways in which, over the course of Anderson's first film, the act of gambling becomes a central metaphor for the film's characters as they negotiate the randomness of the world. As a veteran gambler, Sydney "knows chance cannot be beaten, so he lives out his life in a way that demonstrates a degree of control over his own limitations," just as effective gambling can be an attempt at controlling one's exposure to random chance. Even more provocatively, this explicit thematic and narrative emphasis in *Hard Eight* on the role that chance and unpredictability play in people's lives proved to be a major factor for many of Anderson's later characters.

While the first twenty-plus minutes of the film establish John and Sydney, the main story and mood of *Hard Eight* begins after the jump ahead two years. Here, we're introduced to Jimmy and Clementine, and a more clearly defined noirish narrative arc begins to emerge. However, the ambiguity is still largely intact—we don't know what Sydney's intentions are toward Clementine, and we don't know what narrative function Jimmy seems to serve, other than annoying Sydney. The entrance of the two other main characters brings into relief the father-son relationship between John and Sydney, while also highlighting how they threaten the equilibrium established between them. That it is a woman and a black man who upset the balance is not insignificant—Anderson has left open the question of whether Sydney's dislike of Jimmy is on some level motivated by his race, and Clementine's role begins a strand of misogyny that runs throughout his movies. John and Sydney's first discussion about Clementine revolves around John wanting to know whether the older man slept with her already, as though a territorial issue were at stake.

There are three prominent Steadicam shots in *Hard Eight*, setting a template for Anderson's now-distinctive visual style. Despite the filmmaker's own acknowledgment that the Steadicam can be overused out of convenience, it's effectively deployed throughout his films to evoke the dreamy, affective mise-en-scène he has often privileged. Two variations on the same Steadicam shot are used when Sydney arrives at the seedy motel where Clementine and John are hiding with the hostage. Here, the camera finds Sydney as he exits his car and then follows him up the stairs and down a series of corridors to the room door—often, though not exclusively, framed from Sydney's point of view. After the extended sequence inside the motel room, meanwhile, the same Steadicam shot is repeated in reverse when all three leave the room together.

After the lounge scene with Jimmy and Clementine earlier in the film is a remarkable Steadicam long take of Sydney as he walks through the casino floor. The camera pulls with Sydney, then trails him, and even loses him to reveal other patrons at the tables and

1.7. One of *Hard Eight*'s remarkable Steadicam shots—following Sydney as he wanders through the Reno casino. Periodically, the camera loses Sydney in the crowd, suggesting a point of view greater than the main character (common with Anderson's use of the Steadicam). Also note the "Hit It Big" sign in the background, highlighting the theme of random chance so common in the filmmaker's body of work.

slots before finding the elder gambler as he emerges from the casino crowd again. The shot's only occasional interest in Sydney anticipates the kind of subjectless Steadicam shot Anderson would use in the celebrated opening of *Boogie Nights*, as well as in *Magnolia*, *Punch-Drunk Love*, and *There Will Be Blood*. Part of the shot's surreal, dreamy feeling depends upon how disconnected it is from any one point of view, while Michael Penn's hypnotic xylophone score heightens its otherworldly feel.

CLEMENTINE

As often occurs throughout the film, we are left to wonder what Sydney is searching for as he wanders through this hectic and vacuous world. Perhaps it's Clementine, since the next scene shows him waiting for her as she leaves a motel room—the first indication (hinted at earlier by Jimmy) that Clementine is a part-time prostitute. Like his first encounter with John, Sydney's motive in the encounter is unclear. Their earlier conversation about how much she was "required" to flirt with male customers as a cocktail waitress foregrounds Sydney's sympathy for her difficult position while revealing the film's noir ambivalence toward the potential femme fatale. Although she is not actively plotting to threaten or double-cross others, Clementine's professional choices nonetheless present difficulties for Sydney and John.

Mirroring the opening scene, Sydney invites Clementine to a diner for coffee to find out more about her and to make another largely unmotivated connection. However, this time, it is Clementine who gradually begins to find out more about Sydney's mysterious past—asking about his relationship with John, as well as the biological family he apparently abandoned. "Do you have *real* kids?" she asks, referring to John, "Kids of your own?" At one point, Sydney cannot keep up with the questions, answering them out of order. As Clementine probes more deeply about Sydney's relationship with his wife and children, their quiet discussion is interrupted by a symbolic incident in the corner of the diner—a father gets angry, pounds the table, loudly curses his wife and daughter, and then leaves them in the booth. This suggests to the attentive viewer that Sydney probably did something similar in his past.

The narrative ambiguity in the relationship between these two characters, meanwhile, is heightened by a cut to the next scene, where Clementine inexplicably shows up with Sydney at his hotel room. The inclination for the viewer is to believe, as A.G. Har-

1.8. The diner scene with Clementine and Sydney mirrors the opening
sequence with John—only this time Clementine is the more inquisitive one,
while Sydney somewhat defensively answers questions about his past.

mon has noted,[31] that she is being paid for her sexual services—a
point made explicit when she asks him, "do you wanna fuck me?"
The abruptness of this vulgar moment, and the narrative clarity it
seeks regarding Sydney's undefined intentions, echoes John's earlier warning to him that "I don't suck dick." Clementine's line is an
awkward come-on as she begins to assume the role she thinks Sydney wants, but he firmly rebuffs her.

Clementine's sense of the intersection between sex and money
anticipates much of the interaction in *Boogie Nights*, Claudia's introduction in *Magnolia*, and the phone-sex service in *Punch-Drunk Love*,
where human compassion is reduced to exchanging money and
other goods for sexual favors. As he did upon first meeting John,
Sydney is shown towering over Clementine. She sits, embarrassed,
on the bed—his head pokes just out of frame, while she looks down
in the middle of the image (the composition was influenced by a
much more terrifying scene of domination in *The Hustler* [1961]). Always cool and commanding, Sydney is at once sympathetic, in control of the situation, and also refusing to tip his hand.

That Sydney's goals are undefined gives Jimmy's persistent presence added significance. We know that Sydney doesn't like him and
that Jimmy remembers him from Vegas years ago, but we don't
know why. Jimmy's big-mouthed misogyny is one factor, but Sydney
is not interested in exploring his own dislike of Jimmy—he only acknowledges it when John passively asks him about it. Anderson has
hinted that Sydney's dislike of Jimmy is partially old-school racism,
but it is also tied to the fact that Jimmy represents a part of his past

he cannot control. We realize in the end that Sydney is trying to outrun his criminal past and make amends for the actions that he cannot personally let go of (i.e., killing John's father). Jimmy embodies that past and the threat it represents to him.

Yet it would be premature to say that Sydney necessarily feels much deep-seated guilt about his often-criminal life choices. Even though he plays the part of the harmless, if gruff, old-timer spending his final days doing little but hanging out in casinos and coffee shops, Sydney still resorts to extreme physical violence when necessary. As the quiet montages throughout *Hard Eight* make clear, he seems content to live a generally uneventful life. But he does not hesitate to engage in criminal behavior if the situation demands it—such as when Clementine and John foolishly try to kidnap and ransom one of her clients, or when Jimmy blackmails him.

Much of the film's quiet second act, however, is the setup to a third act in which Sydney's life spirals out of control. This act opens with the intense sequence in the motel room involving Sydney, John, Clementine, and the nameless client who refused to pay her. On one level, this is another sharp shift in tone. The quiet and moody film suddenly becomes a chaotic shouting match, revealing a glimpse into Sydney's capacity for ruthlessness. The scene itself nicely encapsulates *Hard Eight*'s careful ambiguity, while also ratcheting up the suspense that drives the rest of the film. The long sequence begins with Sydney outside the door talking to John, who refuses initially to open the door, building anticipation for what's inside. It also foregrounds the father-son relationship, as John reverts to the behavior of a child who wants to make sure his parent won't be mad at him for something he's done.

Once Sydney is inside, the sequence becomes a remarkable demonstration of how to build suspense simply by refusing to cut. An extended two-shot frames Sydney's silent reaction and John's guilty expression. Importantly, the audience is not shown what they are looking at, and the fact that we have not yet seen or heard from Clementine further highlights the troubling possibilities. As John and Sydney begin to talk about the "hostage," our narrative curiosity is both acknowledged and intensified. The dialogue reveals in layers what is occurring, but it's another minute before the film finally cuts to a long shot of the room, with Clementine crouched in a corner, an unconscious man lying on the double bed, and blood on the pillow.

This pivotal scene in the motel room serves several key func-

1.9. An extended long take of John and Sydney inside the motel room during the botched hostage situation. Refusing to cut in favor of focusing on Sydney's near-speechless reaction effectively builds anticipation.

tions in *Hard Eight*—it is a moment of narrative revelation, but also of closure. We discover that John and Clementine had been seeing each other for a couple of months and that they impulsively got married. We also find out that just because of the marriage, Clementine isn't inclined to give up her side profession. We also see that each character is capable of losing his or her cool. For example, this is one of only two scenes to provide us with any flash of emotion from Sydney (the other being when he's threatened in the car by Jimmy). Clementine yells about wanting her money from the man, while John breaks down in tears at several points. He also exhibits violent tendencies, out of character for the generally soft and passive man-child. He strikes his wife in a fit of rage and assaults the unconscious man as he begins to awaken.

At this point, too, we see for the first time how familiar Sydney is with a crime scene and with how to address the issue so that involved parties can get away with it. After verbally and physically fighting with John and Clementine, Sydney returns to his fatherly demeanor and agrees to help them out—talking Clementine into leaving without the cash, removing fingerprints, uncuffing the hostage, and getting rid of the gun and handcuffs. Yet it is also a moment of closure—once they flee the scene, John and Clementine are forced to leave for Niagara Falls, removing her from the story just as we become aware of her full investment in it. It also splits up the main relationship we have followed up to this point: father and surrogate son.

The primary story ends right as it picks up momentum, and we quickly return to Sydney's uneventful life as a full-time gambler. Several minutes later, John and Sydney have one final conversation on the phone. John calls to touch base and to ask if there might be complications arising from their criminal act. The scene works primarily as closure to their friendship while also foregrounding what is at stake in Sydney's confrontation with Jimmy. John thanks Sydney for everything, while Sydney admits to him that "I love you, John. I love you like you were my own son." The surrogate-father storyline is made explicit by Sydney's declaration, and the line has added weight since at this point we know that Sydney killed John's biological dad. Sydney's expressions seem genuine, but it is hard ultimately to know for sure, especially given his past and his subsequent deception and cold-hearted treatment of Jimmy. At the very least, Sydney's admission of paternal love for John is mitigated by the fact that Sydney is once again alone, having lost his surrogate children much as he had previously lost his real ones.

"I KNOW SOME THINGS ABOUT ATLANTIC CITY"

The character of Jimmy returns to provide motivation and framework for the final act. His return also brings the larger story of *Hard Eight* full circle—indicating why Sydney insisted two years earlier on helping John, at a point when some audiences are likely to have forgotten the ambiguous origins of their friendship. Sydney and Jimmy's scene in the car at first concerns clarifying the outcome of the botched hostage situation—Jimmy says he's seen the unnamed man in the casino and there's no way he called the cops. However, it turns out to be a more ominous situation—"I know some things about Atlantic City" (i.e., the thus-far unrevealed plot point that Sydney murdered John's dad in cold blood). Jimmy turns directly to the camera (while it is Sydney who keeps looking away), and Jackson's cold, straight stare reminds us of Sydney's authority in the opening. Jimmy takes over the narrative with what had been Sydney's calm control.

When Sydney realizes Jimmy's intentions, the older character attempts to gain control back—first by laughing off Jimmy's attempts at intimidation, and then by walking away entirely. We begin to see Sydney losing his edge; he snaps at Jimmy's passive-aggressive accusations and then fumbles with his keys once inside his car, trying to drive away. Yet Sydney's impulsive flight only unravels the situation further—Jimmy follows him, smashes the car window, and points a gun in his face. At this point in the narrative, Jimmy's control be-

1.10. Another threat to Sydney and John's relationship, Jimmy's narrative function doesn't become clear until the third act.

comes explicit—he tells Sydney to turn off the car, and to give him $10,000 to stay quiet, both demands to which Sydney agrees. This is in sharp contrast to moments earlier, when Sydney refuses to put out his cigarette despite Jimmy's repeated insistence.

The uncharacteristic loss of control is apparent in Sydney himself—his behavior is panicked and flustered, and his speech is uneven and rushed. That blank slate of ambiguity Hall's face projected so well gives way to an expression of genuine fear for his physical safety. Suddenly, Sydney looks like an old man in way over his head against the unrelenting hostility and constant threats of Jimmy. The scene ends with appropriate symbolism—Jimmy forces Sydney over to the passenger seat of his own car and drives the old man's vehicle away. Off to get all the money Sydney has with him, Jimmy is literally in the driver's seat.

Yet if the audience is supposed to believe Sydney is truly weak after all—despite the revelation that he once ruthlessly shot a man in the face—it's only to set up the film's final turn of events. Slowly, Sydney regains his cool and begins to assert himself. They return to his hotel room to wait for the bank to open in the morning. Jimmy tells Sydney all he knows about his past behavior and reputation, which doesn't shake the stoic old man. Sydney finally speaks up to admit that he has the money with him. The monologue is shot in one continuous take that slowly tracks from behind Jimmy, across the room, to a medium shot on Sydney's face:

I have the money to give you right now, in this moment. I will give you all that I have. Maybe before you were gonna kill me. Maybe. I don't know. I know John and I love him like he was my own child. But I can tell you this: I don't want to die. I killed his father. I can tell you what it was. This is not an excuse. I'm not begging for clemency. All that matters—I do not wish to sacrifice my life for John's well-being. But I will sacrifice this money for mine. Because you have asked me. Because after this, I will have done all I can for John and for myself. I'm going to ask you with all the heart and sincerity that I have—please do not put a bullet in me . . . and please do not tell John what I have done. I trust that once I give you this money, you and I will take separate paths and that this negotiation will settle everything. That is my hope. I don't want to die.

Sydney is both recomposed and still exposed. He attempts to talk his way calmly out of the mess at hand, to set the conditions for this "negotiation," while his feelings, his safety, and his money are still laid bare. This monologue, and the deeper truths underlying it, encapsulates the cool contradictions embodied in the character of Sydney—plain speaking, but also deceptive; regretful of his past, but only to a point; cool but also capable of great violence.

Given *Hard Eight*'s violent ending, however, Sydney's monologue is also clearly a ruse. The old man's pleas, in retrospect, are sincere to a point, but also partially designed to deceive Jimmy into not taking him seriously as a threat. While Sydney appears helpless in his plea, he is also already planning in his head to give Jimmy the money then kill him and take his money back. His interest in killing Jimmy may also result from the manner in which the extortionist made Sydney feel out of control and vulnerable in a way that he usually doesn't.

The long take of Sydney sitting on his couch during the monologue is echoed by another shot of him later. This time Sydney sits silently as he waits with a gun in Jimmy's home. Jimmy's error in judgment was to mistake Sydney's courtesy—his perceived status as an old-time hood wasting away in retirement—as weakness. Sydney is every bit as ruthless, cunning, and unforgiving as anyone in the world of *Hard Eight*. Hiding in the shadows, Sydney stares quietly at the door. The audience is invited again to study his blank face and left to wonder if we are any closer to understanding him now than we were in the beginning of the film. Sydney's outward affection for John is complicated by the hidden knowledge of his father's murder; his noble attempts to atone for past sins are complicated by the present recognition that he remains perfectly capable of resorting to the ultimate crime when it serves his purpose; his old-school generosity and excessive politeness throughout are offset by the

1.11. Sydney back in charge, giving an elaborate speech about not dying, which is ultimately a ruse as he secretly plots Jimmy's murder in revenge. Behind him, the fill light imperceptibly dims—a stylistic nod to Jonathan Demme's *Silence of the Lambs*.

fact that he is no less morally suspect than Jimmy. One is quiet and one is loud, but both are opportunistic, shady men who have survived their whole criminal lives as bottom feeders amid the moral ambiguity of casino life. Even his seeming helplessness with Jimmy is complicated by an awareness of the methodical way he plots to get his money back and exact bloody revenge. Sydney is one of Anderson's finest characters—but he's not necessarily an admirable man.

Hard Eight's climax gives the audience another sudden, remarkable burst of the decisive violence Sydney is capable of. When Jimmy arrives with a prostitute (Melora Walters, who also appears in *Boogie Nights* and *Magnolia*), Sydney does not even hesitate to shoot him dead. Gone are the long speeches and drawn-out conversations over cigarettes and coffee in favor of a man who gets right to the point. His execution of Jimmy does not show the slightest attention to clemency, sympathy, or even hesitation. An experienced killer, Sydney simply shoots and then retrieves his money from the body.

Anderson originally wrote the scene so that Sydney gave him two chances to return the money, before finally shooting a defiant Jimmy—but later realized that Sydney would not mess around. The suspense was in the crosscutting earlier, while waiting with Sydney for Jimmy to return home, not in the act of killing itself. Sydney lets the hooker out alive, despite the fact she's a direct witness. The old gambler takes his money, quickly leaves the house, and drives out of Reno. The question of whether he will be caught is left open, but we are given the vague impression that Sydney is probably quite

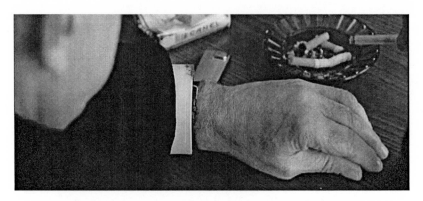

1.12. The end is the beginning. Sydney returns to the same coffee shop where he met John in a nice moment of narrative symmetry. Note Sydney's bloodstained cuff, which he quickly, calmly covers. The character's relationship to his violent past remains ambiguous at best.

experienced and comfortable with going unpunished for such criminal activities.

Hence, the film's remarkably powerful, but all too brief, final moments. In classical narrative form, *Hard Eight* ends at the beginning—Sydney returns to the same roadside coffee shop where he first met John, sits at the booth, drinks coffee and smokes cigarettes. Yet Sydney is now quietly alone, and we have a more direct sense of the immediate and long-term baggage that the character carries with him. However, it's problematic to assume that we "know" Sydney that much better than we did in the beginning—he is still the lonely, ambiguous stranger at a coffee shop, and his behavior throughout the film has consistently contradicted expectations.

Hard Eight ends with Sydney noticing a blood stain on the cuff of his left dress-shirt sleeve, which he quickly covers by pulling his black suit sleeve forward. Harmon noted that, "A darker part of himself, his own history, is dead, but only by virtue of an act which is of a piece with that very past. On one level there is an eradication of evil, on another, the perpetuation of it."[32] In the end, he is an ironic noir antihero, someone who is consistently forced to deal with his troubled past but also someone who never has to pay for the things he's done. This ending is completely different from the more traditionally noirish final scene in Anderson's script, where Sydney is gunned down in revenge by the man that Clementine and John had held hostage in the motel.

However, this less clichéd ending effectively captures the quiet, haunting ambiguity and unshakeable sense of control that emanate from Sydney's character and essentially structure the entire film—while still acknowledging his own history of violence. The efficient manner in which Sydney addresses the sight of his bloody sleeve and then moves on suggests, moreover, that he may not even feel very guilty. In his waning days, the always-calm Sydney is neither redeemed nor punished, only haunted. He is the same mess of contradictions he has always been. And one of the most consistently interesting aspects of Anderson's films over the next decade would be those rich characters, like Sydney, who embody an unresolved jumble of conflicts and idiosyncrasies.

IN RETROSPECT

The new ending was one way in which less is more in Anderson's first film. In hindsight, the shorter version of *Hard Eight* is more powerful, even if the director resisted changes for so long. Though *Hard Eight* lacks *Magnolia*'s thematic scope and ambition or *Boogie Nights*'s historical and metatextual cleverness, it has a quiet narrative drive and accumulative mood that lingers long after the film ends. *Hard Eight* also has a deep commitment to one of Anderson's most iconic characters, Sydney himself. Yet the production of the film also suggests that Anderson was not yet the polished, increasingly self-critical auteur that he would be a decade later. In retrospect, the experience of *Hard Eight* made Anderson a better filmmaker down the road—though not necessarily in the ways one might think. Certainly, he learned more about the craft and intricacies of writing and directing a feature-length film. He also came to believe that studio executives could never be trusted again, though there's little evidence that he ever trusted them in the first place.

A self-fulfilling prophecy, the title change from *Sydney* to *Hard Eight* cemented the idea historically that *Anderson was the auteur* all along, because it solidified the perception that he had somehow been forced unfairly to compromise his artistic vision. Indeed, the shift to the more provocative title was an unnecessary sacrifice. Yet the title change burnished Anderson's credentials as an independent director fighting for "his" film. The battle over *Sydney* would become that core component to his origin story every auteur needs. It proved to be that moment he and his followers could always point to as a means to "prove" his need for absolute control over everything.

ever seen star wars?
people tell me i look like han solo.

For these directors, the "anachronistic" becomes . . . subjected to different aesthetic and narrative strategies, in which reference to "outdated" historical periods and objects invites spectators to engage affectively, though not necessarily uncritically, with history. . . . The poignancy of the irrecoverable gap between past and present—between the 1950s, the 1970s and today, and between childhood and adulthood—becomes the subject of these films.

ELENA GORFINKEL, "THE FUTURE OF ANACHRONISM"[1]

CHAPTER 2

i dreamed i was in a hollywood movie

STARS, HYPERREAL SOUNDS OF THE 1970S,
AND CINEPHILIAC PASTICHE IN *BOOGIE NIGHTS* (1997)

Three temptations emerge when analyzing *Boogie Nights* today. The most suspect is to see the film as the symbolic beginning of Anderson's career—the first auteur film resulting strictly from the stubborn determination of the young director himself. Another is to simply critique the film's lack of historical realism as pertains to representations of Southern California, shifts in media technologies, and the porn industry in the 1970s and 1980s. The final temptation is to see *Boogie Nights* as ultimately a "film about porn." There's quite a bit more beneath the surface of an otherwise straightforward, if also ironic, *A Star is Born*–type epic about a kid with a giant penis who just wants to be a "big, bright, shining [porn] star."

Like *Hard Eight*, *Boogie Nights* is structured around jarringly different sections. Whereas Anderson's first film broke down into three distinct parts, *Boogie Nights* has two halves. The first takes place during the light, celebratory mood of the 1970s and features an effective retro soundtrack, material prosperity, and the endless consumption of sex and drugs without consequence. The 1980s bring the culture of Reagan, videotape's cheap aesthetics, shocking moments of violence, and the inevitable fall from grace for all characters involved, accompanied by a somber musical score that is less

2.1. An image "inside" the camera during one of the film's diegetic porn shots. Beneath the narrative investment in pornography is a deeper fascination with the history of media technologies.

dependent on upbeat recycled pop songs. The movie concludes on a melancholic note, even as almost everyone is happily reunited. The stark tonal split in *Boogie Nights* reflected Anderson's own ambivalence about pornography as well as larger cultural histories of the 1990s.

To get the movie made, Anderson benefitted tremendously from a studio that ignored the rumors about his difficulty on *Hard Eight*, had faith in his talent, and remained admirably open-minded about making such a bleak epic with porn as its primary subject matter. New Line Studios wanted to support an up-and-coming director, and Anderson happened to come along at the right time. Studio executive Mike De Luca was looking for a break after missing out on Quentin Tarantino, Wes Anderson, and others, and the studio was intrigued by the prospects of another hip, pop-song-driven retro film. Like *Pulp Fiction* (1994), *Boogie Nights* had the potential to make profits on soundtrack sales alone. Thus, the ultimate decision to brand Paul Thomas Anderson as "the next Tarantino" was not an aesthetic evaluation. Anderson's short tenure at New Line with *Boogie Nights* and *Magnolia* (1999) was part of a conscious business strategy to break into a particular niche of the art film marketplace, which promised potentially huge box office returns on a product that cost little money up front. It didn't necessarily matter to New Line how talented or determined Anderson was. Without Tarantino, De Luca, and New Line, *Boogie Nights* might never have been made.

Beyond textual and historical negotiations with the limited genre of pornography, *Boogie Nights*'s relationship to cinema in the wider sense is better understood critically as a work of cinephilia—a love of film's material and symbolic ephemerality, of its pastiche relationship to history, of the ways in which it mediates human relationships, and a love for the very tangible materiality of the medium itself. At the core of cinephilia is often, paradoxically, an anxiety over technological change—expressions of cinephilia are habitually most intense when a newer medium (television, video, digital media, and so forth) emerges to threaten the older medium of film. Yet such simplistic narratives inevitably work to affirm the resilience of film. *Boogie Nights*'s idealized representation of media history presents the utopic era of 1970s cinema as an art form and exhibition practice that narratively gives way to the cheaper, less artistic 1980s era of videotape. In this regard, those who criticize the movie's (mis) understanding of history, media transitions, or pornography aren't necessarily wrong, as it's a remarkably erratic and superficial film upon close scrutiny. For all its technical craft, *Boogie Nights* doesn't quite make any thematic or narrative sense unless we see it as a generational allegory reflecting Anderson's media-saturated childhood.

As an overtly cinephiliac film, *Boogie Nights*'s self-reflexive strengths are also its biggest weaknesses. Technically accomplished, it often feels like a superficial film school experiment, showing off all the flashy movie references and camera and editing tricks it knows. *Boogie Nights* depends upon extensive long takes and Steadicam shots until they are practically clichéd, while also throwing in clever editing devices like the iris circle and elaborate split-screen montages, all of which scream a thin kind of youthful swagger. An effect like dropping the camera into the pool and back out again may be attention-grabbing (while also showing off knowledge of the little-seen *I am Cuba* [1964]), but the trick also perfectly exemplifies the film's cinephiliac hollowness.

Structurally, *Boogie Nights* is clever, but one-note—taking the standard arc of the formulaic biopic (rising, falling, and rising again) and giving it an ironic twist. Much of the film's winking humor—just add porn—is already built into the story a priori. Meanwhile, by setting *Boogie Nights* in the 1970s and 1980s, the film is able to appeal to nostalgia and a preexisting set of historical film conventions through the use of an informed soundtrack. For all its flair, the film never transcends this prebuilt structure. While *Boogie Nights* clearly has a great deal of affection for its wealth of characters, Eddie Adams (Mark Wahlberg) is a problematic lead. The fact that he has no personality or attractive attributes other than a large penis makes him an amusingly ironic subject. But that emptiness also makes him wholly unengaging as the empathetic focus for such a long epic, while other more interesting characters are underdeveloped and/or secondary. The product of a certain cinephiliac self-glorification, *Boogie Nights* is, as Ryan Gilbey aptly noted in 2003, a "movie movie," one "driven more by technical prowess than life."[2] On many technical, narrative, and historical levels, the film is all show.

More sympathetically, *Boogie Nights*'s self-aware logic is best defined as "cinephiliac pastiche"—its love of the film medium, its belief in the artistic superiority of film over the cheaper and more degraded video, its fascination with history as seen through cinematic representations of the past, and its perception of history as less a coherent chronological narrative than a visualized soundtrack. To understand *Boogie Nights*, one must appreciate how the film works through a deeply affective logic that reflects Anderson's own experience of the nostalgic impulses generated by his cinephiliac childhood.

All of *Boogie Nights*'s potential faults—its idiosyncratic understanding of media histories in America during the 1970s and 1980s, its insistence on seeing pop songs as synonymous with historical referents, its obsession with the pleasures and guilt of porn, its irrational disintegration of the (suburban) nuclear family, coupled with the utopian belief in the filmmaking community as surrogate family (though ironically some within the porn industry criticized it for presenting people in the business as criminally minded and socially ill-adjusted), its overtly nostalgic affection in general for the decade in which Anderson was born, along with the more complicated ambivalence toward the subsequent decade of his teen years—makes the internal textual logic of *Boogie Nights* completely incomprehensible without reading it symbolically as an allegory for Anderson's own cinephiliac life to that point.

But *Boogie Nights* is not simply autobiographical—its emphasis on the politics of the personal reveals larger questions about the decade in which it was made. As Elena Gorfinkel argued in relation to both *Boogie Nights* and *Magnolia*, "Anderson utilizes anachronistic forms and themes in order to renegotiate a relationship to his audience—forcing the 1990s viewer to reconsider their own historical positioning in relation to film history and popular cultural memory."[3] *Boogie Nights* doesn't simply allude to the past, Gorfinkel noted—it creates a cinephiliac relationship to the 1970s that uses a "film historical imaginary"[4] to transcend mere homage and instead celebrate the jarring gap between past and present. Earlier cinephile directors (such as Steven Spielberg and Martin Scorsese) recycled past cinematic images, alluding to the work of Orson Welles, John Ford, and others. Anderson is interested in a cinematic vision of the past that keeps the viewer constantly focused on cinematic representations of history that are defined as the surfaces, and not the depths, of history.

Structuring the film, finally, is a persistent focus on emergent forms of celebrity. *Boogie Nights* evokes issues of stardom on at least three levels: its narrative meditation on the nature of celebrity (as embodied in the emergence of "Dirk Diggler"); its playful meta-negotiations with the larger star persona of lead actor Mark Wahlberg; and, finally, Anderson's own role as the hot new director to watch on the heels of *Hard Eight*. Dirk's premature rise to fame in the first half of *Boogie Nights* unintentionally mirrors Anderson's at this point in his career. His emergence reflected the circumstances of the film's production, since Anderson was able to make the film he wanted because of New Line's interest in supporting a hot young director, just as Miramax had with Tarantino. Ultimately, though, *Boogie Nights* would not match the success of *Pulp Fiction* commercially or critically. *Boogie Nights* would be a much bigger hit on home video, including VHS, Laserdisc, and the emergent new platform of the digital video disc (DVD). The comparison to *Pulp Fiction* may have been inaccurate and unfair, but the immense industrial shadow of Tarantino was paradoxically needed to get Anderson's film made in the first place.

THE DIRK DIGGLER STORY

For all its stylistic innovations, character affection, and historical ambition, *Boogie Nights* still begins and ends with pornography and Anderson's own nostalgic relationship to it. "I always thought," he said, "the subtitle for *Boogie Nights* should be, 'it's all fun and games until someone gets hurt.'"[5] Like most adolescent boys, the young Anderson was obsessed with porn. He would comb through his father's rather extensive collection, which included the first one he claimed to ever see, *The Opening of Misty Beethoven* (1976). "My dad had an early VCR, and he had [*Beethoven*] on videocassette," recalled Anderson, "and I snuck it when I was nine or ten. I didn't really watch it, though. I only watched it for a moment or two before I got freaked out."[6] In time, Anderson's exposure to porn films increased to the point that he had his own personal favorites, such as *The Jade Pussycat* (1977), *3AM* (1975), and *Amanda By Night* (1981), which was "really well-done, and it's got a little murder-mystery element to it, which is always good in porn."[7]

Aspects of porn were everywhere in Anderson's life. During his childhood, local porn shoots down the street were the open neighborhood secret. "In general porn movie productions were a part of the landscape in the Valley," wrote Sharon Waxman; "all the kids in the neighborhood knew that the white van that pulled up to a house down the street was shooting porn."[8] Later, when Anderson was working at Sundance, he raided Robert Redford's personal stash of movies, including porn, screening them with friends late at night. One such title included a woman on roller skates (the inspiration for Rollergirl [Heather Graham]) who, according to Anderson, would "go from house to house, look in and watch these people fucking. One of my strongest memories [at Sundance] is just us howling with laughter—and probably getting a little horny—watching this porn film."[9]

For a high school project when he was eighteen, Anderson wrote and directed *The Dirk Diggler Story*, which would inspire *Boogie Nights*. *Dirk* was far from the only film the ambitious teenager made with friends, but thanks largely to *Boogie Nights* it's now his most famous. Shot in mockumentary style on videotape, *Dirk* featured the title character (Michael Stein), Reed Rothchild (Eddie Delcore), and Jack Horner (Bob Ridgely, who would play the Colonel in *Boogie Nights*). The relatively tame movie consists of interviews with characters and scenes videotaped "on location" during a motel-room porn shoot. A few scenes are similar to *Boogie Nights*, such as Dirk recording "You've Got the Touch" in studio, and he and Horner having a fight while Dirk is amped up on cocaine.

Yet the film feels very different than *Boogie Nights*, despite the similar subject matter, ironic tone, and affectionate attitude toward its characters. *Boogie Nights* ditched the mockumentary format for a more traditional narrative arc and much darker tone. Beyond the jarring VHS look, there are more substantive differences. In *Dirk*, Dirk is a massive bodybuilder who can't get his lines right, let alone act, and is barely coherent as a speaker. For another, Dirk dies at the end of the film from a coke overdose, and the whole documentary is presented as a memorial to his life. Unlike John C. Reilly's character in *Boogie Nights*, meanwhile, Reed is Dirk's gay lover—on and off-screen, which gives the tragic ending greater poignancy. In fact, a whole section of the half-hour film is dedicated to Dirk's bisexual and gay porn period. This is conspicuously absent in *Boogie Nights*, which has more than a few homophobic overtones. Finally, the modern setting of *The Dirk Diggler Story* isn't interested in disco or narratives of video's ascendancy.

More than *Dirk*, *Boogie Nights* would reflect Anderson's own personal ambivalence towards porn. "I love pornography," he said in 1999, "just as much as it completely disgusts me and completely depresses me."[10] This contradiction isn't reflected in the early amateur film. Despite its tragic ending, *Dirk* maintains a consistently lighter tone and avoids the dark turns of the second half of *Boogie Nights*. Anderson believed later that partly why *Boogie Nights* wasn't more commercially successful was because, unlike *Dirk*, it was more serious and judgmental about porn than audiences could handle. "The first half of the movie is all fun and games," he admitted in an observation that would be reflected later by critics, "but the back-half of the movie is a sort of punishment for those fun and games. It's my own guilty feelings about pornography."[11] Despite the playful embrace of porn Anderson expressed in interviews, he ultimately made a film that condemned much of that life.

THE NEW LINE TO *BOOGIE NIGHTS*

Anderson's obsession with porn certainly wasn't enough to get *Boogie Nights* made. How it came to be is as illuminating as the more notorious production history underlying *Hard Eight*. In *The Sundance Kids*, James Mottram perpetuates the common myth that Anderson's increased creative independence on *Boogie Nights* was simply the result of the young director's resolve on the heels of a traumatic experience with Rysher. "Anderson was not about to let the same thing happen again . . . ," he writes. *Boogie Nights* "starts with the camera squarely focused on the title, glimpsed as a neon-lit sign adorning a Van Nuys Boulevard theatre. The message from Anderson was clear: hands off my title, hands off my film."[12] Mottram reiterates Anderson's sense of having been wronged by others, a belief the director insisted upon in numerous interviews throughout the 1990s. "I wrote my first two movies fuelled by a desire for revenge on all the people who told me I'd never amount to anything, and those movies came from a place of 'I'll show you,'" Anderson told *Creative Screenwriting* in 1997.[13]

It's a seductively common romanticization of the unappreciated artist driven to prove that he's deserving of greater respect—one that followers such as Mottram further highlighted.[14] Yet such self-righteous feelings of victimization are historically suspect and inevitably obscure the other numerous contexts involved in Anderson's gradual rise to auteur status within the industry. They also leave in their wake more questions about what really happened than they answer. Not everyone was sold on Anderson, for example. Famed *New Republic* critic Stanley Kauffmann wrote that *Hard Eight* "was one of those strained independent films whose threadbare central idea wears out very soon," and suggested, in retrospect, that *Boogie Nights*'s quality was due to an increased budget and crew.[15] Even with the typical narrative of Anderson as the rising star generally trending his way, the young director's emergence benefitted tremendously from other factors beyond his control.

Still, Anderson's growing *reputation* was undeniable. Before *Hard Eight* even debuted in late 1996, Anderson and his agent, John Lesher, hoped to utilize the positive critical buzz to get his next script quickly into production. With the aura around *Hard Eight* receiving more circulation than the film itself, Anderson's own emergent status as a "star" name was crucial to getting *Boogie Nights* made. Despite *Hard Eight*'s relatively small theatrical circulation, the film was still well received in the festival circles that, in the long run, would matter most. Ultimately, *Hard Eight* was Rysher's lowest-grossing film in the course of its brief existence.[16] Yet the critical visibility had served its purpose, particularly at a time when being the "next big thing" out of Sundance was just as attractive to Hollywood as being a proven talent. With one promising film now under his belt, Anderson successfully positioned himself for greater creative control over his next project.

Yet, as previewed above, the story of *Boogie Nights*'s production history didn't begin with Anderson—it started with Tarantino, Miramax, and an ambitious New Line studio executive, De Luca. In the early 1990s, Tarantino debuted *Reservoir Dogs* at Sundance, supplanting Soderbergh as the hot up-and-coming film director that everyone wanted to work with. Miramax, meanwhile, was successfully building an empire by acquiring film properties through the festival circuit. In addition to distributing Soderbergh's *Sex, Lies, and Videotape* (1989), its big coup was securing a partnership with Tarantino. By supporting his artistic vision, they formed a relationship that paid off a couple of years later with the critical and commercial success of *Pulp Fiction* (1994). The film made money despite its little production cost; won awards everywhere it went; resonated deeply with a new generation of cinephiles; ushered in a new (mercifully short-lived) subgenre of flashy, soundtrack-driven crime films featuring hip, self-reflexive killers; and, along with *Reservoir Dogs*, established a distinct new auteur brand in Tarantino himself. *Pulp Fiction* dramatically altered the quasi-independent American film scene, while the Miramax-Tarantino partnership affected how smaller production companies imagined future business models.

One such visionary then was New Line's De Luca, who was interested in forming that kind of business relationship with another director coming out of Sundance. The executive, writes Waxman, "quietly noted a reemergence of the writer-director, a departure from the director-for-hire system that reigned on most Hollywood films."[17] He imagined a new era of American cinema around embracing and commodifying the auteur. Waxman adds:

De Luca didn't tell his superiors that he was quietly nurturing a dream of building a stable of visionary filmmakers who would make New Line the address of young, hip talent, like Paramount had become in the 1970s when Robert Evans smoothed the path for Francis Ford Coppola, Peter Bogdanovich, and others.

De Luca was also looking to make amends, having specifically passed on *Pulp Fiction* when he had the chance. He also lost out on the likes of Spike Jonze and Wes Anderson—New Line rejected the pitch for what would eventually become *Rushmore* (1998). Meanwhile, everyone else at the studio focused on how *Pulp Fiction* proved to be "a $100 million hit out of a film that had cost less than one-tenth that amount; that was a formula that New Line liked."[18] Thus, Anderson would find an unusually welcoming environment at New Line.

Anderson's script for *Boogie Nights* presented New Line and De Luca with a chance to emulate the Miramax trend. The story was original, hip, and soundtrack-driven; moreover, Anderson's first film was similar in promise to *Reservoir Dogs*—a small-scale, neo-noir crime film that had been a hit on the festival circuit. Although New Line itself was ambivalent about the project, De Luca was determined to create the kind of creative environment that Anderson and hopefully other directors would find attractive. Moreover, the failure of New Line to support De Luca's interest in *Rushmore* played a part in giving him the opening to push through any project he wanted. "This time," notes Waxman, "New Line owed De Luca his shot,"[19] which he decided to use on Anderson.

Anderson had a much different experience with the shooting and editing of *Boogie Nights* than he'd had with *Hard Eight*, one he'd be hard-pressed to complain about. Anderson had had more experience on set, dealing with the many people involved in front of and behind the camera. He was also working from a more polished, if still bloated, script that he'd spent more time (two months) structuring, writing, and revising than the three weeks he'd had to compose *Sydney*'s more stream-of-conscious first draft. Anderson originally pitched *Boogie Nights* as a "four-hour movie with a disco intermission,"[20] which would be a disastrous description 99 percent of the time. But Anderson had a studio that largely supported the type and scale of movie he had wanted rather than expecting it to fit a preexisting genre formula, as Rysher had on *Hard Eight*.

Nevertheless, Anderson still didn't feel the studio was all that supportive. "There were a few people within New Line who didn't think *Boogie Nights* was a great movie," he said later.[21] Indeed, there remained specific limitations to his agreement with the studio. Part of the fallout from *Hard Eight*'s troubled production was that others, such as studio head Bob Shaye, worried Anderson was difficult to deal with. "He's very talented," one unnamed *Hard Eight* producer told Shaye at Sundance in 1995, "and very hard to work with."[22] While De Luca was supportive, others were skeptical. The script itself ran 185 pages, and even the accommodating De Luca promised higher-ups—as John Lyons had on *Hard Eight*—that Anderson would eventually trim it. Anderson had to promise that *Boogie Nights* wouldn't run over three hours, wouldn't receive an NC-17 rating, and wouldn't go over the $15 million budget. Those were pretty generous terms for a second-time director with a tricky personal reputation who was making an often-dark epic about the porn industry.

New Line was admirably lenient in terms of allowing him to make the kind of large-scale, character-driven epic he'd tried to make with *Sydney*. The changes the studio initially pushed for were minimal. He still didn't yet have final cut on *Boogie Nights*, which was probably the heart of the matter. Even Anderson admitted later that the main reason New Line asked for changes wasn't because they were unhappy with his first cut, but because test audiences hated it:

When I showed *Boogie Nights* to the studio the first time, they came out and hugged me and shook my hand and said, 'This is the greatest movie we've ever made at New Line' . . . Then when we went and tested the movie, and when the movie did not test well (because there's no way in hell a movie like that is going to test well), they got cold feet and were real confused about their own opinions.[23]

There was the unspoken possibility that people were afraid to admit they liked a porn movie, but more often *Boogie Nights*'s dark, violent second half was what hurt it with audiences. However, Anderson argued that "he had to show the repercussions of a life in the porn industry, that if he portrayed only the warm, supportive, side of porn stars, the movie would have no emotional underpinning. It would not be honest."[24] New Line felt, in contrast, that *Boogie Nights* was a good but quite possibly unmarketable, film. De Luca tried to remain calm, negotiating Anderson's perpetually bruised ego with New Line's increasing panic—"You can't trust the test numbers," he said; "I know it's a good movie. Keep working."[25] Then positive critical buzz began to build, starting with the profuse praise of *Newsweek*'s David Ansen, who previewed an early screening. Others at New Line slowly came back onboard, but with the expectation that *Boogie Nights* would in turn approach the type of critical and commercial hit that *Pulp Fiction* became.

THE SOUNDTRACK FILM

Like *Pulp Fiction*, *Boogie Nights* was sold as both an auteur film and a soundtrack movie—a film that told its story through the recycling of popular music. This take provided the narrative with a particular kind of historical referent as well as potentially lucrative forms of additional revenue. One of the main reasons why *Boogie Nights* found a receptive audience at New Line, even among those who resisted the subject, was because many in the studio believed the film's appeal would be its 1970s pastiche and retro soundtrack. Specifically, head of marketing at New Line Mitch Goldman supported *Boogie Nights* early on: "I thought that with a great music track, the era of the seventies, I could sell it that way, as a worst case scenario."[26] When Anderson's film was made, the nostalgic (financial) appeal of the soundtrack for any historical film set between the 1950s and 1980s was a big incentive to get such films made, providing studios with an excuse to repackage existing music. The ideal hope would be that the film and soundtrack enjoyed mutually beneficial financial success within their respective marketplaces.

The economic logic of the retro soundtrack pervaded most every type of Hollywood film—its distribution and production—

2.2. In addition to its nostalgic image of the 1970s as a time of disco and free love, *Boogie Nights*'s appeal to New Line was in its incorporation of a retro soundtrack.

by the late 1990s. Estella Tincknell argued that, by the last decade of the millennium, the soundtrack movie had essentially replaced the modern Hollywood musical of the 1950s and 1960s. "In place of (and sometimes as well as) the diegetically produced and visibly *performed* numbers of the traditional musical," Tincknell writes, "the cinema audience now increasingly encounters a film soundtrack composed of discrete and previously released pop songs."[27] Audiences still wanted popular music in the film, but rather than have characters break into song, the music is relegated to the space of the soundtrack.

Moreover, the use of existing pop music often went hand in hand with representations of the same period that those songs affectively evoked. Kelly Ritter highlighted a range of nostalgia films from the late 1990s that depended upon older songs to foreground the viewer's own memories of the past—*Romy and Michelle's High School Reunion* (1997), *The Wedding Singer* (1998), *54* (1998), *The Last Days of Disco* (1998), and so forth. Colin Tait added that numerous 1990s films "obsess over and imitate distinctly 1970s film style, iconography and content." These obsessions could be localized in particular on what he terms the film's obligatory "70s Sequence," a montage of cinematic pastiche that "is essentially a music video [set] to a 70s song."[28]

For Ritter, some of these films, such as *Boogie Nights*, transcended the simple reuse of pop songs for commercial purposes and embraced the ways songs could be used to create historical meaning. *Boogie Nights* was a musical, she argued, "that not only privileges sound over image, but one that discounts locating all participation in the image, instead locating those identical impulses in sound."[29] What makes Anderson's film distinctive is that the use of music creates an affective bond with a mainstream audience that would otherwise resist identification with the porn-related subject matter depicted visually on screen. *Boogie Nights*, she writes,

evokes a popular response from viewers in relation to its soundtrack, while simultaneously pulling its viewers in *only* through this soundtrack, as the images presented are neither utopian, desirable, nor even *familiar* to the viewer as images per se.[30]

Audiences can immerse themselves in *Boogie Nights*'s diegetic world through the familiarity of its soundtrack rather than visualize themselves in a world full of pornographers, criminals, and drug addicts. Still, the divide between sound and image is complicated. The songs selected invite an affective relationship with the historical periods represented, but they also serve specific narrative functions in the film.

Pop music in *Boogie Nights* conveys both historical referents and thematic meaning in often-astute ways. When Dirk first arrives at Horner's house, in a nice match cut with the closing of his mom's (Joanna Gleason) door, we hear Three Dog Night's "Mama Told Me Not to Come." Later, Andrew Gold's "Lonely Boy" accompanies the failed attempts by Maggie's son (Maggie is Amber Waves's [Julianne Moore] real name; the boy is also called "Andy") to reach her on the phone—while the song extends to a sequence of her watching Dirk on the diving board, symbolically suggesting that he is now her (surrogate) son. Meanwhile, Floyd Gondolli's (Philip Baker Hall) introduction is complemented by Sniff 'n' the Tears' "Driver's Seat," subtly calling attention to Gondolli's immense power as a movie producer, symbolically in the driver's seat. Being anxiously greeted by the usually cool Colonel (Bob Ridgley) indicates his considerable importance, as he will later be the central force in the industry shift to video.

As another example, the remarkably staged botched robbery at Rahad Jackson's (Alfred Molina) house in the end is paced as a musical with three songs (Nena's "99 Luftballons," Night Ranger's "Sister Christian," and Rick Springfield's "Jessie's Girl"), which Rahad sings along to while his partner, Cosmo (Joe G. M. Chan), sets off firecrackers in the background. The songs form part of both the diegetic narrative and the three acts within the scene. As a story

2.3. Diggler finds a loving surrogate family in Jack Horner's porn company, which is explicitly highlighted by a shot of Jack's opening door . . .

2.4. . . . matched graphically to the preceding shot of Dirk's mom shutting the door on him.

2.5. Floyd Gondolli's dramatic entrance—filled with overlaps, jump cuts, and dissolves—set to Sniff 'n' Tears' "Driver's Seat." Representing the (financial) future of videotape's role in porn production, he is, as the Colonel's anxious introduction shows, the most powerful man at the party.

about a woman growing up too fast, "Sister Christian" becomes re-appropriated as a meditation on the depths to which the once naïve and polite Dirk has sunk: "There's so much in life / Don't you give it up." Meanwhile, Springfield's line, "there doesn't seem to be a reason to change," plays over the extended take of Dirk, in a moment of apparent self-reflection that leads to him turning his life around, while the longing in "Jessie's Girl" suggests Todd's (Thomas Jane) desire for Rahad's materialistic life, which motivated the robbery in the first place. Finally, the original German version of "99 Luftballons," about how a fictional misunderstanding at the Berlin Wall set off a spectacular war between the United States and the Soviet Union (a quintessential 1980s context), begins after the sequence descends into chaos and violence.

As the retro-nostalgic content foregrounds, *Boogie Nights* uses recycled pop tunes to create a historical index for its audience. Yet such music-as-history reinforces depoliticized representations of the past, where utopian sounds of nostalgia suggest the idealized version of history for which *Boogie Nights* is often criticized. By seeing the idyllic 1970s as prefeminist and pre-AIDS, Tincknell argues, "phallic masculinity can be celebrated rather than problematized."[31] Tincknell adds

In its use of musical quotation and pastiche, in its knowingness about textuality and the relationship between texts, and above all, in its restructuring of the past at the level of style, I would add that the soundtrack film's nostalgia may be read as close to instant—and depoliticized—history.[32]

Boogie Nights creates an affective feel for the 1970s by "deploy[ing] the music of The Commodores, The Emotions, Marvin Gaye and other soul-inflected performers to emphasise a very particular reading of 'the seventies' in which the disco becomes the site of a kind of innocent excess."[33] Much of the film's sense of the 1970s is rooted in a *cinematic vision of the 1970s*—embodied by films such as *Saturday Night Fever* (1977), referenced in a disco dancing montage in the middle of the film. But this problematic idea throughout *Boogie Nights* of media-history-as-history demands closer attention.

NOSTALGIA FOR A PERIOD THAT NEVER EXISTED

Boogie Nights "isn't about LA in the 1970s any more than *LA Confidential* is about LA in the 1950s," wrote Thomas Doherty in a review; "the film is about the appropriation of a style and the evocation of a

Sunday, December 11th, 1983

2.6. The cheap, degraded aesthetics of videotape serve as a metaphor for the ugly turn of events that befalls Jack Horner and company in the 1980s.

mood, the adoption of music, clothes, habits, and the ethos of a different time, an exercise in the creation of a useful cinematic, as opposed to historical, past."[34] But rather than focus on accuracy, we see that *Boogie Nights* evokes and perpetuates a larger historical imaginary constructed through popular film—i.e., the idyllic 1970s now resemble the blissful disco dancing of *Saturday Night Fever* while the 1980s turn out more like the bloody, coked-out finale of Brian De Palma's *Scarface* (1983). *Boogie Nights* works as a form of postmodern cinephiliac pastiche—the film sees the past less as a documentable, verifiable series of historical events and more as a loose, largely apolitical, hyperreal collage of sights and sounds meant to evoke an affective sense of (cinematic) history.

In *Boogie Nights*, history is defined by, and inseparable from, the medium of film. Not only does the movie reference other films (*Saturday Night Fever, Scarface, Star Wars, Blazing Saddles, Nashville,* and so forth), it also internalizes other audiovisual media within the movie itself to create a similar effect. The split-screen montage of Dirk's rise to fame, accompanied by the Commodores' "Machine Gun," was based on a trailer for the John Holmes film *Eruption* (1977). The pornographic movie scenes and Amber Waves's loving documentary tribute to Dirk Diggler are shot and presented in their original 16mm format. Meanwhile, the film's ugliest sequence—Dirk's homophobic beating and Jack (Burt Reynolds) and Rollergirl's ill-conceived *On the Lookout* project (based on a similar real-life series called *On the Prowl*)—features ugly video footage, reflecting its perception of the degraded artistic and cultural landscape of the 1980s.

2.7. Gondolli's meeting with Jack during the New Year's Eve party foregrounds
Boogie Nights's thematic tension between the polished artistry of film and the
amateurish convenience of video, as well as the idyllic 1970s and the darker 1980s.

More broadly, history becomes thematized as a battle between
film and video. In the New Year's scene that pits one decade against
the other, Jack and Floyd Gondolli symbolically argue over the historical role of video in pornography production and distribution.
The visionary producer explicitly posits the new medium as "the future" and film is seen as an outdated relic from the past. Jack's nostalgia for film echoes *Boogie Nights*'s nostalgia for the 1970s, while
the artistry of film, which he so passionately defends, mirrors the
blissful, simple pleasures of the passing decade. Whether or not
there's any historical truth to *Boogie Nights*'s perception of media
history (and of film's perception of history) is lost amid the nostalgic symbolism.

Elena Gorfinkel has argued that what Anderson's film negotiates
is neither the 1970s as pastiche nor the 1990s fascination with the
past but rather the historical gap between the two. An anachronism
exists within the space between the film's historical setting and the
"present" day in which the film was made. "The visibility of anachronism" is used, she writes, "as a means of highlighting the pathos of
historical difference."[35] Audiences engage with the unavoidable divide between past and present on an affective level—the sights and
sounds of *Boogie Nights*, she suggests, self-reflexively engage people
in the historical anachronism itself. In a sense, the film is meant
to *feel always already out-of-date.* "In *Boogie Nights*," writes Gorfinkel, "anachronism, obsolescence, and failure get thematized in the
emergence of video, and the extinction of porn on film."[36] By the

late 1970s, the dream of narrative-driven porn (e.g., *Deep Throat* [1972]) had already passed, and what Anderson does instead is conflate that early moment in porn with the disco scene later in the 1970s.

Much of *Boogie Nights*'s appeal was rooted in the ways it negotiated a collective nostalgia for the 1970s. Anderson himself was born in the first year of the decade and no doubt saw the era at least partially through the inherent idealization of childhood. Yet Robert Sickels noted a larger late 1990s trend of cinematic nostalgia for the 1970s, to which the soundtrack films also spoke. At that time, he wrote

the 1970s are enjoying a public reevaluation that often overlooks things such as the horrors of Vietnam, Watergate, the failure of the E.R.A., and the selfishness inherent to a decade labeled 'the ME generation.' Instead we choose to revel in the tackiness of the clothes . . . bask in the sheer cathartic joy at the root of Disco . . . and revere the apparent freedoms of the sexual revolution.[37]

Sickels and Tom Simmons, respectively, have argued that *Boogie Nights*'s implicit political commentary was located in its negotiation of the 1980s. For Simmons, the subculture of pornography works against the dominant ideologies of Reaganism, and thus the characters are punished for their deviation from the cultural norms. Sickels argues that the historical transition from film to video in *Boogie Nights* serves as "a metaphor for a fundamental shift in the values of American culture at large"[38] in the conservative 1980s.

Simmons argues that Eddie suffers for his selflessness in an individualistic society, "pitted against his culture's notion of self. Against the 'every man for himself' mentality of post-Vietnam America, he gladly contributes what he has to the greater good . . . he is always polite and courteous, demonstrating a practiced graciousness."[39] When *Boogie Nights*'s narrative reaches the 1980s, argued Sickels, Diggler is immersed "into unfounded self-importance and rampant coke use [and] he begins his slide into self-destruction."[40] *Boogie Nights*'s presentation of the 1970s emerges as

every conservative politician's worst nightmare. Rather than presenting the porn industry as exploitative and tawdry, [Anderson] presents it as a world populated with people with perhaps more than their fair share of problems who still manage to peacefully coexist in an alternative version of the traditional nuclear family.[41]

One of the most surprising aspects of the film for critics was how generally sweet-natured the presentation was of the surrogate porn family that takes Eddie in not once, but twice. Yet this too seems ultimately rooted in a certain kind of cinephiliac history—the idea that the love of the filmmaking process (regardless of genre) will bring and keep a "family" together. Ultimately, these two versions of the traditional nuclear family—both Reagan's conservative 1950s illusion and Anderson's more liberal 1970s pastiche—are equally cinephiliac. Both nostalgic utopias appeal to the imagined simplicity of past eras as they were mediated through film (and television). What redeems the 1980s in *Boogie Nights* is that porn filmmakers still remain and keep working, even if the medium of film doesn't.

PORN CHIC

When the film was released in 1997, *Boogie Nights* spoke to a renewed cultural interest in pornography. Sickels noted *Boogie Nights*'s status as another film that reflected the 1990s rebirth of "porn chic,"[42] a trend where mainstream audiences take porn more seriously, or at least more publicly, as a topic for discussion. The U.S. obsession with porn then was not dissimilar from *Boogie Nights*'s romanticized vision of porn's theatrical popularity in the prevideo era of the 1970s. Just as Anderson's film simplifies the historical narrative of film versus video, the reemergence of porn chic was a complicated one. Not merely a reflection of America's (endless) interest in sex, the return of this moment was also rooted in a range of events involving U.S. President Bill Clinton, technological changes in media delivery, ratings controversies over sexually explicit films, and a general cinematic romanticizing of the 1970s as a moment of greater sexual freedom. They were all factors that *Boogie Nights* in some way responded to.

At the time, *Boogie Nights* was often compared to Milos Forman's First Amendment polemic, *The People Vs. Larry Flynt* (1996), a film about *Hustler* magazine's fight against censorship. The connection was twofold: both films were period pieces largely set in the 1970s and 1980s that negotiated the questions of porn's cultural role and aesthetic representation. They also won over progressive critics, but otherwise generally struggled to find a commercial audience despite the provocative subject matter. With both films, the debate was complicated—did the film show enough sex, or too much, for a mainstream audience? And did people even want to go out in public to see a film about porn?

2.8. *Boogie Nights*'s nostalgia for the 1970s is also for an imagined moment in the history of porn's exhibition when those types of films were part of a mainstream theatrical experience (the movie conflates early 1970s porn chic with late 1970s disco).

On one hand, explicit discussions of sex were a big topic in the American media during the late 1990s, starting primarily with the sex scandal surrounding President Clinton. In late 1997 and early 1998, rumors began to circulate that Clinton had had an extramarital affair with one of his interns, Monica Lewinsky. When initially asked about this relationship under oath, Clinton lied and infamously said that he had "not had sexual relations with that woman." As a result of this, conservative members of Congress, still smarting from having failed to beat the slippery, charismatic Democrat at the ballot box, attempted to impeach Clinton for the crime of lying under oath—a drama that played out on the nightly news coverage for a whole year. A very explicit account of the degree to which Clinton and Lewinsky engaged in sexual activity was the heart of the news coverage, including many lurid details. Rather than tastefully negotiate around the ugly details, the media generally embraced the opportunity to boost ratings by engaging in a sustained conversation about Clinton's penis.

The connection between the Clinton scandal, a crisis in masculinity, and the exposure of Diggler's penis in *Boogie Nights* was explicitly drawn by Loren Glass in an essay for *American Imago*. In "After the Phallus," Glass highlighted the recent obsession with explicit references to the penis in film and television during the late 1990s, after decades of more implicit appeals to phallic power. The exposure of the male reproductive organ in films such as *There's Something About Mary* (1998), seemingly endless fascinations with male masturbation in *American Beauty* (1999), *Election* (1999), and *Amer-*

ican Pie (1999), and even direct references to the penis on network television programs such as *Seinfeld* suggested a new moment in American popular culture. "It seems undeniable," he argued, "that this preoccupation, so often cloaked in goofball humor and satirical savvy, must indicate some larger shift in the protocols of American masculinity and patriarchal authority."[43] The crisis of masculine authority, according to Glass, was directly reflected in the extensive coverage of Clinton's member. In particular, he argued, "all this attention to the President's penis reveals that the patriarchy is in trouble, that traditional discourses of masculine symbolic authority are disintegrating."[44] Such an observation about the status of patriarchy in 1990s America becomes particularly intriguing when considering how pervasive (especially with *Magnolia* two years later) a crisis in masculinity remained in Anderson's films.

The obsession with the penis and issues in masculinity, as Glass noted, wasn't restricted to *Boogie Nights*. Two other 1997 movies, *The Full Monty* and *GI Jane*, were similarly obsessed with the penis—inarguably, the most infamous image in Anderson's film. These three movies "represent cultural anxieties about where versions of masculinity are headed; about what is sex, and what is gender; and about cultural representations of the male body."[45] Yet *Boogie Nights*'s explicit display of the penis becomes symbolic of a larger cinematic attempt to reclaim masculinity from that anxiety rather than show it in a state of crisis. In a 1999 article, Judi Addelston argued that men "who used to be in the center, despite their valued physical and social identities, may suddenly find themselves displaced to the margins. . . . [They] must publicly show their penis (real or metaphorical) in order to either achieve or reify masculinity."[46] *Boogie Nights*'s emphasis on masculinity as first marginalized and then reclaimed through the character of Diggler coincided with the growth of men's studies, a sign of white masculinity's perceived relationship to trends in feminism and multiculturalism at the end of the millennium.

Sex has always remained a controversial topic in American film production and distribution practices; however, it was given added visibility in this particular decade by the infamous change in Hollywood's rating system for identifying the sexual and violent content in films. The Motion Picture Association of America introduced the NC-17 rating in 1990 as a substitute for X to identify films with explicit material, which was more often used to highlight sex than violence. However, this attempt to deflect the cultural stigma of the X only created more controversy than it avoided—countless films, including *Boogie Nights*, were still trimmed to avoid the rating. Originally, Anderson wanted an NC-17 rating for the movie—perhaps the single biggest concession he ultimately made to New Line. Before presenting to the ratings board, Anderson deliberately put more sexually explicit images in the film than he wanted, just so he'd have room to negotiate down to an R rating. Showing the penis, in particular, was nearly a guarantee of an NC-17 rating then, as Richard Rush's *The Color of Night* discovered in 1994—for all the explicit sexual scenes, it was star Bruce Willis's member that generated the most attention. By the mid-1990s, some films even attempted to exploit the rating for ticket sales, such as David Cronenberg's *Crash* (1996) and Paul Verhoven's *Showgirls* (1995), but without any luck. Still others, such as Larry Clark's controversial *Kids* (1995) and the necrophiliac *Kissed* (1996), were at least initially released in some markets without any rating at all to avoid the stigma of the otherwise inevitable NC-17. Yet not a single one of these films saw much theatrical success.

However, *Showgirls* and *The Color of Night* turned out to be big hits once they hit the home video market—either out of audience titillation, ironic curiosity, camp appeal, or most likely a combination of all three. The success of Verhoven's film and other titles on the intimate format indicated that people were more willing to check out controversial and potentially embarrassing material in the privacy of their own homes than in the awkward public space of the local multiplex. This fate would ultimately play out for Anderson's film as well. *Boogie Nights* was released with much critical fanfare, but the film's reception and popularity intensified over the course of the subsequent year, the height of the Clinton sex scandal. Just as important to its success were various home video formats such as VHS, Laserdisc, and the emergent DVD, which was first introduced in 1996.

This twist, of course, became an ironic final commentary on the historical narrative of media and its sense of porn's decline as represented in *Boogie Nights* itself. So much of the renewed attention to sex in the 1990s was due to the emergence of new and/or increasingly popular media platforms. This was, for Sickels, the impetus of porn chic's rebirth. In the year prior to *Boogie Nights*'s appearance,

Americans spent more than $8 billion on hard-core videos, peep shows, live sex acts, adult cable programming, sexual devices, computer porn, and sex magazines—an amount larger than Hollywood's domestic box office receipts and larger than all the revenues generated by rock and country music recordings.[47]

With consumers building considerable personal film libraries and with the novelty of the internet making a range of content more available, the appeal of accessing pornographic and porn-themed content increased in the privacy of home.

THE NARRATIVIZATION OF PORN

The other question became whether *Boogie Nights* succeeds in realistically (or tastefully) presenting pornographic material that was as much a commercial liability as a strength. For all the buzz around *Boogie Nights* and its sympathetic, nonjudgmental portrayal of pornographers, even some porn filmmakers weren't particularly happy with the final product. "The porn industry, which might have been flattered to be the subject of a serious, feature-length Hollywood movie," wrote Waxman, "was upset at what many insiders considered to be a negative depiction"—too dark, but also unrealistic in relation to industry practices.[48]

On the other hand, the visual representation of pornography itself in *Boogie Nights* was not especially graphic compared to its hardcore alternative. This may have been another reason why audiences were disappointed when it first appeared. As a movie "about porn," *Boogie Nights* was in a contradictory position—promoting the pornographic angle as part of its potential appeal, while also not actually *being* pornographic for fear of alienating that same audience. "When Hollywood makes a film about the Titanic, spectators expect to see the ship sink," speculated Peter Lehman; "when Hollywood makes a film about porn, spectators don't usually expect to see porn."[49]

Boogie Nights maintains a fine balance that acknowledges such images, but doesn't threaten the narrative movement of the film. Catherine Zuromskis explored what she called the "porn-in-film" aesthetic in films from the 1980s and 1990s such as *Videodrome* (1983), *8MM* (1999), and *The People vs. Larry Flynt*. These films neutralize and moralize pornographic content as an affective spectacle within the narrative. Pornography threatens mainstream film because of its explicit visual content as well as its disinterest in narrative. Yet the porn-in-film aesthetic creates a distance from this threat by embedding pornographic texts within the film's diegetic space. In *Boogie Nights*, the representation of explicit pornographic content is presented as grainy 16mm "film within a film," or side-stepped in favor of diegetic audiences or camera technology. The "moralizing distance sets in"[50] in the darker second half of the film:

As with [Laura] Mulvey's formulation of the male gaze, the audience for porn-in-film is often offered a measure of sexual pleasure in viewing the pornographic text embedded within the film. In *Boogie Nights* in particular the audience is allowed a full hour of reveling in the erotic kitsch of the seventies porn scene, complete with sex, nudity, and real porn stars in cameo roles. But this pleasure is always followed by the punishment of the porn producers and consumers.[51]

The film's shocking violence and depressing turn of events are intended to punish not only the main characters, but also the audience for being potentially tempted. Instead of sexual titillation, Zuromskis argues, the audience receives gratification ultimately from the feeling of moral superiority—watching these transgressive characters pay for their extravagance and self-indulgence.

Despite the inherent misogyny of its content, *Boogie Nights* is relatively restrained, and even at times brilliant, in its representation of intercourse itself. The paradox of *Boogie Nights*, as a mainstream dramatic feature, lies in foregrounding the very genre (pornography) that it cannot ethically, economically, narratively, or visually replicate for any extensive period of time. After being picked up by Horner and his entourage late one night at the club (and being sold on the business at a twenty-four-hour diner), Eddie is brought back to the producer's house to have sex with Rollergirl. As with the character's first filmed sex scene later, the camera and the editing emphasize the diegetic spectator in the scene. An extended shot of Horner watching them lasts longer than the initial shot of Eddie and Rollergirl together on the couch. This desexualizes the potential effect of the sequence, avoiding the temptation to stop the narrative's progression in favor of lewd spectacle. The long take on Horner also self-reflexively calls attention to the act of voyeurism by *Boogie Nights*'s own audience—we are, in a sense, watching ourselves in the process of watching.

The first actual moment of porn "filmmaking" in *Boogie Nights*, Dirk's "interview" with Amber Waves, similarly reinforces this self-reflexive representation by way of the film's visual emphasis on both voyeuristic audiences and media technologies, as opposed to pornography's emphasis on simply shooting the act itself. As the crew gets ready for the shoot, we wait with the nervous Dirk behind

2.9. Jack Horner, as he watches Dirk's audition. *Boogie Nights* spends more screen time on the film's diegetic spectators than on the porn itself. In addition to sidestepping concerns regarding adult ratings and narrative momentum, this decision calls attention to the audience itself as voyeurs.

the door. After Jack calls "action, Dirk," the camera follows him onto set and into Amber's line of vision as she waits for him. The point-of-view shot here aligns the audience with Dirk's nervousness upon entering a movie for the first time. But this extremely subjective shot is then jarringly juxtaposed with the more removed, objective perspective of the crew's 16mm camera as it quietly records the scene.

This stylistic decision takes us inside the "look" of an old-fashioned 1970s porn film (though in reality the camera used is already outdated by late 1970s standards). It paradoxically isolates us from any potential intimacy in the interaction between Amber and Dirk, while also "removing" the pornographic content in a way from the dramatic narrative proper. As the sex scene begins, *Boogie Nights* uses 16mm footage to distinguish the "pornographic" content from the rest of the movie—meanwhile, when the film cuts back to the standard 35mm, the images of Dirk and Amber are shot in a series of disorienting extreme close-ups that are largely out of sync with the rest of the film's framing and spacing. But the uncomfortably close shots intentionally decontextualize the act of sex further, taking away the audience's sense of diegetic perspective, and keeping most of the more pornographic images out of the camera's point of view.

Equally effective in defusing the sexuality of the sequence are the subsequent reaction shots, which also comment on the film's larger

2.10. The 16mm footage of Dirk's first porn scene, literalizing what Catherine
Zuromskis has called the "porn-in-film" aesthetic, where nonpornographic
movies incorporate pornographic content without interrupting the story
momentum and restrained visual expectations of mainstream narrative films.

metatextual relationship to pornography. As soon as Dirk unzips
his pants, *Boogie Nights* cuts to several shots of cast and crew watching him perform (the obvious intent is also to indicate his noteworthy size via their nonverbal responses). The cameraman (Ricky Jay)
sneaks a peek with his own eyes (as though the camera doesn't do
justice to the spectacle), Scotty (Philip Seymour Hoffman) anxiously
holds the mike, clearly aroused by the sight, and Reed (John C.
Reilly) and Becky (Nicole Ari Parker) tilt their heads in unison. As
with the sequence of Dirk's couch audition with Rollergirl, where
Jack watches indifferently, Anderson spends as much screen time
on the people watching the sex as on representing the act itself. Finally, Anderson's self-reflexive focus on film technology is privileged when *Boogie Nights* tracks into the diegetic camera and cuts to
footage from "inside" the lens—Amber and Dirk are barely visible,
upside down, at the other end. The emphasis on diegetic reactions
here, along with the use of 16mm footage and shots inside the camera itself, desexualizes the content by foregrounding the artificial,
manipulative nature in which pornography is constructed and then
received by audiences.

Boogie Nights's most explicit (and infamous) sexual scene is also
the one most ambivalent about its own obsession with narrativ-
izing pornography. In the last shot, we finally see Diggler's penis.
It was not Anderson's first choice to keep the big reveal until the
very end. In the original script, the penis is shown during the first

porn shoot. Yet the decision to defer paid off artistically. As Dirk once again looks in the mirror, his head is cut off while the camera zooms in on his crotch—accompanied by the Electric Light Orchestra's "Living Thing" (*"it's a livin' thing / it's a terrible thing to lose"*). The shot is amusing but also depressingly anticlimatic. After its tremendous buildup, the spectacle reveals a melancholic letdown. Dirk is still not a real actor; he's still not even "Dirk," but Eddie Adams from Torrance. And the shot of this remarkable (and prosthetic) penis reinforces the idea that, at the end of the day, he's still just the same naïve kid perceived by those around him as nothing more than an empty personality with a giant penis. That this part of his anatomy makes him "a big, bright, shining star" is as sad as it may be empowering.

"I PLAN ON BEING A STAR"

Appropriately, Dirk's first "scene" involves being cast by Amber for a major part in a movie, because the fascination with stardom is another layer to the film's cinephiliac pastiche. As a movie about movies, *Boogie Nights* is an overt interrogation of celebrity. Dirk is obsessed with being a star. When Eddie first arrives home and enters his bedroom, the camera pans 360 degrees to reveal a space dominated by celebrity obsession—posters of Al Pacino, pictures of Bruce Lee, and other objects. Diggler's lowest moment comes when he's beaten by a group of homophobic strangers in a parking lot. This is preceded a few moments earlier by his inability to perform sexually and by the failure of another person to recognize his celebrity ("Do you know who I am?")—the two qualities that define "Dirk Diggler." On a basic level, *Boogie Nights* revolves around finding a sense of stardom, losing it, and then finding it again.

Like its influence *Nashville* (1975), *Boogie Nights* is a film about those celebrity subcultures one might not consider when thinking about stardom. In Robert Altman's classic, it was the country music scene; in *Boogie Nights*, it's the porn industry. The obsession with stardom in Anderson's film is established early in Eddie's one scene with his girlfriend. Here, his ambitions are the subject of a speech that reveals a larger narrative of destiny, which structures the film:

Everyone has one special thing, you think? I mean, everyone's given one special thing, right? That's right. Everyone's blessed with one special thing. I want you to know that I plan on being a star. A big, bright shining star. That's what I want. That's what I'm going to get.

2.11. The posters in Eddie's bedroom explicitly reflect his desire for both celebrity status and conspicuous consumption.

Eddie leaves Eddie Adams from Torrance behind in an ironic "baptismal" scene in Horner's hot tub. The power of his newfound stardom is so intense, he believes, that a neon "Dirk Diggler" sign explodes into flames when lit. In *The Power of Myth* (one of Anderson's favorite books), Joseph Campbell discusses the notion that happiness in life is following one's bliss—finding the one thing in life that one is passionate about, or talented at, and committing one's life to doing it well. *Boogie Nights*, writes Waxman, "was all about being really good at one thing and one thing only."[52] Thanks to his remarkable endowment and apparent sexual abilities, Eddie is destined to be a star. As Horner says, "I got a feeling, beneath those jeans, there's something wonderful just waiting to get out." What then is initiated is Campbell's classic journey of the hero—the one who goes out into a strange world, overcomes obstacles and challenges, and finally returns home stronger to his (surrogate) family, for the betterment of the larger community.

Wahlberg, the former rapper turned actor, anchors the complex narrative and cast of characters in *Boogie Nights*. Anderson wanted Leonardo DeCaprio for the part of Diggler, but he dropped out to do James Cameron's *Titanic* (1997). Anderson's second choice, however, commented on Wahlberg's own star persona at that point in his career. Wahlberg, who helped form the boy band New Kids on the Block but left before it achieved success, initially came to fame in the early 1990s as a rapper with the group Marky Mark and the Funky Bunch. Diggler's humorously bad vocals and subsequently brief and failed singing career after a fallout with Horner comment ironically on Wahlberg's own short stint as a singer.

Wahlberg was also known for his chiseled physique and overt heterosexuality, which was prominently displayed in music videos, in his own Marky Mark workout videos, and in his work as a fashion model for companies such as Calvin Klein and photographers such as Annie Leibovitz. Like his costar Burt Reynolds had twenty years earlier, Wahlberg made headlines as much for his seminude posing as for his acting. With this in mind, the casting of the relatively untested film actor Wahlberg in *Boogie Nights* is particularly fascinating. Wahlberg dedicated his 1992 autobiography (*Marky Mark*) to his own penis. The actor's presence gives the story of an unusually well-endowed young man, and its notorious final image, a humorous extratextual dimension.

As someone who exploited his own physical appearance for celebrity gain, even Wahlberg himself picked up on the connections with Dirk. While first reading the script, Wahlberg stopped and called up Anderson. "Listen, I love these thirty pages, and I know I'm going to love the rest of it," Wahlberg asked Anderson while reading an early draft of the screenplay, "but I just want to make sure that you don't want me because I'm the guy who will get in his underwear."[53] Anderson told him "no" to placate his insecurities, but in retrospect it's easy to read Wahlberg's casting in this light. Also intriguing was the casting of 1970s sex symbol Reynolds in the role of a 1970s porn director. Anderson's first choice for the role, director-actor Warren Beatty, was also a prominent 1970s sex symbol. Beatty turned the part down because he was unsure what the point of *Boogie Nights* was supposed to be (Waxman claims that Beatty wanted the part of Dirk Diggler instead of the Horner role[54]).

Boogie Nights's opening image of the marquee establishes the film's primary preoccupation with celebrity culture—a marquee title still in search of its star (it foreshadows the use of the marquee later to introduce "Dirk Diggler"). The Steadicam tilts and swoops down to street level in one continuous shot that will take us down the road, through the crowds, past Jack Horner and his crew, and into Maurice Rodriguez's nightclub, Hot Traxx—all while "The Best of My Love" plays over the soundtrack. In the background in all caps, a sign reads BOX OFFICE, anticipating Maurice's line a few seconds later: "I'm talking box office, Jack, box office." It also highlights the film's primary focus on selling stardom and the importance of being recognized. The uninterrupted take then follows Jack, Maurice, and Amber into the club before wandering off with Maurice to the dance floor to find other characters, including Buck Swope (Don Cheadle)

2.12. Like *Hard Eight*, *Boogie Nights* begins with an older man approaching a younger man under mysterious circumstances, engaging in a conversation that explicitly touches on sexual favors for money.

and Reed Rothchild, before finding Jack and Amber again—after which we are introduced to Rollergirl and finally Eddie Adams. Only Little Bill (William H. Macy) is introduced later, when he interrupts Jack's eyeline with Eddie. The film cuts only at the moment of Eddie's emergence—jumping back to Horner, who discovers his future star for the first time. Only when *Boogie Nights* finds its star does the restless, subjectless Steadicam finally stop wandering.

This remarkable shot pulls us into a world that revolves around disco dancing, 1970s music, and sex. But there are two worlds here—the glamorous, fun one in the club itself and the more ambiguous one that exists just beyond, in the kitchen; one filled with money and status, and one without. When Jack first awkwardly approaches Dirk in the dishwashing room, the sounds of the club quickly fade. We're initially unsure of the direction the conversation will take. Our hesitation is intensified by the CAUTION sign just over Eddie's right shoulder. This echoes the narrative ambiguity during the first time Sydney and John meet in *Hard Eight* (both conversations carry homophobic undertones). Like John, Eddie assumes the unplanned encounter involves trading sexual favors for money, to the point that he offers said services up front only to be rebuffed. Jack (like Sydney) never quite tips his hand as to his intentions. Jack's vision of Eddie as a porn star isn't yet made explicit—we don't know if Jack is just hitting on him, or if he sees genuine star quality. What is established is that Eddie is comfortable with sex as a vehicle for gaining material wealth.

At the root of Anderson's vision of American postmodern culture are stardom and celebrity, but also the everyday role of salesmen and sales pitches—both are driven by materialism and the commodification of everyday life, just as Eddie's final fight with his mom centers on who paid for the stuff in his bedroom when he leaves. The material differences between Eddie's and Jack's different lives are further drawn out by the parallel scenes of them returning to their respective homes. Jack drives to his place nearby, while Eddie has to walk to a bus stop, and then ride all the way to his parents' house in Torrance. Jack lives in a huge, sprawling ranch house—the camera leaves him for a moment to survey his spread-out recreational room before finding him by the record player. Eddie, meanwhile, sneaks quietly into his home, navigating a series of narrow corridors before entering his cluttered bedroom filled with celebrity posters and fan memorabilia. As with Jack's homecoming scene a few minutes earlier, the camera leaves the main subject for a moment to pan around the room, this time in a complete 360-degree movement (this shot also offers a first glimpse at his penis, bulging out of his underwear). While Jack's open living room suggests a life of luxury, Eddie's room is a claustrophobic monument to the celebrity and consumer lifestyle he only wishes he could afford. When the camera finds him again, he is appropriately looking into a full-length mirror—Eddie is good-natured but incredibly vain, imagining himself as another star poster on the wall.

The connection between stardom, sales pitches, and commodities is made explicit early on in *Boogie Nights*. At an all-night diner, Horner seduces Eddie into the porn lifestyle. The first moment catches Horner in mid-pitch, with an image that doesn't necessarily seem glamorous at first:

What I'm trying to tell you is it takes a lot of the good old American green stuff to make one of these things. You've got your camera, you got your film, you got your lights, your sound, your lab costs, your developing, your synching and your editing. Before you turn around, you spent maybe $20,000, $25,000, $30,000 on a movie. . . . But if you make a good one, there's practically no end to how much money you can make.

His sales pitch to the young dishwasher centers not on endless sex with beautiful women, but on the potential financial windfall involved with such a lifestyle. Horner's primary pitch is about the eco-

2.13. In an all-night diner, Jack sells Eddie on being a porn star, focusing on the economics of filmmaking and the dream of narrative-driven pornography rather than the opportunity for sex itself.

nomic side of porn. He tries to sell Eddie on the idea of making a great film, too—one with such an engaging story that people will stay in the theatre, even after they've finished masturbating, just to see the supposedly riveting narrative's resolution. However, this utopian view of filmmaking is presented as Horner's unrealistic authorial vision, rather than something tangibly connected to the daily realities of the porn lifestyle. Later, more directly, Horner says to Eddie right before his "audition" with Rollergirl that "I'm thinking I want to be in business with you"—Jack sees Eddie's services as something to be negotiated over. Once on board with Horner's company, Eddie is recruited to help "sell" the Colonel—the one who "puts up all the money for our features; it's an important part of the process." Horner's artistic ambitions, however sincere, always come back to the issue of funding, including selling out his love of film once the Colonel goes to jail and video's big proponent, Floyd Gondolli, enters the picture.

Moreover, there is another salesman in *Boogie Nights*—one whose day-to-day life is focused on selling commodities. Buck Swope is the first in a long line of professional salesmen to appear in Anderson's films—people who exist at the margins of consumer culture and whose worth is defined by their ability to pawn off superficial material needs, trivial commodities, service upgrades, and so forth on others who invariably don't need the junk (Becky's husband, we discover, is a Pep Boys store manager, which he passes off as working "in the auto industry"). Invariably, there is a certain kind of pitiful presence to Anderson's salesmen. For instance, Buck isn't a particu-

2.14. Buck Swope: the first of many salesmen in Anderson's films. His black cowboy look is based on similar characters in Mel Brooks's *Blazing Saddles* and Altman's *Nashville*, both of which were released shortly before *Boogie Nights* is set (1977).

larly good salesman—we encounter him early on at his day job, selling stereo equipment without much luck. He attempts to sell one customer on the "TK421" modification, the first of several references to *Star Wars* (1977) in *Boogie Nights*[55] (one of the many subtle reinforcements of the subtext of 1970s cinephilia running throughout the film). He knows the standard pitch ("I have this very unit in my home") and at one point was apparently employee of the month, though this might be related to the manager's interest in his porn connections. Yet his choice of loud country music to show off the "bass" as a sound sampling immediately alienates a prospective client (played by the original Dirk Diggler, Michael Stein), who politely walks away without committing to a purchase. Much of Buck's sense of feeling out of place in the film's first two-thirds is related to this initial failure as a salesman unable to anticipate consumer needs. Just as important is his refusal to conform to—as his manager notes—the white expectations of what his interests in music should be as a "brother."

Buck is the most complicated African American character in any of Anderson's films to date. His very name encapsulates the contradictions involving the historical representations of blacks in Hollywood film. His first name is a reference to the old Hollywood stereotype of the "buck," an African American male known for his sexual prowess. For a porn star, this would make some sense. Yet the buck was historically presented in a negative way (e.g., Gus in *Birth of a Nation* [1915])—a sexual threat to white women who must therefore be killed. Buck's last name, meanwhile, is an homage to one of

2.15. A poor salesman, Buck uses obnoxious country music to demonstrate the stereo equipment, only to alienate a prospective customer (played by the original Dirk Diggler, Michael Stein).

2.16. Director of the influential *Putney Swope* (1969), Robert Downey Sr. appears briefly in *Boogie Nights* as the recording studio manager (composer Michael Penn also appears as the technician during this scene). An old friend and mentor, Downey also appeared very briefly as one of the TV producers in *Magnolia*.

Anderson's favorite films, *Putney Swope* (1969), directed by Robert Downey Sr., who also appears in *Boogie Nights* as the studio manager who refuses to give over the demo tapes to Reed and Dirk. The random firecrackers in the Rahad Jackson scene were also taken from a similar non sequitur sequence in *Putney Swope*. Downey's film was a more biting critique of inherent racism, deception, and manipulation in the American advertising industry and is a more direct and sharp social satire than anything Anderson has ever done, addressing corporate hypocrisy and social inequality in a remarkably experimental style.

Buck, though, is perhaps the closest Anderson has yet come to anything resembling a coherent critique of whiteness and institutional racism, particularly when compared to the at-best-clichéd African American criminals that populate *Hard Eight* and later *Magnolia*. Much of Buck's search for an identity comes from other people's stereotypical expectations of what a black man should look like and what type of music he should listen to. It's also likely that he was denied the loan he needs to open his own stereo-equipment store in part because of his race (he's the only black person in the bank), even though the loan officer keeps bringing up his pornographic past. Thus, when he has a chance at the money from the botched donut shop robbery, any serendipity at work (more common in other Anderson films) is karmic redistribution for the earlier act of discrimination. In the end of *Boogie Nights*, though, Buck ultimately adopts a more stereotypical persona to succeed as a businessman, playing the part of a rapper while shooting the commercial for his new stereo store—what an African American media celebrity "should" look like in 1984 for a presumed white audience. That look serves as an ambivalent bookend to his rejected "black cowboy" persona in the film's beginning.

REPRESENTATIONS OF MISOGYNY

Eddie's speech about how "everyone has one special thing" is also explicitly about his penis, as the heavily masculine, even misogynist, structure of *Boogie Nights* is also foregrounded. Inside New Line, even supporters of the film such as studio executive Karen Hermelin noticed its sexist undertones—it is essentially a movie about the journey of a particularly well-endowed man. After her first read-through of Anderson's massive screenplay, Hermelin came away with the response that it "was completely misogynistic," but liked it anyway.[56] The film begins by positing that a household dominated by a strong woman will implode, thus leading the main character to seek out the reassurance of a surrogate family dominated by an authoritative father figure, Jack Horner.

Boogie Nights never really overcomes the gender tensions presented by this representational issue. The film is already saddled with considerable baggage on the issue of misogyny, given that it's a film about pornography—a genre traditionally criticized for its exploitation of women, reducing them to nothing more than sexual objects for a presumed male spectator. Pornographic material shot for an assumed heterosexual audience always diegetically privileges

2.17. In a rare scene not featuring the film's male characters, a coked-up Amber agrees to be mother to Rollergirl, literalizing the surrogate family that is Jack's production company. As in Anderson's other films, the female characters barely exist outside their exchange-value as sexual commodities.

the sexual needs of the male character. Porn is an inherently misogynistic genre, even though some scholars have noted that it's impossible to universalize pornography's many audiences or the source of their voyeuristic satisfaction. In any event, the narrative premise of *Boogie Nights*, creating an entire business structured around Diggler's penis, hardly avoids the most misogynistic assumptions about pornography. The film's final moment foregrounds the restoration of the patriarchal order in very explicit (visual) terms.

Boogie Nights attempts to problematize its own evocation of pornography's misogyny. Dirk Diggler attempts to make a distinction between classy pornographic films that he thinks treat women with respect and more trashy ones that exhibit overt violence towards women. The latter type is clearly embodied by the repulsive Johnny Wadd, Dirk's eventual replacement as Horner's main star, who finds sexual gratification in holding a gun to women's heads while forcing them to have sex in a transparent glorification of rape. However, Dirk's insistence on a more respectable form of pornography comes across as hypocritical and naïve, expressed in the sexist lines he himself utters in Horner's movies. His speech about treating women right is amusingly ironic as Dirk becomes increasingly self-absorbed and delusional over the course of the narrative.

The female characters are central in any discussion of *Boogie Nights*'s misogyny. Eddie's mom creates a tension that never really goes away—namely, the film's apparent discomfort with strong women. However, Amber Waves and Rollergirl, while not assertive, are still relatively complicated characters not merely reduced to their sexual use-value for the men around them. In fact, one of the film's best scenes involves the two of them doing coke, with Rollergirl asking Amber to be her mom. Not only well written and well paced, the scene is also noticeable in that the conversation does not revolve exclusively around a man. In the end, though, Amber and Rollergirl are both still porn stars who are referred to exclusively by their porn names—their livelihood remains dependent on selling their bodies.

Most troubling are the destructive tendencies of *Boogie Nights's* only assertive female characters—Little Bill's wife and, more famously, Eddie's mom. An early breakfast scene establishes the failed biological family Eddie is ready to leave for greener pastures. Their problems revolve around his angry, controlling mother, who was notoriously based on Anderson's own mom, Edwina. The character's irrational outbursts of verbal abuse make no narrative sense without an awareness of this information, since her intense animosity toward her own son is really given no reasoning. Even Anderson himself, while avoiding the autobiographical issue, admitted the character didn't work:

When his mom comes at him like that, she's really crazy and out of control. She's kind of without motivation to a certain extent. . . . That woman is pretty nuts, and I think it's sometimes hard for an audience to grab hold of a character whose intentions aren't clear. You don't really know what the fuck she's yelling about. You know she has an odd jealousy towards him or towards the neighborhood girl that he's banging, so she's upset about that, but her actions are so manic, you can't get a hold of them.[57]

Some people can relate to the experience of unsupportive parents and broken homes, but as written the character really comes out of nowhere. At best, she works as a plot device, forcing Eddie out of his home and into Jack's waiting arms—a turn also anticipated by the utter lack of strength exhibited by his biological father (Lawrence Hudd), who can't even bring himself to look up from the table while sitting quietly next to his son. Eddie and his father, whose affections are also rebuffed by his wife, barely share two words with one another during the breakfast scene, while Mom verbally abuses both of them—Dad for not shaving before he tries to kiss her and Eddie for not going back to school.

Eddie's mom's role in the disintegration of his home life comes to

2.18. Eddie's irrationally angry mom. Although the empty bottle clearly suggests that she's drunk here, the character still is largely unmotivated in her unrelenting contempt for her son.

a head shortly thereafter, when she drunkenly confronts him upon coming home late. Irrationally angry, she is partially motivated by the alcohol, the late hour, and jealousy toward his trashy girlfriend, Sheryl Lynn (Laurel Holloman), who has already disappeared from the narrative. Yet the root of her anger is structured around her disappointment in Eddie's lack of potential to amount to anything in life. This, however, muddles more than clarifies why she would take it so personally. His mom doesn't even believe in him enough to think he's capable of doing something: "You'll never do anything! You'll always be a loser." The mom insistently picks a fight with Eddie, despite his own reluctance to take the bait by walking away. Undeterred, she follows him into the bedroom, becoming increasingly abusive. Finally, Eddie defends himself in tears: "I'll do something! I'll do it! I'll go somewhere and I'll do something. . . . You don't know what I could do, what I'm going to do, what I'm going to be. You don't know. I'm good. I have good things you don't know about and I'm going to be something! I am!" Ultimately, the mom exists not only to progress the story, but to clarify Eddie's imagined sense of isolation and betrayal. His mom tears down his posters, symbolically stripping him of his ambitious dreams: his materialistic desires (the red Corvette) and his goal to be a star (Bruce Lee). Both of these desires will be met by Jack, who—in a nice match cut—is waiting at his door to welcome Eddie as soon as his mother slams hers.

Ultimately, there is no way around the more troubling aspects of *Boogie Nights*'s gender dynamics. As in Anderson's other films to date (with the arguable exception of *The Master*), a complicated de-

construction of masculinity does not offset the simplistic representation of women, who are largely restricted to one-dimensional,
sexist roles (the selfless mother, the un/redeemable whore) defined
by the needs of men. *Boogie Nights* makes this fact even more problematic with its central content. Other than Eddie's shrieking mom,
every major female character is a porn star in *Boogie Nights*—Amber
Waves, Rollergirl, Becky, and Little Bill's unfaithful wife (Nina Hart-
ley). Meanwhile, there are major male characters in the film who
are not directly involved with porn filmmaking, including Maurice,
Todd Parker, and Rahad Jackson.[58] Additionally, there are several
substantial male characters involved in the industry itself: Horner,
the Colonel, and Floyd Gondolli, whose respective roles in the narrative are not related to or defined by any presumed sexual value.
Clearly, Eddie/Dirk is sexually objectified as well, but the power dynamic is very different—rather than be submissive to the needs of
the opposite sex, Dirk draws power from being the room's dominant
presence, an opportunity explicitly derived from that greatest symbol of male authority: his phallus. Moreover, the relatively eclectic
mix of male characters in *Boogie Nights* offsets the objectification
of Dirk's penis, meaning that men clearly aren't *only* sex objects in
the film.

Scotty, the most prominent gay character in *Boogie Nights*, is just
as troubling as the domineering mom. It's never quite clear what
narrative or thematic function he serves—in the beginning, as he
lusts after Dirk, he is largely intended as a source of comic relief
(whether or not one finds it "funny"). His obsession with Dirk extends from watching him with lust during shoots to emulating the
porn star's material lifestyle—buying an identical car and clothes.
But when he works up the courage to make his move during the generally dark New Year's scene, only to be awkwardly rejected by Dirk,
he becomes pathetic. He sits alone in his Corvette and descends into
a crying spiral of self-loathing. Afterward, he does little more than
stand in the background.

The representation of homosexuality here would be less troubling had Anderson not eliminated a key aspect of the original *Dirk
Diggler Story*—Dirk's comfort with his bisexuality, which is arguably the most important aspect dropped in the adaptation (along
with Dirk's death from an overdose). There's a big difference between Dirk rejecting Scotty because he's not attracted to him and
Dirk rejecting him because he may be repulsed by the idea of homosexuality (intensified by rumors of Wahlberg's own homopho-

2.19. When Scotty is reduced to drunken despair by Dirk's rejection, his pathetic fate anticipates a very similar fate for Donnie Smith (played by William H. Macy) in *Magnolia*.

bia early in his career). Keeping Dirk's bisexuality intact would have made *Boogie Nights* less marketable to mainstream audiences (not that the film would have ever appealed to that rhizomatic demographic), but it would have made the film's representation of sexuality much more complex than the overt, intense heteromasculinity it ultimately celebrates.

THE CONTRADICTIONS OF THE NEXT TARANTINO

Boogie Nights was technically impressive, if historically and culturally problematic. Yet it was destined to struggle with audiences who weren't inclined to go to the multiplex for a movie "about porn"—or, at least, a wide enough audience to justify the film's budget. Yet New Line stuck with Anderson and the project, finding alternate ways to market *Boogie Nights* by following Miramax's approach to *Pulp Fiction* a few years earlier: highlighting the appeal of its retro soundtrack and the critical ideal of the auteur more generally. Playing to the proven appeal of Tarantino did work to the studio's advantage initially. Anderson was a hot name by the time *Boogie Nights* premiered at the Toronto and New York Film Festivals in 1997, generating exactly the kind of strong critical buzz that New Line had been strategizing for by supporting Anderson so closely. "By the middle of the Toronto Film Festival, hope sprang eternal [after a run of bad or uninspired films]," Daryl Chin and Larry Qualls wrote skeptically in early 1998, "and *Paul Thomas Anderson was being talked about as the next Tarantino* for his 'epic' *Boogie Nights*, so that the appearance of the film at the New York Film Festival was greeted with wild anticipation."[59]

Along with David Ansen's glowing *Newsweek* review, the Toronto and New York Film Festivals saved Anderson's film with the studio after disastrous test screenings by putting the attention back squarely on what New Line had hoped for all along—critical praise. With positive buzz pouring in, writes Waxman: "suddenly a new marketing campaign was born, but it was based on free publicity—interviews with prominent journalists, glowing reviews in glossy magazines—rather than paid advertising."[60] Given the tricky, even impossible, subject matter (many theatres refused to show it), *Boogie Nights*'s strategy was based upon appealing to critical prestige, the upcoming awards season, and word of mouth rather than an extensive ad campaign.

Yet this buzz was not always particularly well intended toward Anderson himself or *Boogie Nights*, as the attention to the writer-director's emergence was met with some resistance, particularly in the festival circuit. The lack of support wasn't from frustrated studio executives or prudish audiences. Rather, fellow cinephiles were upset with media coverage that created the effect of Anderson dominating the spotlight. Chin and Qualls's larger point in 1998 was to lament the ways in which the obsessive media search of festivals for the "next Tarantino" was preventing a more thoughtful and detailed discussion of the wide range of masterpieces also circulating during this time—Abbas Kiarostami's *Taste of Cherry*, Wong Kar-wai's *Happy Together*, Atom Egoyan's *The Sweet Hereafter*, and so forth. Rather than a sustained critical commitment to seeking out and rewarding the best of a large, rich field, they wrote, "we're stuck in a climate where the important critical issue is to be in on the start of a hot young career."[61] This opposition to Anderson's quick rise points toward a larger critical ambivalence toward the director for much of the first ten years of his career. The resistance to Anderson and *Boogie Nights* was not without merit, particularly since the director hadn't really done much yet, and talk of the "next" Tarantino was already a tired topic by 1997.

However, the attention also reinforced the notion that Anderson's reputation was gaining considerable traction. *Boogie Nights* underwhelmed at the box office but still received generally strong reviews and even award consideration, including Oscar nominations for Julianne Moore, Burt Reynolds, and Anderson himself (for the screenplay). Then, in 1998, the new platform of the DVD, of which New Line was an early supporter, increased attention to a home video market already crowded with VHS and Laserdisc formats. *Boogie Nights* quietly became a proven money earner and even cult hit amid a new generation of young American cinephiles. Meanwhile, New Line executive Mitch Goldman was proven right on the other score—like *Pulp Fiction*, *Boogie Nights*'s soundtrack was a huge hit in the fall of 1997. Listeners often indifferent to the film itself embraced its clever collection of 1970s and 1980s pop songs. So popular was the soundtrack that a second volume, featuring some of the featured songs from the movie that hadn't been included in the original album (such as "Jessie's Girl" and "Mama Told Me Not to Come"), was released in January of 1998. Whatever the reason, New Line was sufficiently convinced that Anderson was worth further investing in as potentially the next great American filmmaker, or at least the "next Tarantino."

In the niche market (Sundance, smart film, soundtrack movie) in which *Boogie Nights* fortunately found itself, Anderson ironically benefitted from the trail blazed by Tarantino. As the next decade would reveal, Anderson's films were nothing like Tarantino's. Anderson's cinematic vision was not ultimately as interested in the criminal world; as a filmmaker, he didn't show much interest in experimenting with narrative or chronological structure; his thematic emphasis on compassion, guilt, and redemption directly contradicts Tarantino's relentless (if often thrilling) nihilism; and, unlike Tarantino's ironic examination of an endless roster of despicable low-lifes, Anderson's affection for his characters is at times embarrassingly sincere. Anderson was more thematically ambitious than his predecessor, and when New Line finally handed him his coveted final-cut status after *Boogie Nights*'s modest success, Anderson would prove it—for better and for worse.

i like it. it's long. it's indulgent. let's leave it.

ANDERSON, 1999

Paul Thomas Anderson says he doesn't know "if I'm the type of guy who'd want to run the world like Spielberg or retreat to a mansion in London like Kubrick. I haven't got it figured out yet." It takes a lot of hubris for a twenty-nine-year-old director with three films behind him to presume that either route presents a viable option.

FILM CRITIC TODD MCCARTHY, "THE NEXT SCORSESE" (1999)[1]

CHAPTER 3

if that was in a movie, i wouldn't believe it

MELODRAMATIC AMBIVALENCE, HYPERMASCULINITY, AND THE AUTOBIOGRAPHICAL IMPULSE IN *MAGNOLIA* (1999)

At the end of the last millennium, American multiplexes everywhere celebrated the auteurist potential of numerous cinematic talents—particularly rare since they emerged largely from the major studios. The success of these young directors was so widespread that *Esquire* magazine took the time to ask several respected film critics (Andrew Sarris, Kenneth Turan, Elvis Mitchell, McCarthy, and others) who they thought was "the next [Martin] Scorsese." A silly exercise on the surface, it reflected a powerfully complicated moment in the historical intersection of Hollywood and the indie film scene. Early 1999 alone saw the general theatrical releases of Wes Anderson's *Rushmore*, Doug Liman's *Go*, Alexander Payne's *Election*, and Terrence Malick's *The Thin Red Line*. By the summer, U.S. audiences were treated to Stanley Kubrick's final opus, *Eyes Wide Shut*; M. Night Shyamalan's breakout phenomenon, *The Sixth Sense*; Steven Soderbergh's revenge neo-noir, *The Limey*; and a pair of hugely influential genre films, *The Matrix* and *The Blair Witch Project*—both of which clearly spelled the beginning of significant new trends in cinema. Meanwhile, Sofia Coppola's debut *The Virgin Suicides* was generating intense buzz across film festivals in Europe. In the fall, U.S. mainstream cinemas everywhere had shown David Fincher's landmark *Fight Club*, Michael Mann's riveting *The Insider*, David O. Russell's eerily prescient Iraq War film *Three Kings*, Spike Jonze and Charlie Kaufman's brain-twister *Being John Malkovich*, Kimberly Peirce's haunting *Boys Don't Cry*, Kevin Smith's thoughtful *Dogma*, Martin Scorsese's underrated *Bringing Out the Dead*, Sam Mendes's Oscar-winner *American Beauty*, and Anthony Minghella's *The Talented Mister Ripley*. In every respect, 1999 was one of the truly seminal years for American cinema in the post-classical Hollywood era.

At that moment another unique auteurist vision found its way through the Hollywood system—Anderson's Southern California epic *Magnolia*, an ambitious, sprawling story about the intersection of several lives during one day in the San Fernando Valley. The film begins with a series of bizarre vignettes involving a pharmacist's murder by vagrants, a scuba diver's freak death, and a man's accidental murder/suicide. These incidents have nothing to do with the rest of the film, but they establish the general theme of random fate, which pays off in the film's even more bizarre finale. There is no dominant plot in *Magnolia* per se, but the characters all directly or indirectly relate to a popular game show called *What Do Kids Know?*—an ironic reference to the abuse and neglect that several children throughout the film suffer at the hands of their respective parents. The fictional show was based on a short-lived real program, *Quiz Kids Challenge*, on which Anderson served as a production assistant in the early 1990s. As Anderson himself admitted later, one big difference from the fictional version was that, in real life, the kids didn't "know" nearly enough, and the show was cancelled after a month because the adults won pretty handily every week.[2] The main patriarchs are host Jimmy Gator (Philip Baker Hall) and producer Earl Partridge (Jason Robards)—both of whom are dying from cancer. The stars of the show include former Quiz Kid Donnie Smith (William H. Macy), now a broke and lonely middle-aged man, and current champ Stanley Spector (Jeremy Blackman). Along the way, we are introduced to Jimmy's coke-addict daughter Claudia (Melora Walters) and her would-be boyfriend, Jim Kurring (John C. Reilly). On Earl's side, meanwhile, is his bedside nurse Phil Parma (Philip Seymour Hoffman), his cheating trophy wife Linda (Julianne Moore), and his estranged son, Frank T. J. Mackey (Tom Cruise), a self-help guru who profits from the sexual misery of men who feel unappreciated by women. Over the course of the Altmanesque narrative, characters cross paths and then leave again. The story is largely driven by overlapping encounters and by secrets

3.1. A brief image at the end of the *What Do Kids Know?* credits is the only clue that draws together all the disparate narrative threads in *Magnolia*, as we discover that the dying Earl Partridge is producer of the long-running show. His iconography evokes a general nostalgia for TV history (*Partridge Family*, the NBC "peacock").

3.2. Frogs falling from the sky in *Magnolia*'s bizarre finale.

eventually revealed and clearly relies more on emotional resonance than narrative cues to keep the momentum going. The film's famous climax features frogs inexplicably falling from the sky—based on weird scientific phenomena researched by journalist Charles Fort.

Despite underwhelming at the box office, the film developed a cult following among those who found resonance with its melodrama, the Aimee Mann soundtrack, and themes of guilt, chance and redemption in the San Fernando Valley. It was also a personal achievement for Anderson himself. Having earned final-cut authority, engaged the services of the world's then-biggest box-office star (Cruise), and worked within a generous budget, the twenty-eight-year-old writer-director was able to tell a story on par with the ambitions of his biggest influence, Robert Altman (especially *Nashville* [1975] and *Short Cuts* [1993]).

Anderson benefited from the critical and home-video success of *Boogie Nights* as well as a larger tendency within Hollywood to embrace the newest iteration of the auteur. While hardly revolutionary, movies such as *Election, Three Kings, Magnolia, Fight Club,* and others collectively spoke to a post-Sundance moment in the industry where a certain level of creative independence for upcoming directors was readily embraced by the studios. Moreover, the resulting themes in these movies, as rhizomatic and populist as they were, offered a surprisingly consistent thematic preoccupation with gender politics, media consumption, stardom, and commodity culture in America at the end of the millennium. A perfect embodiment of the contradictions and erratic promise of this Hollywood trend was *Magnolia.*

It is indelicate—not to mention methodologically suspect—to place so much emphasis on Anderson's personal life when closely examining *Magnolia.* His biography or his "intentions" (both difficult to pinpoint) only tell us so much about the film's production and reception. Yet this third film most clearly reflects Anderson's explicit and unapologetic life experiences. "I consider *Magnolia* a kind of beautiful accident," Anderson explained later. "It gets me. I put my heart—every embarrassing thing that I wanted to say—in *Magnolia.*"[3] Add this to his creative freedom as a final-cut director, and *Magnolia* cannot be fully considered without sustained attention to its many autobiographical impulses. Framing *Magnolia* in relation to Anderson's personal experiences extends beyond the narrative content of finding love, dealing with cancer, growing up in the shadow of the television industry, and so forth. It also pertains to the film's intensely affective logic, how it operates on an emotional level much more than a narrative one. *Magnolia* worked for Anderson when he wrote, shot, and cut it because he was in that emotional place represented in the film—and his personal passion for the story sold everyone around him on the project, including pop music star Fiona Apple (his girlfriend at the time) and movie people like producer JoAnne Sellar, executive Mike De Luca, and editor Dylan Tichenor. When *Magnolia* does work for audiences, the connection depends more on whether they can relate to those intimate spaces from which Anderson also worked.

Magnolia, in more ways than one, was all Anderson's. Having final cut for the first time, Anderson got pretty much every scene up on the screen as written (with the exception of one minor story-line). The director could not retrospectively blame Rysher, New Line, meddling producers, test audiences, or anyone else for compromising the creative integrity of the end result. The critical question in the film's reception would no longer be whether Anderson finally had the freedom to make the movie he wanted. Instead the question was what he would actually *do* with that freedom. Thus, when read as the purely personal expression of a talented director finally achieving complete creative freedom and unapologetically pushing that independence to its limits, *Magnolia* may indeed be a triumph of *pure*, unencumbered film authorship. Yet as a claim to critical respectability, as a test of Anderson's cinematic talent, as a matter of simple old-fashioned evaluation (is it ultimately a "great" film?), *Magnolia* left open as many questions as it answered. For instance, did the hypothetically powerful emotional connection that Anderson structured the whole film around make *Magnolia* the masterpiece that everyone at New Line had hoped for? Unlike critical reaction to his two previous films, reviews were mixed, if generally more positive than not. *Magnolia* tested Anderson's critical support, which had been so crucial to the success of both *Hard Eight* and *Boogie Nights*.

Trying to conceptualize the affective potential of *Magnolia* becomes irretrievably entangled with any attempt at an objective account of whether the film is effective. Anyone who has experienced the pain of cancer tearing through a family, the blissful moment of love at first sight, the loss of unrequited love, or the challenge of reuniting with a parent could empathize with particularly powerful moments in *Magnolia*. But the same could be said of thousands of other films and television shows over the last fifty years that explore similar themes, characters, and premises through any number of genres and narrative strategies. What made *Magnolia* so raw and profound was also what made it generic. Thus, audiences who were not pulled into the film's emotional logic were likely to dismiss its indulgences as the work of an ambitious and overconfident filmmaker who couldn't see the narrative forest for the thematic trees, or who arrogantly thought that his own abstract, emotional whims would easily translate to a broader audience that needed stronger narrative hooks and more original characterizations to become invested in the film's progression.

Many of *Magnolia*'s characters—the cancer patient, noble cop, trophy wife, repressed homosexual, child genius, and so forth—

3.3. Linda in angry tears. *Magnolia* is better understood within the televisual traditions of the melodramatic soap opera, and its emotional excesses are situated in autobiographical impulses—ambivalent father figures, the facades of TV, dealing with cancer.

bump up against one-dimensional stereotypes. They betray a thin characterization that the film's crowded structure and didactic tone manage to intensify rather than hide. For the former audience, it was enough to feel lost within the film's intense, even hysterical, emotional displays, irrespective of narrative concerns. But for others, cut adrift from emotional resonance, *Magnolia* was a directionless film framed by pretentious mediations on fate and filled with uninteresting characters and bloated, obvious monologues about life—as though it were the first movie in Hollywood history to have uncovered the hard truth that the world can be cruel, lonely, intense, and even crazy. Between those two critical extremes *Magnolia* still resists easy categorization, and perhaps the irresolvable contradiction is that the film is really both.

Indeed, what is *Magnolia* ultimately *about*? While affectively powerful, the film's cracks (like those of *Hard Eight*) are more easily seen the closer one looks—Anderson's film is thematically and narratively schizophrenic, a jumbled mess of contradictions that might have been more effective had the film not been so insistent on its own deep importance. Anderson's ambitious epic is a film that never quite finds itself: its rhythms (fast, slow), its themes (serendipity vs. guilt), its storylines (narrative framing, the number of characters). There is too much urgency for such a rambling story—as though it tries to push its audience toward an ultimately undefined goal. Most everyone, even sympathetic friends and critics, agreed that *Magnolia* was too long. And its indulgent length became, justifiably, a metaphor for Anderson's lack of restraint as a writer and director at that point in his career.

Magnolia's excesses make sense when the film is read more sympathetically as the product of a very specific moment in Anderson's career—involving his relationship to the industry, the sense of his critical reputation, and the negotiation with his personal experiences. He had successfully pushed for complete creative control and modestly expanded financial means for the project to follow *Boogie Nights*. New Line agreed (particularly after Cruise was on board) because of its own goals of critical prestige and, hopefully, a few awards. Critically, Anderson was in a position to make a major artistic statement, to write and direct a film—free of interference—that would cement his status as the next great American auteur. In a circular way, final cut was itself an indication of having achieved that status, but with it came the added pressure to deliver something memorable—a film not only epic in scope, but profound in its thematic reflections and transparently award-craving in its motivations. In his personal life, Anderson was going through his own transitions—grieving the loss of his father to cancer, falling in love with pop singer Fiona Apple, and establishing friendships, deep and fleeting, with several respected Hollywood actors. When Anderson sat down to write his third feature-length film, *Magnolia*'s ambitions, to a fault, reflected all these different historical factors.

Thus, there are two fascinating stories to the creation of *Magnolia*, both related to his attainment of final-cut approval: the private one that details Anderson's attempts at making his most personal film and the more public one regarding the way his film speaks to the thematic and industrial status of Hollywood at the end of the twentieth century. *Magnolia* is perhaps more interesting as a reflection of its particular historical moment than it is an engaging film to sit through. The film embodies Anderson's internal struggles as a filmmaker to that point—genuine talent in tension with a self-fulfilling sense of purpose that blinded immense creative gifts from the self-reflexivity, maturity, and patience needed for them to emerge. Like its writer and director at the time, *Magnolia* had flashes of genius but lacked the discipline to make it the masterpiece that would cement his auteur status. *Magnolia* did not end Anderson's career, but it was the end of the first chapter, the end to Anderson's (at times overstated) personal search for critical visibility and creative authority in the industry. *Magnolia*'s struggles also provide clues to the next chapter—once Anderson was a final-cut director (in the sense that he was accountable only to himself), the real challenge of fulfilling his own premature auteur mythology would begin.

STAR POWER

While *Boogie Nights* did not make a significant box-office impact, the film's critical and subsequent home-video success convinced New Line to stick with Anderson. The promise extending from the Valley porn epic made such an impact that they agreed to purchase his next project without a script—giving him complete freedom from scratch (though they reserved the right not to produce the end result). Ever more empowered and confident, the young director pushed further—for final cut. Anderson was well aware of his own press, embarrassingly so—in the introduction to *Magnolia*'s script, he referred to himself as "being a 'new, hot young director,'" and bragged about not having to cut anything.[4] Anderson's plan was selling New Line on the idea of cornering the market for the trendiest filmmakers in a post-Sundance Hollywood, or "that cool niche of the [film] world."[5] Irrespective of *Magnolia*'s final box office, the studio could at least brag it was home to edgy young directors with complete creative control.

The chance to gain a reputation with new auteurist talent sold De Luca in particular on Anderson, since he saw himself as the "blank check guy"[6] to a new generation of Orson Welles–like figures. New Line could create in Anderson's wake a comfort zone of independence that other directors would be eager to embrace. New Line chief Bob Shaye, on the other hand, was not sold on giving Anderson increased control, but neither did he want to lose the rising star to another "hip" studio like Miramax. However, he felt differently once Anderson secured the verbal commitment of Cruise, who was arguably the biggest box-office draw in the world. With Cruise headlining (from a marketing if not a narrative perspective), there could be no subject New Line would refuse to fund—not even one that ends with frogs inexplicably falling from the sky.

Aside from getting *Magnolia* made, Cruise gave Anderson the chance to create one of his most distinctive characters. In early 1998, *Boogie Nights* screened in England for Cruise, then-wife Nicole Kidman, and famed auteur Stanley Kubrick during a break in the lengthy shoot of his final film, *Eyes Wide Shut* (1999). Aware of the value in working with top-level directors such as Kubrick, Oliver Stone, Brian De Palma, Cameron Crowe, and Barry Levinson, the movie star invited Anderson to the set. Once Anderson was there,

3.4. Frank's televisual introduction. Mackey remains one of Anderson's most complex and distinctive characters.

Cruise insisted he wanted to be involved in the director's next project.[7] In Kubrick's literal presence, such an offer was no doubt intoxicating to Anderson. He subsequently committed to writing Cruise a "show-offy role"[8] that would be "a real gold mine for an actor to work with."[9] Cruise added yet another layer to *Magnolia's* expansive mosaic, since Anderson had already committed to writing parts for Walters, Hall, Reilly, Moore, Hoffman, and Macy.

Yet as Anderson recognized, there was more to writing for someone of Cruise's stature. Writing a part like Frank T. J. Mackey was a first—Anderson wasn't just writing for another actor he was friends with, he was writing for a marquee star. While Mark Wahlberg's role in *Boogie Nights* commented humorously on his persona as a failed rapper and former underwear model, it was not initially written for the actor. Structuring whole narratives around stars would be central to *Punch-Drunk Love* and *There Will Be Blood*. When Anderson challenged himself as a writer to work with a star's existing persona, the result was uniformly memorable. Like those subsequent roles for Adam Sandler and Daniel Day-Lewis, Mackey was Anderson's commentary on Cruise's existing persona, rather than a role that challenged the actor to play against type.

Cruise's performance in *Eyes Wide Shut*, for example, exemplified an established formula for stars looking to expand and solidify their cinematic presence—playing an idiosyncratic role *against* type for an established auteur. In the late 1990s, Cruise attempted to reimagine his already thriving career by taking a break from high-octane action films (*Mission Impossible*) and romantic comedies (*Jerry Maguire*)—two reliable box-office genres at which he excelled.

Cruise jumped at the chance to appear in Kubrick's first film in over a decade, *Eyes Wide Shut*. The film offered Cruise not only a high-profile prestige project but the desirable chance to play against type. While Cruise was more often known for his characters' cockiness and sexual charm, the character of doctor Bill Harford allowed him to play someone so sexually repressed that he was completely oblivious to his own desires. And his offbeat work in *Eyes Wide Shut* just as importantly ensured that demand remained when he returned the following year with the big-budget franchise spectacle *Mission Impossible II* (2000)—which itself allowed him to work with one of the premiere action auteurs, John Woo.

Though the project itself was still coming into focus, Anderson's *Magnolia*, like *Eyes Wide Shut*, was a chance for Cruise to both expand his range as an actor beyond the usual mainstream commercial fare and reaffirm his critical status by working with another big-name director. Cruise's first appearance in *Magnolia*, unmediated by television, appropriately shows the actor alone on a stage, basking in the spotlight. We have an explicit commentary on Cruise's considerable presence as by far the biggest star in the film's eminent ensemble. Meanwhile, the use of Strauss's *Also sprach Zarathustra*, and the preceding image of an old man (Earl) on his deathbed, is also a clever reference to Kubrick's most famous film, *2001: A Space Odyssey* (1968), and to the biographical origins of the character himself.

Yet the character Cruise played in *Magnolia* was distinctly different from that which he played in *Eyes Wide Shut*—rather than another sexually repressed middle-aged man, Mackey is a character who wears his heterosexuality on his sleeve, to the point of blatant misogyny. Mackey is a self-help guru who profits by selling middle-aged losers on the secrets of how to "seduce and destroy" women. In other words, Mackey is an extreme, grotesque intensification of Cruise's star persona. His methods for manipulating women are barely removed from his characters' more "playful" seductions of women in movies such as *Top Gun* (1986), *Cocktail* (1988), or *Days of Thunder* (1990). Those roles often required little beyond that trademark cockiness and smile to win over a woman's affections. Although Mackey is uncomfortably close to the dark side of Cruise's persona, the actor was eager to play such an external part after a year of keeping it all in for Kubrick.

Getting *Magnolia* off the ground was very much the direct result of star power. Given *Boogie Nights*'s modest success, Anderson's

3.5. Anderson with William H. Macy during the promotional tour. More than any other film, *Magnolia* was Anderson's most transparently autobiographical film to date.

emergent reputation, De Luca's continued faith at New Line in his potential, and the highly desirable Cruise as the star attraction, the studio signed off on the relatively low-risk gamble giving Anderson final cut on *Magnolia*. The director did not have to screen the film for test audiences, either—a process of consistent rejection that had made the final months of *Boogie Nights*'s post-production a nightmare for everyone involved. From the script to principal shooting to final editing, Anderson could largely do whatever he wanted with *Magnolia*. It is little wonder, then, that principal photography alone took six months—beginning with all of Cruise's scenes in January 1999 and going until early June.

THE AUTOBIOGRAPHICAL IMPULSE

Even before the shoot, Anderson took eight months on the writing process—composing parts for all his actor friends and putting "every embarrassing thing" about his personal life on the page. Aside from being set in his beloved Valley, *Magnolia* is specifically about childhood, love, and cancer within the celebrity culture of Los Angeles's television industry. As Reilly told an interviewer in 2000, "without getting too specific, because he specifically asked me not to, a lot of the things that happen to the characters in the movie come directly out of his life."[10] The clear inspiration for Big Earl Partridge, and the two cancer subplots, was his father Ernie, whom Anderson took care of in his final days. A major television celebrity, Ernie died from cancer in February 1997, just a few months before his son began writing *Magnolia*. Writing Earl's story was no doubt an attempt to work through that loss, while Frank's anger with his estranged father suggests ambivalence toward losing a beloved family member who was never as emotionally close as one would have liked. (In general, Frank's avoidance of his family recalls Anderson's more abstract responses to questions about the origin of Eddie's mom in *Boogie Nights*.)

Although Anderson, understandably, did not talk a lot about his father's death, he was quite open with reporters about the more general subject of cancer. His sensitivity to the subject extended to open contempt for Fincher's *Fight Club*, where cancer survival plays a somewhat comedic function. In that movie, narrator Jack (Edward Norton) finds emotional comfort in attending a support group for the survivors of testicular cancer, even though he never suffered it. Anderson told *Rolling Stone* that

I saw thirty minutes of [*Fight Club*] only because our trailer is playing in front of it. And I would love to go on railing about the movie, but I'm just going to pretend as if I haven't seen it. It's just unbearable. I wish David Fincher testicular cancer, for all of his jokes about it, I wish him fucking testicular cancer.[11]

Ironically, *Fight Club*'s symbolic use of testicular cancer was a more creative meditation on the same late 1990s U.S. crisis in masculinity and materialist alienation that *Magnolia* was also attempting with its critique of patriarchy. Even Anderson's own editor, Tichenor, loved *Fight Club*, calling it "the first film of the twenty-first century."[12] The always-competitive Anderson was selling Fincher's talent and richly complicated film short. Yet his visceral response to that aspect of the movie laid bare the intense feelings Anderson had on the subject of cancer, and on how powerful its cinematic representation was.

In addition to dealing with his father's death, Anderson was also vocal about his new romantic life. In late 1997, Anderson met Apple around the time they did a music video together for her cover of the Beatles song "Across the Universe" for *Pleasantville* (1998). As

Anderson himself admitted in 1999: "I was falling in love and writing a movie [*Magnolia*] at the same time, and all that that implies."[13] The affective logic of *Magnolia* is structured around the indescribable emotions at play when you *feel* like you've met "the one"—the bliss, uncertainty, passion, fears, and exhilaration. Apple's experiences as a child star also, according to Mim Udovitch, inspired scenes for Quiz Kid champion Stanley, including the scene where he is not allowed to use the bathroom.[14] It is foolish to speculate with too much detail on how Anderson's personal life shaped the finished product—but it's just as problematic to ignore it. *Magnolia* is an intensely affective experience and one that Anderson vocally, if also imprecisely, celebrated as autobiographical. Moreover, the film was produced during an especially emotional period in Anderson's life involving profound personal and professional transitions.

AIMEE MANN AND WRITING "FROM THE GUT"

"For better or for worse," Anderson observed after the film's release, "consider this screenplay written completely from the gut."[15] This was often his defense for *Magnolia*, believing that the film's indulgences and eccentricities were the product of a specific creative zone that he entered while pounding out the script. He started in November 1997 and worked on the project sporadically over the next several months. Most of the script was written while Anderson was locked in a self-imposed summer exile in Macy's Vermont cabin. Anderson believed that the truth of *Magnolia* was somewhere in that 190-page draft. "You have to sit in the movie and really absorb it," Anderson told the *New York Times*. "I am always looking for that nuance, that moment of truth, and you can't really do that fast."[16] Later, he reflected further on his self-indulgent writing process during an interview with *Creative Screenwriting*: "I've just got to decide whether I'm being lazy or whether my gut's truly taking me to a proper place."[17] In some ways, *Magnolia*'s strengths and weaknesses ultimately reflected this uncertainty.

Anderson first discovered Aimee Mann around the time he was making *Hard Eight* (whose composer, Michael Penn, is Mann's husband). Mann's role in preproduction, and in the film, demands closer attention. "I write to music," Anderson explained in 1999, "so I better own up to stealing quite a few lines from Aimee Mann, who provides all the songs in the film,"[18] which was symbolically true. Her career, in turn, was revitalized by the attention the film and its soundtrack brought her. Anderson was specifically inspired

3.6. Aimee Mann in the music video for "Save Me." Her music—both older songs and new recordings—inspired Anderson while he wrote *Magnolia*.

by Mann's line from the song "Deathly"—"Now that I've met you / Would you object to never seeing me again?" Claudia repeats this line verbatim to Jim late in the film. "I heard that line," Anderson said, "and I wrote backwards."[19] Much of the resulting screenplay was also written while he was listening to Mann's albums, which resulted most famously in the whole cast singing along in unison to "Wise Up." This distinctive moment echoes *Boogie Nights*'s musical sensibilities and anticipates the implicit musicality of *Punch-Drunk Love*.

Mann's presence brings up several interesting ideas. For the first time, there's another "author" at work in a Paul Thomas Anderson film. Just as Jeremy Blake's artwork (along with Jon Brion's discordant score) would spontaneously erupt and overcome the later *Punch-Drunk Love*, Mann's voice reflects many of the choices throughout *Magnolia*. Anderson joked as much at the time—"this 'original' screenplay could, for all intents and purposes, be called an adaptation of Aimee Mann songs," he wrote in the screenplay's introduction; "I owe her some cash, probably."[20] Lucy Fischer read Anderson's comment here as an awkward admission that the filmmaker was working through the larger anxiety of conceding control over his ambitious final cut. "It may betray," she argued, "Anderson's discomfort (as a male auteur) with 'owing' Mann anything or with having his 'original' work reduced by collaboration."[21] At the very least, Mann's musical presence—influencing the writing process as well as composing new songs—problematizes the young filmmaker's authorial control.

Yet the extensive use of Mann's music fits the larger autobio-

3.7. As the lonesome Donnie stares longingly at Brad, the computer deals a game of solitaire—the lonely man's game.

graphical impulse underlying *Magnolia*. In addition to being close friends at the time with both her and her husband (who scored *Boogie Nights* as well as *Hard Eight*), Anderson was obsessed with Mann's music—even singing one of her lyrics at the beginning of the *Hard Eight* DVD's audio commentary. Mann's presence reinforces the idea of a single voice guiding, rather than disrupting, the film's multiple storylines. Unlike the eclectic soundtrack in *Boogie Nights*, *Magnolia* is composed of Aimee Mann songs and little else. One exception is a remarkable sequence of slow-motion shots accompanied by Supertramp's "Goodbye Stranger," during the moment when Donnie visits the bar to gaze longingly at Brad (Craig Kvinsland).

The heavy diegetic emphasis on Mann's songs throughout *Magnolia* reminds the audience of Anderson's dependence (as both he and Fischer noted) on the singer while he was rushing through the production of the script. The centerpiece of her contribution, the much-discussed "Wise Up" sequence, meanwhile, highlights the film's at times careless indulgence—Anderson included it at that moment in the film because "Wise Up" just happened to be playing as he finished writing the monologue that occurs just before it. As he described later:

I had reached the end of Earl's monologue and was searching for a little vibe—I was lost a bit, and on the headphones came Aimee singing "Wise Up." I wrote as I listened—and the most natural course of action was that everyone should sing—sing how they feel. [. . .] This is one of those things that just happens, and I was either too stupid or not scared enough to hit "delete" once done.[22]

The musical logic was also grounded in the idea that people often sing along with the radio at times of great emotional excess—sadness, joy, anger, and/or release. The "Wise Up" sequence embodies the film's larger narrative logic—trying to find a moment, more than a structure, and unapologetically going with it, hoping that that moment somehow points to a deeper emotional truth. The group sing-along paradoxically foregrounds the occasional strength of *Magnolia*'s idiosyncratic ambitions. As straightforwardly melodramatic and emotionally limp as it often is, the "Wise Up" ensemble nonetheless represents one of *Magnolia*'s truly daring artistic decisions.

Mann's voice in the film begins with Claudia. The young coke addict listens to her music constantly and repeats the lyrics in everyday conversations. Her lip-syncing to "Wise Up" later gives way to everyone else doing likewise. With Claudia, Anderson envisioned a character who believed that she was "so disastrously fucked up that you have no chance of loving" her.[23] Thus, the movie did not originally focus on Earl or Frank, despite the father-son/cancer plotline that had also played out in real life. Rather, Anderson's focus was on the relationship between Claudia and Jimmy—the first scene Anderson envisioned was the sick television-host father returning to his estranged daughter to tell her that he has cancer and will die soon. *Magnolia*'s heart rested with Claudia, who was his "love. My affection is just massive. . . . I wanted to be, in a way, her lover in the moviemaking way. And it turned out to be my personal favorite performance [Walters]."[24]

3.8. Linda sings along to "Wise Up" while sitting in her car. Anderson has said one of the influences for this ambitious sequence was when he one day observed a woman in her car singing Whitney Houston's "I Will Always Love You" at the top of her lungs.

3.9. Claudia was the emotional heart of the film for Anderson. One of the first scenes he envisioned for *Magnolia* was when Jimmy Gator returns to his estranged daughter to tell her he has terminal cancer. The framing and actor positioning here echoes Sydney's first meeting with John in *Hard Eight*.

The well-known backstory is that Anderson did not intend to write a three-hour film with *Magnolia*, but rather a small-scale, intimate character piece that could be done cheaply and swiftly. "*Boogie Nights* was this massive, two-and-a-half hour epic," he explained in an interview shortly after *Magnolia*'s premiere, "and I thought, 'You know what? I wanna bury my head in the sand and just make a little small movie.'"[25] It was to be something Anderson didn't want to overthink, something written directly from that raw personal place—a film focused on following elusive emotional truths as opposed to plotting out a neo-noir or an epic along the lines of *A Star is Born.*

On the other hand, Anderson also wanted to compose something to showcase his rapidly expanding Altmanesque network of friends. Overall, Anderson's logic was to make something quick, low-key, and emotionally powerful before the imagined critical and artistic expectations following *Boogie Nights* had caught up with him. Yet the pressure he had brought upon himself by demanding creative control from New Line had made a low-key *Magnolia* impossible. Anderson, consciously or otherwise, had to justify the studio's considerable faith in him. Added to that, Anderson's desire to write from the gut while also providing parts for his friends created a momentum that ensured his latest film would be far from modest in scope.

The result was a bloated narrative structure that, in retrospect, only superficially paid homage to Anderson's primary influence, Robert Altman. There's no question that Anderson's greatest strength as writer—as with Altman as director—is a deep affection for the characters, thus partially explaining *Magnolia*'s ambitions. From there, the similarities between, for example, *Magnolia* and Altman epics like *Nashville* or *Short Cuts* largely diverge. Altman rarely wrote his own scripts, preferring actors who largely improvised, a practice that was all but banished in the production of *Magnolia*. Altman had a far more cool approach to his ensemble epics—characters wandered in and out of scenes without clear functions, actors were crowded into a more observational frame, audible strands of dialogue come and go, conversations are picked up or dropped off halfway through. For Altman, there was no necessary urgency to get somewhere thematically or narratively important.

But with Anderson, particularly as a director, the opposite was often true, especially on an early film like *Magnolia*. The dialogue he had written from his gut was meant to be delivered as written, his characters served clearly defined narrative and thematic functions, and the camera and editing had little patience for an actor's potential improvisation. To a greater extent than on *Hard Eight* or *Boogie Nights*, virtually every line in *Magnolia* appeared as written. Reflecting on the extensive rewrites he did while drafting *There Will Be Blood* in 2008, Anderson noted that "I didn't have any desire I might have had 10 years ago to shoot every single word that I wrote."[26] While Anderson clearly respected the actors' abilities to find the scene on their own during rehearsals, he still maintained tight control over the bigger picture—the film's scenes, framing, narrative plotting, and thematic progression. Insisting that *Magnolia* ultimately be a profound story about life in the Valley, Anderson forced his film to show an urgency to its structure that Altman, with his more laid-back approach to storytelling, never really insisted on.

Altman held the camera on actors and improvised dialogue because that's how he felt moments in life often were—fleeting, incomplete, perhaps even ultimately insignificant. Anderson, though, let the camera run on his actors and his lines of dialogue only because he felt that, somewhere in there, a deeper truth about life would emerge. He couldn't bear to cut a second of any of it for fear of compromising the development of that elusive truth. And he even went so far as to frame the film with larger references to the Bible, accounts of weird scientific phenomena, and even a voice-over about the quirkiness of random fate—all to make sure that, at the end of the day, his sprawling mosaic of characters in Southern California would *mean* something.

As *Magnolia's* story ballooned, Anderson's self-indulgence and personal defiance would once again test his support with people around him, specifically as the film moved into post-production. Even Tichener, his editor, "thought [*Magnolia*] was too long,"[27] but had the right perspective on it when pressured by an increasingly nervous De Luca. If the executive was so frustrated by the length, Tichener asked him, "why did you greenlight a 192-page script?"[28] As this suggested, even De Luca, then Anderson's biggest industry supporter, eventually lost patience with the arrogant director he had repeatedly defended. At one point, he went so far as to snap and curse at the rebellious Anderson in front of an entire collection of New Line executives[29]—a group that, in retrospect, was eager to throw both of them overboard once *Magnolia* began to sink. But, unlike on *Hard Eight* and *Boogie Nights*, Anderson could for the moment blow it all off without repercussion, and he did. Shaye, the studio chief, once leaned on Anderson at a party, asking him to trim *Magnolia*. According to Sharon Waxman, Anderson said, "Bob, I have two words for you: final cut." Then he walked away.[30] Such arrogance would empower Anderson in the short term but cost him later.

AMERICAN CINEMA AT THE END OF THE MILLENNIUM

While *Magnolia* was a deeply personal film, Anderson's contempt for *Fight Club* reminds us that it did not exist in a historical vacuum. Indeed, *Magnolia* was typical of its time. Many of 1999's so-called "maverick" films—*Magnolia, Fight Club, Being John Malkovich, Election, American Beauty*, and even traditional genre fare like *Office Space*—showed remarkably consistent themes. In particular, all focused on existential dilemmas stemming from a perceived crisis in masculinity and an anxiety regarding historical emptiness in a country that was drowning in media saturation and consumerist materialism. Before 9/11 and the "war on terror," constructed media notions of masculinity were perceived as being in crisis, no longer defined by roles such as fighting in military conflicts or working jobs that required intensive manual labor.

In a sympathetic *Newsweek* column on *Fight Club*, journalist Susan Faludi (author of such controversial books as *Backlash: The Undeclared War Against American Women* [1992]) argued that Fincher's film was an especially potent reflection of this moment in American culture. "An incisive gender drama," she argued, *Fight Club* showed that:

behind the extremities of [Edward Norton's] character is the modern male predicament: he's fatherless, trapped in a cubicle in an anonymous corporate job,
trying to glean an identity from Ikea brochures, entertainment magazines and
self-help gatherings. Jack traverses a barren landscape familiar to many men
who must contend with a world stripped of socially useful male roles and saturated with commercial images of masculinity. "We are the middle children of
history," his doppelganger, Tyler Durden ([Brad] Pitt), says, "with no purpose or
place. We have no great war, no great depression . . . We have been raised by
television to believe that we'll be millionaires and movie gods and rock stars—
but we won't . . . And we're very, very pissed off." . . . For men facing an increasingly hollow, consumerized world, that path lies not in conquering women but
in uniting with them against the hollowness.[31]

While impossibly utopian, such perspective was reflected in the
young-auteur-driven films of the time that confronted questions
of gender construction directly, even violently. As Faludi argued in
Stiffed: The Betrayal of the American Male (1999), modern masculinity was largely defined by shifting gender roles in the wake of corporate downsizing, reduced military infrastructure, and a feminiz-
ing celebrity culture. *Fight Club* romanticized older masculine ideals
as defined through the strong, quiet dignity of active fathers, proud
military veterans, and lifelong factory workers. This nostalgic ideal
was lost through media images of easy charisma and perfect phy-
siques as well as a postwar, postindustrial culture that left many
such hard-working, soft-spoken men behind.

Moreover, other films, such as *Magnolia*, also spoke to that distinct pre-9/11 moment in shifting gender expectations. In these
late-1990s movies, filmmakers represented ideal notions of masculinity as constantly problematized by the presence of failed fathers,
the opportunism of reactionary self-help gurus preying on men's
most misogynistic tendencies, and the negotiation of impossible celebrity ideals. Much of this intense self-introspection also spoke to
the larger cultural and political void of a prosperous 1990s America.
With the U.S. economy and feelings of domestic security relatively
stable, the biggest national crisis was, as I noted in the previous
chapter, the attempt by petty Republicans in Congress to impeach
the President for having an affair and lying about it. The older medi-

ated gender ideals of a dominant masculinity, however, returned in the wake of the United States's "war on terror."

WHICH IS WHICH AND WHO ONLY KNOWS?

In a *seemingly* carefree environment prior to 9/11, though, it would be easy to imagine a world in which (for some) the most urgent question was something as self-indulgent as uncovering the meaning of life, or where the biggest problem was feeling stifled by too many material resources rather than too few—thus coming to see one's parents as the oppressors. As a result, it's no coincidence that many of these philosophical excesses focused on the breakdown of white middle-class families, a perceived "personal" crisis in the absence of more meaningful political ones. In his discussion of late 1990s "smart films" like *Magnolia*, Jeffrey Sconce observed that often the "focus [was] on the white middle-class family as a crucible of miscommunication and emotional dysfunction."[32]

Thus, the best way to understand the abstract, muddled philosophical dilemmas that frame *Magnolia* is to see them as the product of someone with too much time on his hands, pondering grand questions of life's purpose in place of more urgent matters such as where the next paycheck or meal will come from. Such existential inquiries can still have a potentially powerful affective impact. Yet causal ponderings on their own, and without an engaging plot to anchor them, can land with a big thud for audiences. Of course, the same criticism could apply to most every one of the smart films mentioned earlier. Sconce argued that notions of narrative and thematic serendipity were one of the defining characteristics of many American films during this time, identified by "a fascination with 'synchronicity' as a principle of narrative organization" and "a related thematic interest in random fate."[33] He highlighted *Magnolia* (along with *Boogie Nights*) as a strong instance of the focus on people "fucked by fate," and wherein "the centrality of coincidence and synchronicity [became] an organizing principle."[34] In *Magnolia*, such a reading strategy feels particularly acute because the three-hour search for "that moment of truth"—as Anderson himself put it[35]— in all its vague, undefined glory, is so transparently the film's primary thematic and narrative preoccupation.

Even if one accepts the theme of random fate—coincidence and serendipity's power in everyday lives—it's still in tension with *Magnolia*'s other explicit thematic preoccupation—the often-repeated idea that "we may be through with the past, but the past ain't

3.10. A rather transparent attempt to explain the random events of *Magnolia*, highlighting the unresolved tension in the film between foregrounding narratives of coincidence yet also explicitly insisting it all adds up to something.

3.11. As Sydney Barringer prepares to commit suicide, a group of wires spell out one of the film's many 82s, though they largely appear in the beginning montage.

through with us." In other words, *Magnolia* isn't ultimately about strange, random occurrences of fate; it focuses on a much more fatalistic notion directly opposed to serendipity: *people will pay for their pasts.* Likewise, the clever use of the number 82, in particular during the opening prologue, speaks to the film's underdeveloped thematic logic. From the roof of Sydney Barringer's apartment complex, to the number of the hanged murderer, to the identification of the fire-fighting airplane in Nevada, the number 82 is littered throughout *Magnolia's* opening—a half-dozen references total in just a few minutes. They appear less frequently in the rest of the film: on a sign in the *What Do Kids Know?* audience and on billboards outside Solomon & Solomon at the very end.

3.12. Another (Exodus) 8:2 in the *What Do Kids Know?* audience, anticipating the film's potentially biblical finale. The page who takes the sign away was Anderson himself.

Like the references to the Freemasons in *Magnolia*, the 82s are a clever inside gag, but what do they really *mean*? On one level, they reference the Exodus material from the Bible about God smiting Egypt with a rain of frogs if Moses and his folk are not allowed to leave (the "children" in the film demand to be freed). This explains the film's bizarre conclusion. But Anderson reportedly didn't know about the biblical frogs until he was informed by actor Henry Gibson of it. In the original script, the use of frogs was drawn from the work of Charles Fort. The 82s were tacked on during production to match the end, but without any clear sense of how they fit with the competing vignettes of random chance initially put forth.

Largely through montage and voice-over, *Magnolia* repeatedly appeals beyond its sprawling cast of characters to this general idea that strange things happen all the time. It is the only such instance of a voice-over narrator in Anderson's films to date—used, like the stories of chance, only at the beginning and end of *Magnolia*. Cinematic voice-overs can be last-minute solutions, designed to fill holes or hide gaps in narrative and thematic logic. The narrator is voiced by Ricky Jay, the actor who plays *What Do Kids Know?* television producer Burt Ramsey. Is Burt the one secretly controlling everything (he does wear the Freemason ring, after all)? Perhaps, but to what end? Except when deployed ironically, the voice-over is a common narrative shortcut for filmmakers to relay important information directly to the audience. The dependence on voice-over in *Magnolia* fits with its abstract appeal to random fate—insofar as both are designed to mask a deeper thematic incoherence to the movie.

Of course, *Magnolia* is rich with allusions: the Bible, Freemasonry,

Charles Fort, etc. Yet such thoughtful references muddle *Magnolia's* thematic arc far more than they offer useful clues to understanding the larger point. Likewise, the inexplicable incidents in the film (Sydney's death, frogs, people singing an Aimee Mann song in unison across time and space, guns falling from the sky, and so forth) lack a clear internal thematic logic to them. Is there any larger (divine) energy at work, dictating what happens and to whom? Or is it all truly just a matter of chance? Is the movie about the sins passed from father to child? If so, why does the one good father, Sir Edmund William Godfrey (Pat Healy), get beaten to death in the film's first two minutes? If it's about the role of fathers, what relevance does Delmer Darion's (Patton Oswalt) freak death have to do with anything? Maybe nothing, but the film is hardly nihilistic, either.

If it's all "just a matter of chance," then why do Jimmy Gator and Earl Partridge have to pay for what they have done? If it can't be just "one of those things," then *what is it?* The film doesn't really know: "And for what I would like to say," the narrator says, evading the question, "I can't." Then, when the narrator returns in the film's conclusion, he speaks in the same obfuscating generalities as he did in the beginning: "There are stories of coincidence and chance and intersections and strange things told and which is which and who only knows?" While it is true that repeated viewings can reward the attentive, informed spectator (e.g., spotting the 82s), the lasting effect of these details is ultimately superficial; they lack the resonance of, for example, Jack's reconciliation at his father's deathbed. Nothing explains its considerable narrative web of characters. In the end, *Magnolia's* main point—that people must confront their pasts—is a common one in Anderson's films, and right there on the surface.

MELODRAMA AND THE SOAP OPERA AESTHETIC

Underneath that grandiose façade rests a more common narrative trope. *Magnolia* is less indebted to the cool improvisations of Altman than to the open-endedness of the soap opera genre—more televisual than cinematic in its structure. Arranged around a sprawling web of characters and deeply emotional sensibilities, *Magnolia* doesn't make sense without understanding its essential dependence on the affective logic of that most traditionally maligned of modern narratives, the melodrama. Joanne Dillman argued that *Magnolia* should not be read in relation to the classic Hollywood structure of clearly defined characters, logical plot progression, and narrative closure. Instead, she suggested, *Magnolia* works as a televisual soap opera in cinematic form. This reading involves a heightened emphasis on melodramatic intensity and emotional hysteria, as well as privileging narrative open-endedness and interruption over transparent character arcs, plot points, and resolution.

Like the soap opera, *Magnolia* is an open-ended text seeking to reveal moments of truth in numerous lives instead of a self-contained story. "The most logical way," Dillman wrote, "to read *Magnolia*—because it clearly offers itself as working outside both mainstream narrative and film conventions—is as television [. . . where] melodrama so 'dominates' the television discourse that few programs, including the news, escape its conventions."[36] Unlike the extensive journey of Dirk Diggler in *Boogie Nights* or John and Sydney's friendship in *Hard Eight*, *Magnolia* picks up on many characters midway through, and sometimes leaves them with minimal, if any, change. We are invited simply to witness ephemeral flashes of charged emotions, sometimes to powerful effect.

Structurally, *Magnolia* evokes a season finale without the season that preceded it. The film works best as serialized melodrama—one that presumes a masculine, rather than traditionally feminine, point of view. What becomes dramatized to excess in *Magnolia* is the presentation of what it means, according to Anderson, to be a white male living an upper-middle-class lifestyle in the San Fernando Valley at the end of the millennium. In a perpetually unhappy emotional state, the male characters' senses of self are constantly under siege from cultural, familial, and professional pressure. Nearly every major character breaks down crying, at one moment or another, from the stress of everyday life. "The film is overwrought," Dillman added:

So much is unmotivated (communal singing, frogs falling from the sky, Jim's gun falling from the sky); much is left unsaid (between Frank and the journalist, Donnie and Brad, Stanley and his father, Jimmy Gator and Rose [Melinda Dillon], Jimmy and Claudia, Linda and Earl, Linda and Phil); much is repressed (especially by Claudia, Linda, and Frank); and much is unanswered (what is the story of the dead man in the closet? Where is the elusive son of Marcie [Cleo King]? Why does Linda try to kill herself?). At the most obvious level of performance, Linda, Claudia, Frank and even Donnie move through the film at a pitch of near hysteria, broken only by outbursts or tears.[37]

Magnolia is a film completely written from the (masculine) gut, without reflection or discipline. Whereas Anderson's first two films

3.13. Scholars have noted that *Magnolia* works best as a masculine melodrama, foregrounded by the consistent emotional breakdowns of figures such as the male nurse, Phil.

privileged narrative, *Magnolia* is driven affectively by the degree to which viewers invest themselves in the passionate, melodramatic circumstances of characters living out another day in their lives. One must empathize with the intensely personal emotional zone from which Anderson was writing—obsessed with Aimee Mann's music, recalling feeling ignored by adults as a child, falling in love with someone who feels unloved, losing a parent to cancer, embracing his actor friends, reinventing his (auteur) self to outrun his past, and/or feeling both empowered and oppressed by the celebrity culture surrounding the television industry. Therein lies the contradiction of *Magnolia* as the (closed) cinematic telling of an (open-ended) televisual story—it either works or it doesn't, and it's difficult to argue how cutting or rewriting it would have made it a stronger film (though the prologue and voice-over could be dropped). Cutting *Boogie Nights* and *Hard Eight* down to their central concerns made them better films, but *Magnolia* doesn't really have just one thread to focus on.

THE FEMINIZED (WHITE) MALE

Magnolia attempts to deconstruct traditional models of masculinity through a (feminine) televisual narrative structure that privileges gaps, eruptions, and interruptions rather than tight narrative structures. Dillman argues that *Magnolia*'s emphasis on disruption and openness, and on emotional excess, presumes a feminine audience as a means to complicate its gender dynamic. The movie also appeals to what Fischer, in her analysis of *Magnolia*, called the "feminized male."[38] Like *Boogie Nights*, representations of gender roles and power dynamics are front and center in *Magnolia*. Yet unlike its predecessor, Anderson's third film does not follow the traditional phallocentric structure that *Boogie Nights*'s premise only intensifies.

Magnolia raises questions about gender construction by presenting a complex picture of multiple masculinities. In "Theory into Practice: En-Gendering Narrative in *Magnolia*," Fischer argues that *Magnolia* is essentially a "dissertation on patriarchy."[39] In contrast to Dillman, she does not focus on the film's assumed audience as symbolically feminine. Rather, *Magnolia* deconstructs masculinity by arguing that the failure of patriarchy is grounded in issues stemming from the larger American media landscape. This is not to say that female characters in *Magnolia* are somehow empowered, however—as Fischer notes, wives are "disempowered appendages to their husbands," while the other female characters seem "demoralized by life in a patriarchal world."[40] With the exception of the two main black women—Marcie and Gwenovier (April Grace)—women are powerless. *Magnolia* nonetheless locates itself within the dynamics of a heavily masculinized world: "despite the presence of 'feminized' males and the film's skewering of patriarchs, it privileges men by the sheer number of them functioning as major characters."[41] Thus, even *Magnolia*'s attempted deconstruction of patriarchy leaves unanswered questions in its wake. After all, as Donna Peberdy has argued, "the recuperation of masculinity for the contemporary man [in *Magnolia* and other 1990s films] ultimately depends on the extrication of the boy from the mother, the husband from the wife, the man from the woman."[42]

How notions of femininity are complicit in the construction of masculinity rests at the heart of *Magnolia*. In an article on Cruise's persona and masculine film roles, Peberdy provocatively argued that *Magnolia*'s representation of men is situated within a larger discourse regarding what she terms "bipolar masculinity"—a cultural logic by which men are expected to be both hypermasculine/"strong," and feminine/"weak." The dichotomy is established around opposing ideals: poet Robert Bly's notions of the "wild man" (the untamed mythical figure who represents the last gasp of manhood in the feminist backlash of the 1980s) and the "wimp" (the ineffectual, passive, failed father figure who demands the presence of the former as an alternative—and vice versa).

Most of the males in *Magnolia* are situated within these two polar opposites. Mackey represents the misogynistic extreme of the wild man, while his seminars seem designed to appeal to the same crowd of frustrated white men that Bly does. Donnie, on the other hand, embodies the opposite extreme, the wimp. He's played particularly well by Macy, who throughout performances in the 1990s "embodied 'the loser' through vocal performance and as a result of his 'given' facial characteristics; the 'whiny' voice, hangdog cheeks, and sagging eyes all contribute to his [wimpy] persona."[43] Characters Macy played in Anderson's films (Donnie, Little Bill in *Boogie Nights*) are situated as wimps in their respective narratives by direct opposition to hypermasculine extremes (Mackey, Dirk Diggler). "Their relationship," Peberdy writes, "is one of interdependence with each masculinity trope reliant on the other for validation and definition."[44] The core of bipolar masculinity rests on the idea that these mutually reaffirming extremes coexist.

The complexities of bipolar masculinity, according to Peberdy, often rest in an actor tasked with "performing" both extremes. In *Magnolia*, this performance becomes particularly evident with Mackey's character. He swings from being the untamable, misogynistic wild man in the film's first half to the weak, crying wimp in the second as he confronts his dying father and cares for his injured stepmother. In the end, Mackey reveals "the softer, gentler identity hidden beneath his wild exterior."[45] But this "softer" side is no less a "performance" than the former. Peberdy adds:

Jack [Mackey's real name] is revealed as authentic, reinforced by his unrestrained emotional episode at his father's bedside. Yet, his emotional outburst is also depicted as excessive and over-the-top, so that rather than moving from a performance of manliness into "authentic" manliness, Jack's childlike weeping demonstrates the shift from excessive hypermasculinity to excessive softness.[46]

Thus, both extremes are equally situated as gender performances. This tremendous shift, moreover, speaks back to Cruise's larger persona. Peberdy argues that Cruise's public-relations self-destruction in the mid-2000s (jumping on the couch with Oprah, verbally assaulting Brooke Shields and Matt Lauer) was the result of such an extreme swing. In a matter of months, Cruise's image went from one of tightly controlled star to unhinged fool, which contrasted too sharply with his expected public performance. A complicated masculine figure, Mackey internalizes the disproportionate extremes of wild-man misogynist and ineffectual, weeping "soft" man. (One could also observe that Barry Egan, Anderson's next major character in *Punch-Drunk Love*, works within similar extremes.)

We are still left with the more extreme wimp: Donnie. As with Scotty (Hoffman in *Boogie Nights*), the representation of homosexuality in *Magnolia* is even more troubling than the passive representation of women. Indeed, Donnie's and Scotty's narrative trajectories are virtually identical: both men lust after another physically perfect man, and both model themselves after the object of their desire. Scotty buys the same clothes and car as Dirk; Donnie dyes his hair and wants to get braces, just like Brad. Both men finally confess their feelings in a sad, drunken display of desperation. Scotty sits in his car, weeping uncontrollably; Donnie stumbles to the bathroom, throwing up in the toilet. Both men are filled with equal amounts of self-loathing and the narrative never shows them recovering from their moment of emotional breakdown. Scotty remains in the margins of *Boogie Nights*; Donnie is reduced to ineffectual criminal behavior. When he is hit by a falling frog and lands face first on the pavement, smashing his teeth, Donnie's final cruel irony is that he will need oral corrective surgery after all. The most disturbing part of *Magnolia*'s "dissertation on patriarchy" is that the furthest extreme from the patriarchal ideal—the socially marginalized gay man—is the one major male character in *Magnolia* most visibly denied a relatively happy ending (not counting those, like Partridge and Gator, who are beyond redemption). Stanley finally stands up to his dad, Phil has completed his charge, Jim returns to Claudia, and Frank is allowed to say goodbye to his father and reunite with his family. But Donnie is left alone with a busted mouth.

Finally, a particularly complex moment of gender construction worth exploring further is Gwenovier's confrontation with Mackey. She aggressively challenges the celebrity salesman on his manufactured educational and family history. Clearly, the assertive Gwenovier serves as a direct counterpoint to Mackey's boisterous misogyny—the first step in Frank's gradual emotional breakdown over the course of the remaining narrative. Their verbal confrontation becomes an ironic replay of the strategic use of careful indifference and arrogance Cruise's character deployed to seduce Kelly McGillis's character in *Top Gun*. Gwenovier, Fischer notes, "gets the better of the male supremacist" by testing him at every turn and eventually forcing Mackey back into his protective shell.[47]

The powerful role that Gwenovier plays in *Magnolia* also paradox-

3.14. Gwenovier is the most assertive female character in the film, ignoring Mackey's misogynistic intimidation and challenging him on his manufactured past.

ically highlights how pervasively Anderson's films focus on white men. In fact, the only major plotline removed from the first cut of *Magnolia* concerned several African American characters involved in a murder by the Worm (Orlando Jones). This brings to mind that the only significant subplot shot and then cut from *Boogie Nights* involved "Chocolate Love" porn star Becky Barnett (Nicole Ari Parker) and her abusive husband (hence, Dirk's car crash remains unexplained). A rare direct negotiation with institutional racism comes with Buck Swope (Don Cheadle) in *Boogie Nights*. His blackness is stated as a factor in others' perceptions about him, and his race is implied to have factored into his loan rejection.

The attention to racial representation has an added significance considering that Southern California—no stranger to complicated histories of race—is home to stories like *Magnolia* that often aspire to negotiate the complicated interactions of characters who might otherwise not interact. As Hsuan L. Hsu notes, "Like previous L.A. ensemble films [*Short Cuts*, *Grand Canyon*], *Magnolia* presents a totalizing image of L.A.'s community by deliberately relegating its black characters to the sidelines."[48] When interviewed on the subject by Cynthia Fuchs years earlier, Anderson's defense was to suggest "spending a couple of days in the Valley: that's how much color would come into your life."[49] Yet this observation seems as damning in its ignorance as it may be enlightening in its explanation. Race is central to Anderson's films precisely because it is so invisible, so overlooked, so unrelenting in the films' collective perpetuation of a larger thematic preoccupation with white, middle-class perspectives.

3.15. No one in *Magnolia* is outside its celebrity media culture; even Jim imagines himself as the star of a *COPS* reality television episode.

"I LENT YOU MY CELEBRITY"

Nearly as important as the complex images of masculinity and whiteness in *Magnolia* is the persistent concern with celebrity, its commodification, and cultural impact. Frank and Donnie not only present two extremes of masculinity—they also offer two extremes of the film's intertwined relationship between the economic role of salesmen and the cultural value of celebrities on society's periphery. Celebrity status is an attempt to sell something, and vice versa. *Magnolia*'s preoccupation with stardom reflects the life Anderson grew up with: in the shadows of the Los Angeles television industry and of minor, mostly television, celebrities, such as his dad, his dad's friends (Bob Ridgely, Tim Conway), and the fathers of childhood friends (Robert Conrad). Celebrities are everywhere in *Magnolia*—Frank, Donnie, Stanley, Jimmy Gator—to the extent that we quickly forget their media status. Even police officer Jim imagines himself as a celebrity. He talks to himself in the squad car, pretending to be the focal point of a *COPS*-type reality show, as though such televisual visibility would make his life more eventful.

As with Dirk Diggler in his lowest moment in *Boogie Nights*, social and economic self-worth are defined for these characters through their celebrity status (or loss thereof). This is made most explicit with Donnie, who is fired early in the film from his job at Solomon & Solomon electronics, where we are again invited to witness the ubiquity of televisions in *Magnolia*. To save his job, Donnie argues with Solomon (Alfred Molina) that his celebrity status as the former Quiz Kid makes him an asset to the store, and that they're obligated to continue employing him because of their use of it. Meanwhile, Frank is the opposite—someone anonymous who became famous by way of his sales skills. Selling middle-aged losers on "seduce and destroy," Mackey has acquired a level of social visibility that suggests he cannot use his own tricks on women who recognize him, inviting a devastating and deserved public exposé by Gwenovier. Mackey agrees to this interview only because he's interested in the further self-promotion it would provide. Both Donnie and Mackey are trying to "sell" something (themselves as proven commodities) that they are also paradoxically trying to outrun.

Similarly, the stars connected to the game show *What Do Kids Know?*—Jimmy, Donnie, and Stanley—reinforce the idea that the attainment and maintenance of celebrity status do not necessarily guarantee happiness. Like Frank, Jimmy's iconic status as a living television legend is a sad façade, as the opening montage cleverly establishes. Jimmy drowns himself in booze and self-hatred, knowing television hides what a miserable and unfulfilling life he has lived. His cancer is the punishment that he must endure for sexually abusing his daughter, just as Earl's cancer embodies the price he must pay for cheating on his first wife and abandoning his son.

Stanley, on the other hand, is trapped by and completely uninterested in the celebrity lifestyle, oblivious to the perks that come with it. Moreover, he has been robbed of his childhood as his phenomenal genius is exploited by his father to the point of child abuse—a fate that also befell the now broke and lonely Donnie. Scarred by stardom, Donnie is a man without an identity. Having missed out on his childhood, he cannot find a comfortable role as an adult other than sticking ambivalently to his fading status as a former Quiz Kid. In the end, Stanley can only run away from the soundstage, fleeing the spotlight that so many others crave. Donnie, meanwhile, is haunted by his lost celebrity—a giant copy of a royalty check hangs over him in his parents' dining room. Frank, Donnie, Stanley, and Jimmy are all celebrities trapped by their high level of social visibility.

The sharp critique of celebrity personas in *Magnolia* fits with Anderson's larger theme of people trying to reinvent themselves, often unsuccessfully. The television industry here is all about deception for short-term gratification—a public, smiling disguise to hide disturbing private demons involving lust, betrayal, abuse, and greed. Such reinvention can be about outrunning the past, as for Mackey. But *Magnolia*'s central thematic preoccupation, beyond the damage inflected on children by their fathers, concerns the inability to do just that. And such fame is entangled with money. Stanley's dad cares more about the cash than about the way celebrity impacts his son's emotional and physical well-being. Meanwhile, Donnie's salesman job is simply about exploiting his past stardom financially—interestingly, he doesn't lean on his celebrity status to impress Brad. Celebrity is always a commodity, one with a detrimental impact, in *Magnolia*.

THE NEW KING AT NEW LINE

Looking closely at *Magnolia* reveals a wealth of thoughtful details and moments of wild melodramatic excess, but in the end it remains unclear what the cumulative goal was. Even Anderson seemed disappointed when finally viewing the first cut with an audience. As documented in *That Moment: Magnolia Video Diary* (2000), Anderson appeared dazed and even melancholy afterward as he stared out the limousine window. Talking to the interviewer, Anderson casually compared the movie to a girlfriend who just wasn't there for him anymore—a metaphor that may have worked on multiple levels.[50] An unabashed labor of love, *Magnolia* didn't end up being quite the film Anderson thought it would be. If *Magnolia* was still more or less that film he envisioned, Anderson himself had since moved on emotionally from that raw space in which he had originally conceived it and embraced its idiosyncrasies. Any film so transparently melodramatic, so unapologetically absorbed into its own one-dimensional excesses, does not leave much room for someone in the audience who can't relate to that moment the movie tries to capture. This may even apply to the person who made it.

In the end, final cut was as much a burden as a blessing to the promising young filmmaker—all kudos, but also all blame, fell squarely on Anderson's suddenly overwhelmed shoulders. Added to this was the pressure to produce a masterpiece for an Oscar-starved studio. In rushing to write and produce *Magnolia* so quickly on the heels of *Boogie Nights*'s success, Anderson tried to do too much—too many storylines for their own sakes, too many characters for too many friends, too many half-developed themes to justify its scope, and too many personal issues laid bare. All came at the expense of more fully developed characterizations and a sustained, focused narrative. In some ways, Anderson's earlier experiences on *Hard Eight* and *Boogie Nights* were blessings in disguise—any negative critical blowback regarding the final product could be deflected by Anderson and his supporters to those other members of production with whom he had publically fought. Thus, having final cut also meant—in time—that it would fall on Anderson himself to be more self-critical, to be his own worst critic. Anderson would increasingly challenge himself after *Magnolia* was not received as the unqualified masterpiece that he felt it would be.

Anderson may have won the battle with New Line—making the film he wanted—but he lost the war. *Magnolia* appeared in theaters in late 1999 and early 2000 as exactly the version that the young director wanted. But the protracted fights with studio executives, and the divisions and animosities created over *Magnolia* (and still lingering from *Boogie Nights*), became irresolvable once the film proved to be a substantial disappointment from an industry standpoint. The film earned only $22 million domestically, nowhere near its budget, which was closer to $40 million. Moreover, the film's award tally was underwhelming for an epic of that ambition and scope. Cruise was nominated for an Oscar—in a role that was designed to *win* an Oscar—Aimee Mann was nominated for "Save Me" (an appropriate nod to the film's muse), and Anderson was nominated for his second Best Original Screenplay award, a nod to his singular, undeniable ambition in making the film.

In the end *Magnolia* didn't win anything, and it certainly let down New Line's hopes of being a legitimate contender by winning that elusive Best Picture Oscar. *Magnolia* did win the Golden Bear Award for Best Picture at the fiftieth annual Berlin Film Festival in February 2000, but that modest accolade appears, in retrospect, to be more bittersweet than vindicating. Overall, *Magnolia* received more positive reviews than negative ones or, more precisely, often mixed reviews that were themselves more positive than negative. However, putting aside the question of awards, there simply was no outpouring of critical praise to justify, from an industry standpoint, Anderson's unprecedented freedom in making *Magnolia*. In that respect, the film was doomed to fail.

If the critical ambivalence toward *Magnolia* was not enough to force Anderson to rethink his industrial etiquette or blinding self-importance, then his subsequent falling out with New Line should have been. The beneficiary of a remarkably supportive creative environment at the studio for two motion pictures, Anderson's tenure there essentially ended after what was perceived, in the eyes of Hollywood and the critical community, as the general failure of *Magnolia*. New Line was contractually a coproducer on his next film, *Punch-Drunk Love* (2002), but that film was really a Revolution

Studios project. After demanding complete control, despite a relative lack of accomplishment, Anderson then erred by shoving that power in the face of powerful people like De Luca and Shaye—no less than the head of the studio. After trying to work on a compromise with New Line over *Boogie Nights*, Anderson quickly reverted to his *Sydney*-era naiveté upon obtaining final cut—effectively shutting out the studio, as if it no longer mattered. Regardless of one's personal opinion of *Magnolia*, there is no question that its reception was generally perceived as a disappointment, even a much-deserved comeuppance for the cocky young director who hadn't yet earned the status to which he felt entitled. De Luca wasn't far behind Anderson in leaving New Line. Taking the fall for a disastrous 2000 fiscal year, the "blank check guy" was forced in 2001 to leave after eighteen years at the studio.

The story had a very happy ending for New Line, once they cut Anderson and other edgy directors loose. By 2003, it was the envy of all of Hollywood, thanks to the monumental success of the *Lord of the Rings* trilogy (2001–2003), which entered production around the same time as *Magnolia*. It would be overreaching to speculate that the failure of intimate auteur films like *Magnolia* led to New Line's subsequent embrace of the big-budget blockbuster. Yet after experimenting with more modest projects in hopes of critical acclaim, New Line followed its support of Anderson by throwing the entire future of the studio behind a very different emergent auteur, Peter Jackson. With *Magnolia* in the rearview mirror, the studio went on to critical acclaim and record box office with Jackson's historic trilogy. New Line even finally won its much-sought-after Academy Award for Best Picture in early 2004—an award that seemed almost preordained by the time the last of the three, *The Return of the King*, hit multiplexes in late 2003.

Anderson's career and reputation hadn't seemed to fare nearly as well by 2004. Having left New Line, the director followed up his massive epic with the modest, quirky little Sandler romantic comedy *Punch-Drunk Love*. While Shaye was busy collecting Oscars, Anderson's fourth film came and went with barely a notice. Like *Magnolia*, *Punch-Drunk Love* baffled some critics and failed once again at the box office despite its star power. The film's idiosyncrasies alienated many die-hard Sandler fans, who were expecting something more mainstream. Even many Anderson devotees weren't anticipating such a sharp deviation from the look and feel of his earlier films.

The initial reception of Anderson's collaboration with Sandler appeared to further cement his creative slide from the hot, young director whose promise was first shown in *Boogie Nights* and then exposed in *Magnolia*. But if it seemed to an outsider like Anderson had been forgotten like many other maverick directors from the 1990s, it was only because people hadn't looked carefully enough at *Punch-Drunk Love*. For his fourth film—a low-key visual and aural masterpiece of modern alienation in the Valley, which concealed much beneath its unassuming surface—would prove to be just the beginning of Anderson's emergence as one of America's premiere young filmmakers.

this is funny.

CHAPTER 4

the art-house adam sandler movie

COMMODITY CULTURE AND THE ETHEREAL EPHEMERALITY OF *PUNCH-DRUNK LOVE* (2002)

The opening shot of Paul Thomas Anderson's *Punch-Drunk Love* (2002) reveals much about that moment in the director's career. The static long shot of its protagonist, Barry Egan (Adam Sandler), as he sits at a desk in an empty warehouse, conveys that powerful sense of personal and material alienation so crucial to the film. It's also the first of countless moments where the safe distance of an old-fashioned telephone is his only acceptable means of interpersonal communication. Barry's blue suit allows him to disappear into the wall—he is both the center of the film's attention and insignificant in the world around him. In the wake of *Boogie Nights* (1997) and *Magnolia*'s (1999) epic canvas, this film focuses intensely on one character and on the star himself, Sandler. *Punch-Drunk Love* is as much a star vehicle as an auteurist one.

As this remarkably simple image lingers, almost completely motionless, it also begins pointing to something else. If the flashy Steadicam shot in *Boogie Nights* and the elaborate montages opening *Magnolia* boisterously announce Anderson's authorship, this strikingly still image in *Punch-Drunk Love* and the moments of eerie silence that follow proclaim a dedication to allowing the possibilities of a particular character, storyline, or star persona to emerge with methodical patience. While *Boogie Nights* insisted stridently

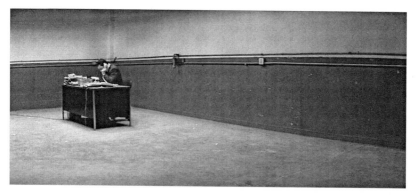

4.1. The film's opening shot boldly and calmly announces the theme of loneliness in a barren commodity culture while also foregrounding the star himself.

4.2. Barry is most comfortable communicating through the distance of telephones— even his first romantic encounter with Lena is initiated over the phone.

on Anderson's status and talent as a filmmaker, *Punch-Drunk Love* suggested a newfound maturity attuned to the aesthetic beauty and creative potential of ephemerality. Fittingly, this film's opening ends with Barry's pitch-perfect declaration, *"I don't know"*—a line he repeats several times that sharply contrasts with the omniscient voice-over of *Magnolia*'s prologue.

There were many accidental moments in the making of *Punch-Drunk Love*. Early on, Egan mumbles that "business is very *food*," rather than "good," when asked by his brother-in-law (Robert Smigel) how things are going with his novelty toilet-plunger business. The line was a typo in the script, but Anderson left it in. "Business is very *food*" fit the socially awkward, ill-spoken character perfectly. Later, as a Steadicam tracks Barry around his apartment while he speaks with a phone-sex operator, the frame briefly shakes when the camera bumps the coffee table. The effect was accidental—a gaffe that occurred during a test-run of the scene. Yet Anderson was pleasantly surprised by the jolting effect created and incorporated the "mistake" into subsequent takes. These unplanned moments in *Punch-Drunk Love* speak to the larger ephemeral aspect of Anderson's film—a certain sense of *unexpectedness*. In so many ways, people didn't see *Punch-Drunk Love* coming and perhaps did not know what to make of it once they did.

Punch-Drunk Love is today the "forgotten" Anderson film (along with *Hard Eight* [1996])—the one that slipped into the cracks between *Boogie Nights* and *Magnolia* in the 1990s and the considerable success of *There Will Be Blood* a decade later. Anderson himself famously referred to *Punch-Drunk Love* as "an art house Adam Sandler film"[2]—a deceptively simple description. The often-repeated phrase is not always meant approvingly by those who use it—though it's a fitting label. *Punch-Drunk Love* was explicitly written as a vehicle for the box-office star; moreover, the film builds directly off the stereotypical roles and plots that Sandler usually inhabits. At the same time, it possesses an offbeat visual and aural aesthetic that echoes elements of the avant-garde. Yet the notion of *Punch-Drunk Love* as simply a variation on the typical Sandler film (*Billy Madison* [1995], *Happy Gilmore* [1996], etc.) also misses much. While working closely with Sandler's persona, Anderson constructed his most unique film up to that point.

Although *Punch-Drunk Love* references many other styles, films, and directors throughout, it's not dictated by any of them. Instead of latching onto the genre of neo-noir (*Hard Eight*), emulating the look of Martin Scorsese (*Boogie Nights*), or mimicking the scope of Robert Altman (*Magnolia*), Anderson created something alarmingly original—something that *felt* unlike anything that either he or anyone else had made before. The initial reaction for some was to hold this against him, as though he were just goofing around with *Saturday Night Live* pals like Sandler and Smigel and wasn't trying hard to do something epic like *Boogie Nights* or *Magnolia*.

Yet *Punch-Drunk Love's unexpectedness* is one of its finest qualities. As Anderson told *The Sunday Times* in 2003, this film is "referenceless. When you start out, you latch onto other styles, to help you get across what you're trying to say. But this one is mine somehow—and I'm proud of that."[3] Given unrestrained creative freedom with *Magnolia* by New Line, Anderson had pushed his narrative and logistical self-indulgence—only hinted at in first cuts of *Hard Eight* and *Boogie Nights*—as far as he could. "I was a madman making [*Magnolia*]," he said at the time. "I put too much pressure on myself, and I was not the person I wanted to be. So with *Punch-Drunk Love* I forced myself to be more compact."[4]

In the process of trying to work within the formulaic confines of something as unassuming and unpretentious as an Adam Sandler movie, Anderson was freed to make a more idiosyncratic film, without the same level of pressure to prove himself artistically, to win awards, or to justify final-cut status. As a result of this newfound patience and a more open mind about the shifts and detours of the creative process, *Punch-Drunk Love* is a remarkably complicated little film, despite its deceptively simple premise. It's just as intricate as *Boogie Nights* and *Magnolia*—two technically impressive but transparent narratives that wear themes on their sleeves. "For all their vitality, Anderson's previous films have been very much 'movie movies,' driven more by technical prowess than life," wrote *Times* critic Ryan Gilbey at the time of *Punch-Drunk Love*'s release, "*Hard Eight* was an exercise in calcified film noir. *Boogie Nights* was all but saturated in stylishness. *Magnolia* sometimes felt like a compilation of weighty, melodramatic Oscar scenes. . . . But *Punch-Drunk Love* is, as Anderson concedes, the first film he has made that is entirely his."[5] And, in this sense, the film became Anderson's true auteurist moment.

On a first look, *Punch-Drunk Love* doesn't reveal much—the simple story of an emotionally unstable toilet-plunger salesman (Barry) whose verbal abuse from his seven sisters and a regrettable encounter with a corrupt phone-sex line complicate his newfound romantic relationship with a mysterious woman named Lena (Emily Watson). The first half of the plot largely revolves around Barry's elaborate plan to exploit a flaw in a Healthy Choice food products' promotional giveaway in order to quickly accumulate frequent-flyer mileage. The plan works, but not in the timely fashion Barry would have liked. Meanwhile, the second half of the film focuses more on a Utah-based phone-sex line that blackmails and physically threatens Barry after he uses the service late one night.

The frequent-flyer mileage thread was inspired by a true story. A few years earlier, David Phillips, an engineer from the University of California, discovered a loophole in Healthy Choice promotions that exploited a discontinuing line of pudding cups for the individual barcodes. Purchasing three thousand dollars' worth of pudding

4.3. One of the film's Steadicam shots culminates—as with the opening of *Hard Eight*—with a truck barreling through the scene. The moving truck reflects the transitional state of Barry's and Lena's respective lives.

eventually netted him one million frequent-flyer miles. Healthy Choice and its parent company ConAgra were initially skeptical about being involved with *Punch-Drunk Love* but ended up embracing the free publicity in an era when product placement in Hollywood films is both ubiquitous and costly.[6] The origin of *Punch-Drunk Love*'s story presents one of several instances regarding the film's ambivalent relationship to the cultural impact of commodities in postmodern America.

Meanwhile, other aspects of the narrative reflect Anderson's experiences, suggesting that *Punch-Drunk Love* was nearly as autobiographical as *Magnolia*. Anderson's past use of phone-sex services, which the filmmaker openly admits to in interviews, is one such aspect. This is unsurprising, given his unabashed obsession with porn that paid off with *The Dirk Diggler Story* and eventually *Boogie Nights*. Sandler later joked that "Paul did all the research for me. . . . Every time I tried to call him, he'd tell me he was on the other line and asked me to wait for two minutes."[7] Anderson claimed to have a playfully cynical perspective on the business. "I think those things can be a turn-on," he said, "if only because of how strange and distant it all is. If you can actually connect with the woman on the phone, then it becomes exciting. When that happens, it can be special. You almost feel like you're beating the system, taking this sleazy setup and making a real human connection."[8] *Punch-Drunk Love* highlights the emptiness of the experience and subsequent guilt, while nicely contrasting the "strange and distant" feeling of

Barry's passive phone-sex activities with his movement toward a more genuine connection with Lena.

Also autobiographical in *Punch-Drunk Love* are Barry's anger issues and his large, sister-dominated family. Anderson grew up the youngest brother to three older sisters, though the director resisted the implication that they were anything like the verbally abusive siblings in the film. Anderson did concede that, like Barry, he struggled with anger issues. "I was prone to fits of violence," he said at the time. "It's scary when I look back at it. What did I think I was achieving?"[9] The film conveys the futility of such anger while also resisting easy moments of resolution to Barry's expressions of violence, which at times are quite shocking. At one point (in the middle of his first date with Lena, no less), Barry completely destroys a restaurant bathroom in a scene that needed four takes—enough for Sandler's hands to start bleeding from the performance.[10]

One way in which *Punch-Drunk Love* works beyond its quirky storyline, operating on a much more complicated set of affective registers, is the intensity of Barry's violent fits. Unlike the nostalgia of *Boogie Nights* or the melodrama of *Magnolia*, *Punch-Drunk Love*'s emotional impact is more akin to the language of pure cinema and not merely a rehearsal of established cinematic techniques. The film reveals itself slowly—through layers of irreducible tension between beauty and violence, bodies in motion and still-framed landscapes, love and anger, harmonious music and unsettling sounds, Jeremy Blake's stunning artwork and Barry's barren world, richly intoxicating soundscapes and long moments of awkward silence, and swooning periods of old Hollywood grandeur unsettled by discordant in-

4.4. Barry's point of view as we first meet face-to-face his numerous sisters together.

stances of experimental disruption. *Punch-Drunk Love* avoids the alternately amusing and horrifying shock value of *Boogie Nights* and the grand, sweeping emotions of *Magnolia*. But what it does provide lasts through repeated viewings—all the more because this richness is irreducible to simplistic thematic observations like the historical rise of video, the ephemeral quality of celebrity, being haunted by one's past, or the serendipity of everyday life.

When Anderson told an international group of reporters at Cannes in 2000 that he wanted to make his next film with Sandler, he was laughed at. No serious director would make a formulaic movie with a Hollywood star known in the 1990s as the king of juvenile humor. Working with someone like Tom Cruise was one thing. Despite the generic fare of *Top Gun* (1986) or *Mission Impossible* (1996), he had also collaborated with nearly every elite director in Hollywood—Martin Scorsese, Oliver Stone, Stanley Kubrick, Francis Ford Coppola, Neil Jordan, Brian De Palma, Ron Howard, Rob Reiner, Barry Levinson, Cameron Crowe, and so forth. But fellow box-office superstar Sandler was another matter. Why, observers asked, make that film? When *Punch-Drunk Love* debuted in late 2002, both Anderson's and Sandler's fans were completely bewildered by something both so unlike *Boogie Nights* and *Magnolia*, and—on the other extreme of American cinema—so different from mainstream hits such as *Happy Gilmore*, *Billy Madison*, or *The Wedding Singer* (1998). *Punch-Drunk Love* came out of nowhere and went back there just as quickly.

In one final respect, *Punch-Drunk Love* is also *unexpected*. During a first viewing of the movie, it's difficult to anticipate where the film is going. At the film's center, Barry is a likeable but distant character whose anger and social awkwardness keeps audiences at arm's length and who inhabits a depressingly barren and colorless urban landscape. The movie begins with a series of bizarre non-sequiturs (like the falling frogs in *Magnolia*)—the car crash, the taxi, the harmonium in the street—that the film never really bothers to explain (*unlike* the frogs; i.e., "it did happen"). The sound design, meanwhile, is constantly toying with its audience, oscillating between asynchronous moments of profound silence, anxiety-inducing effects, and richly moving musical scores.

The actual plot shifts randomly, from Healthy Choice pudding and frequent-flyer scams, to the criminal behavior of phone-sex operators, to horrifying family get-togethers and instances of verbal abuse. It features nonstop phone conversations and a detour to the

4.5. The fine line between comedy and tragedy: Barry breaks down in tears during a scene that initially seems played for laughs, only to become increasingly pathetic and awkward to watch.

colorful richness of Hawaii (as Anderson finally steps outside the continental American West). The movie is anchored, finally, by an awkward love affair involving a man with serious anger management problems and a woman who may well be a stalker. Their courtship features busted-up restrooms, constant miscommunication, a considerable dose of self-loathing, and pillow talk involving affectionate descriptions of human cruelty. "Haven't you ever felt like that, man?" Anderson said. "I know I have. I've said it, too. It's like when you look at a kitten or a puppy and you think: I wanna kick the shit out of that little thing, it's so damn cute!"[11]

So how to account for *Punch-Drunk Love*'s strange affective contradictions? In a 2010 article, "Notes on Quirky," James MacDowell chalked up the balancing act in the film to what he sees as part of a larger, quirky aesthetic in other American art films of the period. In the late 1990s and early 2000s, many films that walked the line between independent and Hollywood productions were labeled rather lazily as "quirky" by critics, journalists, and even some movies' own promotional campaigns, in order to signal offbeat style and content. These films ranged from Wes Anderson movies to those of Michel Gondry, who inhabited the same established art-film niche as Paul Thomas Anderson. Deviating from Jeffrey Sconce's emphasis on irony in his discussion of the smart film, MacDowell argued that the defining characteristic of the quirky aesthetic was how it walked a fine line between comedy and tragedy. In a film such as *Punch-Drunk Love*, we don't know whether to laugh or cry (or both) at Barry's pathetic existence. The indefinable quirkiness comes from that awkward copresence of ironic distance and sincere sympathy.

However we are meant to feel, *Punch-Drunk Love* ends at a brisk 95 minutes (half the length of *Magnolia*). The audience is left with a touching moment of romantic reconnection that is undermined somewhat by its fleeting nature, the off-kilter emotional states of its two partners, and the larger sense that our most intense feelings of affection are often as savage (physically, verbally) as they are reassuring. So what to make of this "romantic comedy" in the end? *Punch-Drunk Love*'s beautiful displays of affection are marred just beneath the surface by a cold, unresolved vision of an emotionally imbalanced life in an alienating consumer world, while its considerable humor reflects profound feelings of sadness. At no point does the film cheat by telling us what to think or feel. There is no "but it did happen." There are no grand speeches about regret or waiting to die. In every way, *Punch-Drunk Love* was, and is, wholly *unexpected*.

AUTEURIST CONTINUITY

Lest the point be understated, *Punch-Drunk Love* nonetheless shares similarities with Anderson's earlier films. In retrospect, *Punch-Drunk Love* is similar thematically to its more bloated, ambitious predecessor, *Magnolia*—both are films about finding ephemeral moments of harmony within a chaotic, even inherently meaningless, postmodern consumer culture. Yet while the prior film directly announces its didactic ambitions, *Punch-Drunk Love* subtly incorporates that fleeting sensibility into its very structure. Anderson returns to a smaller story focused around one clear character (like Sydney in *Hard Eight*). That protagonist is another salesman (Barry) who struggles with a sense of his own identity after years of trying to please others (like Donnie Smith in *Magnolia* and Buck Swope in *Boogie Nights*). Centered on a small-business owner who is deeply unhappy despite the modest financial success he has achieved, *Punch-Drunk Love* is another Anderson movie about isolation and loneliness, about finding a loving environment amid the alienatingly bland, materialistic consumer culture of the American West. The film's playful *intensification* of Sandler's persona extends a similar metacommentary offered by Cruise as the hypermasculine misogynist in *Magnolia*. Finally, the meditation on the nature of a star's persona along with the narrative emphasis on a single, violent salesman anticipates Anderson's next film, the more celebrated *There Will Be Blood* (2007).

Punch-Drunk Love's story of a man harassed by a phone-sex com-

4.6. Barry is lost—often literally—in the anonymous,
generic landscapes of Southern California.

pany continues Anderson's obsession with two interrelated thematic trends: guilt (often sexual) and characters forced to pay for
their mistakes. The line uttered to Barry late in the film by his tor-
mentor, Dean Trumbell (Philip Seymour Hoffman)—"Do you think
you can be a pervert and not pay for it?"—would easily fit into any
of Anderson's first four movies. *Punch-Drunk Love* ends on a hope-
ful note that, as with those earlier films, is complicated by the sense
that such resolution is fleeting at best. Believing that Barry and
Lena will simply live "happily ever after" superficially ignores unresolved problems with both of them raised throughout the film.

Stylistically, Anderson continues his use of long takes—*Punch-
Drunk Love* eschews excessive cutting and montage in favor of pa-
tiently composed shots that last seconds, even minutes, longer than
expected. There are traces of Anderson's fondness for the wandering Steadicam—in particular, a haunting shot that floats through
the patio of the Royal Hawaiian Hotel. More striking is the sudden
attention to the stillness of the frame. In *Punch-Drunk Love*, door-
frames and hallways appear prominently, creating the visual impression of a man utterly trapped by his generic surroundings. The
tranquility of Robert Elswit's composition provides a contrast to
the constantly chaotic state of Barry's emotions. Sandler's character
barely holds himself together, only just keeping his rage and self-
loathing from spilling out into the world. This tenuous equilibrium
is made all the more awkwardly transparent by the ways in which
the camera calmly holds on the tightly wound Barry. The frame's resulting blank effect complicates our relationship to the easily agi-
tated character even more.

As with any film by an intensely cinephiliac director, the outside influences are still there in *Punch-Drunk Love*. The clearest directorial reference is again Altman, whose work is cited more than once. The song ("He Needs Me") that accompanies Barry's impulsive journey to Hawaii is taken directly from the musical *Popeye* (1981). "He Needs Me" was written by Harry Nilsson, the original composer of "One [Is the Loneliest Number]," which is utilized so effectively in the opening montage of *Magnolia*. *Punch-Drunk Love* also pays homage to the phone-sex operator/stay-at-home mom played by Jennifer Jason Leigh in *Short Cuts* (1993).

More broadly, the stark use of color in *Punch-Drunk Love* harks back to classic MGM musicals such as *The Band Wagon* (1953), in which Cyd Charrise wears a white dress identical to that worn by Watson during the Hawaii sequence. Sandler's physical humor, meanwhile, is influenced by the director's and actor's mutual affection for Jerry Lewis comedies. Contrasting such prominent use of color with pale white backdrops, *Punch-Drunk Love*'s barren landscape evokes memories of the empty modern wasteland of Jacques Tati films, such as *Mon Oncle* (1958). Moreover, the sparse sound design, slapstick humor, and barely audible star of the Tati classic also appear to have influenced *Punch-Drunk Love*. Meanwhile, its themes of a dehumanizing consumerist society and of a boy who feels alienated from his parents evoke Anderson's career more generally.

The word LOVE spelled out on Barry's bloody knuckles after he smashes the wall in his office not only beautifully illustrates the

4.7. Barry's arrival in Hawaii is accompanied musically by "He Needs Me," a song from Altman's *Popeye*. When Anderson screened the film privately for the legendary director, he deliberately avoided telling Altman the song had been used because he wanted to watch his spontaneous reaction.

4.8. After Barry punches the wall, the wounds spell out "LOVE" on his fingers. In addition to referencing *Night of the Hunter* (1955), the image also foregrounds the fine line throughout *Punch-Drunk Love* between love and violence.

copresence of affection and violence in *Punch-Drunk Love* but also makes a direct reference to Robert Mitchum's tattooed fingers in *The Night of the Hunter* (1955), which was also referenced in Spike Lee's *Do The Right Thing* (1989). Finally, the story of a harassed man who finds solace in playing a piano and wooing a woman named Lena is a direct homage to François Truffaut's *Don't Shoot the Piano Player* (1960). Yet, as King notes, all these references are fleeting or indirect and don't distract from the overwhelming sense that *Punch-Drunk Love* is, stylistically, more distinctly Anderson's own film than the ones that came before it.

REVOLUTIONS

The production history of *Punch-Drunk Love* proves as illuminating on Anderson's sense of patience as the movie itself. Fresh off *Magnolia*, Anderson quickly committed to *Knuckle Sandwich* (as it was first called, later *Punch-Drunk Knuckle Love*). While Anderson was still personally fond of *Magnolia*, he was eager professionally to go in new creative directions. Additionally, he was motivated by working against the expectations that others had begun to develop about the type of film he was interested in making. As he told James Mottram later:

It's harder to do a stripped-down straightforward story like [*Punch-Drunk Love*]. . . . That's what I found anyway. What it does is help focus in on what you really want to say, on what your real point is. That can get a bit muddled in three hours. I wish I could take ten or fifteen minutes out of *Magnolia*. I don't know where from, but it might help pinpoint what it was saying a bit better. But in ninety minutes you have to get to it, say what you've got to say and get the hell out of there.[12]

The time it took to reach the screen (three years), filled with stops at *Saturday Night Live* and so forth, suggests that Anderson made an effort not to rush his next project into production, showing a greater artistic patience than he had with any of his first three films. For some, this patience was indicative of the typical self-indulgence that long marked his work as a writer/director. Sharon Waxman, for instance, reported that during production of *Punch-Drunk Love*, Anderson

raged around the set like the diva he was, shooting for months and months without much of a script. The movie was weighed down by his overindulgent working style (his longtime collaborator [editor] Dylan Tichenor quit halfway through in frustration) and an overgenerous studio [Revolution].[13]

No doubt, the process was drawn out—shooting halted at one point and then picked up again several months later. However, Anderson and Tichenor eventually repaired their differences in time to reunite on *There Will Be Blood*. And the final product indicated, ultimately, that Anderson's "overindulgent working style" on the project paid off, aesthetically if not commercially.

For the first time, Anderson was invested in disciplining his creative instincts and experimenting with them rather than just following them blindly. Both *Boogie Nights* and *Magnolia* had been in preproduction before their respective predecessors (*Hard Eight* and *Boogie Nights*) had even been released to the general public. After *Magnolia*, Anderson was less focused on getting out his next major film as he experimented with other projects in the meantime. He directed and edited several music videos starring his then-live-in-girlfriend, pop singer Fiona Apple. She had put together her second album, *When the Pawn* (produced by Jon Brion), at the same time Anderson finished *Magnolia*. She and Anderson first did a video for the hit song, "Fast as You Can," in late 1999, followed in 2000 by "Paper Bag" and "Limp."

Similarly, he spent considerable time behind the scenes at *Saturday Night Live*, where he met Smigel and his future partner Maya Rudolph (who appears briefly in *Punch-Drunk Love* as Lena's stand-in). In 2000, *Variety* reported that Anderson did the "writing stint on *Saturday Night Live* [specifically] to learn how to write that kind of picture [an Adam Sandler comedy]."[14] During this time at *Saturday Night Live*, he helped produce a short film—a spoof of MTV's *FANatic* (2000)—that featured Ben Affleck as a young man with an unhealthy obsession with Anna Nicole Smith (Molly Shannon). The young man's desire to call her "Mom" comically echoed Anderson's common theme of people in search of surrogate families. This eclectic mix of short-subject films reflected a new period in his life—not only his brief but intense relationship with Apple, which had ended by 2001,[15] but also a moment of experimentation that the short-subject format afforded him.

In addition to *Magnolia*'s intense production schedule, this hiatus was the result of an underwhelming critical response to his final-cut opus. *Magnolia* received many more mixed and divisive reactions than either of his first two films. The wait was also tied to uncertain circumstances with New Line. As late as September 2000, Anderson was scheduled to do another film with them to follow *Magnolia*,[16] but that project—perhaps an earlier version of *Punch-Drunk Love*—never appeared (although New Line remained legally attached to the final product). Meanwhile, New Line lost interest in supporting edgy directors, investing much of its future into the adaptation of *Lord of the Rings*. This newer, "tamer" New Line was influenced by its corporate buyout by media giant AOL,[17] which signaled an era of less creative risk. By the end of 2000, Mike De Luca, Anderson's biggest supporter at New Line, had been fired by the company—taking the fall for a disastrous financial year that included, but was not limited to, *Magnolia*. Within a few months, however, he landed on his feet at Dreamworks. Anderson didn't follow him but did begin to move away from New Line. By January 2001, Anderson had committed to making his next movie with the logistical support of a new upstart company across town.[18]

No longer enjoying unprecedented creative freedom at Bob Shaye's studio in the wake of *Magnolia*'s disappointment, Anderson ended up at Revolution Studios through a combination of factors. In 2000, Joe Roth started Revolution as a small production company that specialized in relatively low-budget films focused on established stars such as Julia Roberts and Bruce Willis.[19] The company was supported economically by various financial institutions, as well as a five-year distribution deal with Sony Pictures. Roth saw

himself as a supporter, like De Luca, of such aspiring young directors as Anderson, but it would be inaccurate to suggest that his interest in *Punch-Drunk Love* was rooted in a desire to win Oscars.

Rather, Anderson's deal at Revolution was all about Sandler. Like
other marquee stars, he had signed a multipicture deal with Revolution in late 2000.[20] Anderson's collaboration with Sandler and
Revolution echoed his prior agreement with Cruise and New Line—
as long as the box-office star remained onboard with the project,
Anderson was creatively free to do whatever he wanted. And yet,
though he could make *Punch-Drunk Love* on his own terms, Anderson remained very much a kind of hired hand with the movie
studio—he was brought in by Revolution to shepherd an "Adam
Sandler film." It would be the closest yet that Anderson had come to
being an old-fashioned studio auteur—the kind of filmmaker who
chooses to work within preexisting genre confines and expectations
of something like Sandler's frat-boy mode of comedy.

Of course, the idea for *Punch-Drunk Love* still began with Anderson, since he wanted to do an Adam Sandler movie as soon as he
finished *Magnolia*. When asked by *The Guardian*'s John Patterson in
2000 what he planned to do next, the young director gave the interviewer an honest and direct answer. Typical of such skeptical reactions, Patterson's response was amazement, even doubt: "The real
surprise came when I asked him who he'd like to work with," the
interviewer commented. Anderson responded that he'd like to use
Sandler, whose movies make him cry with laughter. Patterson added
derisively, "As far as I can determine he's not being facetious."[21] The
doubting, dismissive tone anticipated some of the film's eventual
critical response.

Nonetheless, Anderson committed to writing a Sandler star vehicle. Around the same time he was hanging out at *Saturday Night
Live*, Anderson was even more emphatic about his passion for working with Sandler in a *Rolling Stone* interview. In a feature article focused mostly on *Magnolia*, reporter Mim Udovitch observed that

It's not the least of Anderson's talents—and he has many, as demonstrated by
1997's dazzling, revved-up *Boogie Nights* and his new movie, the beautiful, ma-
jestic *Magnolia*—that he is a world-class, virtuoso enthusiast who registers his
delight in things with every particle of his being, a person who, if aesthetic pleasures were measured in decibels, would not infrequently be bouncing the nee-
dle all the way to the right. *"Are you aware of Adam Sandler?"* he'll ask, intensely
serious, his tone practically quivering with the joy of discovery. *"I mean, are you truly*

fucking aware? He is headed for a level of genius in creation and acting that I just cannot wait to see keep going."[22]

With his last film still in theaters, Anderson focused on Sandler, proclaiming him to be a comic genius whose potential had yet to be tapped. Meanwhile, a first complete draft of the script was finished as early as September 2000, when the project was still based solely out of New Line. By then, Anderson had already offered parts to Sandler, Emily Watson, and Sean Penn (who was reportedly in line to play Trumbell[23] but was replaced by Hoffman[24]).

The film went through several titles: *Knuckle Sandwich*, *The Denise Show*[25] (probably a tongue-in-cheek reference to Sandler's *Saturday Night Live* skit of the same name), and then *Punch-Drunk Knuckle Love*.[26] Whatever its name, *Punch-Drunk Love* had jumped to Revolution as its primary production company by January 2001,[27] where the studio's agreement with Sandler generated the creative space that Anderson needed to make the movie he had wanted to make after relations with New Line cooled. With Shaye's company in the rearview mirror almost as quickly as they'd invested in him as a final-cut director, Anderson, Sandler, and the new production house moved ahead on an art-house Adam Sandler movie.

VISUAL AND MUSICAL ABSTRACTION

A key notion in *Punch-Drunk Love* is "abstraction"—how the film works visually, aurally, and thematically through nonnarrative, nonrepresentational means. In the film's very first moments, a car flips and crashes, after which a harmonium is dropped off outside Barry's warehouse. Neither receives any narrative explanation (why the car loses control and flips suddenly is visually uncertain), nor is their significance resolved in the end. This continues Anderson's thematic interest in serendipity—moments of random chance that appear in *Hard Eight* and *Boogie Nights* and are central to *Magnolia*. Yet such serendipity in those earlier films occurs within otherwise realistic diegetic worlds. In *Punch-Drunk Love*, these unexplained events force the audience to reject any notion of cinematic realism.

In his seminal book *Only Entertainment*, Richard Dyer argued that the appeal of classic Hollywood films, particularly musicals, rested not in their realistic depictions of everyday life. They were thoroughly *artificial* stories even by Hollywood standards, relying on cavernous set designs, colorful costumes, and melodramatic plots, to say nothing of the music and dancing. Yet, Dyer argued,

4.9. Barry's relationship with the harmonium transparently reflects the character's desire to be in accord with a surrounding world that so clearly makes him uncomfortable. The presence of the harmonium announces the film's nonrepresentational, affective narrative logic. Anderson designed a lot of the film around Jon Brion's music, rather than the reverse.

they employed "real feelings" of intense pleasure to which audiences responded in place of a realism aesthetic. "Utopianism is contained in the feelings it embodies," Dyer writes; "it presents, head-on as it were, what utopia would feel like rather than how it would be organized."[28] They depended—as *Punch-Drunk Love* does—on nonrepresentational signs (colors, sounds, movement) to communicate abstractly rather than literally.

The most explicit form of abstraction in the film is Jeremy Blake's distinctive art work, which has various nonrepresentational images exploding periodically across the screen. Anderson commissioned the avant-garde artist, whose work frequently appeared in art galleries (and who created the cover to Beck's 2002 album *Sea Change*), to compose these remarkable abstract sequences. They serve as colorful musical interludes throughout, accompanied by an eclectic mix of sounds, music, and dialogue that fits the film's larger erratic sound design. Blake's unforgettable images stand in sharp contrast to the film's drab mise-en-scène. They suggest another moment when Anderson conceded authorial control over the film to a fellow artist (Blake's contributions are particularly haunting today, given his tragic suicide in 2007).

In a discussion of color in recent narrative film, Brian Price focuses in particular on *Punch-Drunk Love*: "a series of color abstractions . . . not only interrupt the narrative, but threaten the legibility of the image, and thus narration, altogether."[29] Just as the artwork disrupts Anderson's presumed control momentarily, so too do the abstract images and sounds disrupt the centrality of Barry's journey as the primary narrative focus. Upon the introduction of Blake's artwork, shortly after Barry introduces Lance (Luis Guzman) to the harmonium,

abstraction and narrative separate: as Barry struggles to articulate his interest in the harmonium—in his found object—Anderson cuts to a lush field of Blake's color designs. From the realist space of the image we move to a field of alternating vertical bands of juxtaposed color—pink, red, orange, red, blue, white, yellow. These bands of color, restless in themselves, now dissolve into a field of inexactly rounded, sometimes ovular, color forms—white, pink, blue—against a baby-blue background. These colors shift and dissolve into a celestial abstraction. . . . We might also understand abstraction here as a moment of respite from the banal space of the warehouse; an intrusion of beauty in an otherwise lusterless environment.[30]

Abstraction and narrative never reconcile in *Punch-Drunk Love*—or, if they do, it's because the logic of abstraction becomes the narrative drive of the film. Other aspects of the film's color suggest the move toward abstraction, such as the two-dimensional paint job in Barry's warehouse, containing white and blue neatly separated into strips that run from one end to the other. On the one hand, Barry's blue suit causes him to disappear: "the integration of figure and ground in a three-dimensional space, so central to the production of realism, begins to break down" even prior to the introduction of Blake's work.[31] The film's distinctive use of color in general and

4.10. Jeremy Blake's remarkable artwork emphasizes the film's larger emphasis on visual and aural abstraction.

4.11. The lens flares emerge during Lena's entrance into Barry's world.

Blake's artwork in particular reflect Barry's struggle to find the vitality and beauty of life within his drab surroundings. *Punch-Drunk Love* pushes past any notion of realistic narrative representation and instead toward an affective sense of abstract visual expression.

Moreover, the color patterns within the often colorless film are not always opposed—emphasized in particular during moments when lens flares stretch across the screen, partially obstructing the view of the film's characters. The flares first appear in the shot that introduces us to Lena, as her compact car pulls past the harmonium and into the driveway in front of Barry's business. They remain while Barry and Lena talk, returning suddenly during an eyeline match when Barry looks over at her car later. A correlation is established between the flares and Barry's emerging relationship with her. Price notes that the sequence involving the shot/reverse shots of Barry and Lena after they leave the restaurant is also interrupted by these optical effects: "the mechanistic rhythm of the cutting and the clarifying potential of alternating close-ups is undone by streaks of blue-lit lens-flares that partially erase the figure."[32]

Likewise, King emphasizes the ubiquitous use of lens flares as an abstract continuation of Blake's art, as nonrepresentational moments of intensity that suggest the intrusion of abstract color. They embody the chemistry between Barry and Lena as well as the strength he draws from it. "This systematic use of lens flares," he writes, "show us *visually* that Barry's love for Lena is indeed real and it becomes a physical element of the film itself. The same way in which a poet pens a poem in search of capturing the feeling of love, or a musician sings a song, Anderson uses this aesthetic technique of flaring his lens to hint [at] something which transcends his frame. . . . they confine and display something that is unexplainable and *impossible to physically photograph*: the feeling of love."[33] Lens flares appear when Barry finds the strength to confront Trumbell, and when he and Lena embrace in her doorframe near the end. In their final warehouse embrace, the lens flares streak across the frame yet again, in perfect sync with the sound of Brion's chimes.

Like *Boogie Nights*, with its pop soundtrack, or *Magnolia*, with its Aimee Mann–driven narrative, *Punch-Drunk Love* is an implicit musical, but a complex and subtle one whose lyricism always rests just beneath the surface, momentarily disrupting the film's illusory and ephemeral sense of realism. We see the musical influence in the abstract colors and Brion's often deeply romantic score. This idiosyncratic artifice is also embodied by Barry—his bright blue suit and deliberate, choreographed swaying. An intensely physical role, Barry visually evokes a dancer struggling to find his rhythm. After introducing Lance to the harmonium, Barry backs away, swinging his body from side to side with precise deliberation before turning to face the other synchronized workers who enter the reflection behind him. While bolting through the hallway door in Lena's maze of an apartment complex, Barry's body rotates 360 degrees with impossible grace and control. In the grocery store, he tap dances in the aisles while Lance collects the pudding.

A significant part of *Punch-Drunk Love*'s abstract mode is not merely visual, but just as intensely aural—a point made most explicit through the remixed "He Needs Me" from *Popeye*. Thus, a final component to the film's use of nonrepresentational signs is the music itself. "While *Magnolia* may be the closest thing Anderson has done to a musical, *Punch-Drunk Love* feels like a one-man concert film," Mottram observed with respect to Brion's remarkably schizophrenic sound design—"the perfect expression of Barry's inner turmoil."[34] Brion remains a prolific pop musician and producer (e.g., for Mann's and Apple's albums) who writes movie scores only sparingly. In fact, at the time of the film's production, Anderson was the only filmmaker Brion had worked with—first on *Magnolia* (for which he was nominated for a Grammy) and then on *Punch-Drunk Love* (he also contributed to *Hard Eight* along with Michael Penn). Brion has since gone on to work with Michel Gondry on *Eternal Sunshine of the Spotless Mind* (2004), David O. Russell on *I Heart Huckabees* (2004), and Charlie Kaufman on *Synecdoche, New York* (2008). "There are too many other lovely and interesting things to do," he noted in 2003, "than always writing film scores"[35]—an attitude that explains the distinctiveness of his contributions. "With *Punch-Drunk Love*," says Brion, "we were still drawn to the spirit of musicals, but also to the silent comedies of Keaton and Chaplin, all of which we're both nuts about. Yet we didn't want to be direct and obvious about it, and instead imply these twin spirits."[36] Whereas Brion's score for *Magnolia* was largely secondary to the role Mann's songs played, in *Punch-Drunk Love*, his talents permeate every frame.

PRODUCTION AND IMPROVISATION

Anderson knew early on that he wanted to incorporate a harmonium into the plot of *Punch-Drunk Love* and asked Brion to write much of the music before shooting even began. With cast and crew arranging sequences to match the score, the film and its choreography feel remarkably in sync with a soundtrack that tap dances back and forth between diegesis and something in excess of it. This permeable boundary—between diegetic and nondiegetic space, between Barry's drab world and the abstract, colorful cosmos beyond, between the discomfort of his surroundings and the desire for harmony—is established in the film's opening moments, as the score seems to emanate from Barry's harmonium (the first hint of Brion's chimes emerge when Barry picks up the device in the street). The largely quiet first few minutes are disrupted only by eerie sounds of trains, car crashes, and Barry's heavy breathing in the dark. This silence slowly gives way to a more recognizable musical score after the harmonium appears, bringing a soft glow that contrasts with the harsh outdoor light of which Barry seems so afraid.

The more romanticized component of Brion's score struggles to find itself, just as Barry struggles through interruption to play his newfound instrument. The first time Barry starts to play, Lance suddenly appears, throws open the door (flooding the warehouse with the harsh sunlight), and disrupts Barry's emergent rhythm. Tied to the musical design, the harmonium is a central symbol throughout *Punch-Drunk Love*. King notes that

The entire film Barry pecks notes on the harmonium, as if in search of some secret it possesses; it represents an enigma to him, and ultimately, to the audience as well. But in the final shot of the film the puzzle is solved. Barry plays the exact notes from Jon Brion's score for *Punch-Drunk Love*, playing the harmonium almost concurrently with the music that plays nondiegetically over the scene. The diegetic and nondiegetic music playing together is a moment of cinematic harmony; Barry, Lena, and the harmonium are now in sync.[37]

4.12. Brion's avant-garde score gives way to more traditional Hollywood romanticism as the relationship between Barry and Lena begins to develop.

Yet the ephemeral harmony, both existential and musical, found throughout *Punch-Drunk Love* is just as dependent upon the other, less harmonious half of Brion's remarkable design. In fact, the film's musical score is as frazzled and disorienting as it is reassuring and beautiful. There are several sequences of old-fashioned Hollywood romanticism throughout the score, particularly as the chemistry between Barry and Lena begins to develop. Yet Brion is just as effective in composing off-kilter moments of agitating, anxiety-inducing sound that are tied as tightly to Barry's fragile psychological state as the overtly swooning moments.

One of Brion's biggest influences was not a classic musical composer such as Arthur Schwartz (*The Band Wagon*), but "the decidedly anti-romantic John Cage, the late, great father of avant-garde, whose techniques for prepared piano (including the placing of objects directly on piano strings) were applied throughout the composing and recording."[38] Rather than depend solely on old-fashioned orchestrations, Brion also assembled a large Foley-esque sound "laboratory"[39] of random objects for producing distinctive, experimental sounds that are interspersed throughout. The score becomes another way to disrupt the audience's expectations rather than reassuring them with familiar sound bridges. During a particularly jarring sequence in the warehouse, after Barry is blackmailed by the phone-sex operator, Mottram writes that Brion's "freewheeling score [is] dominated by bleeps, beats, pulses, tics and rattles."[40] The sounds amplify Barry's anxiety as he avoids both the harassment and his own feelings towards Lena. All the while, the warehouse comes unhinged around him—a forklift crashes into the shelves, sending merchandise everywhere, barely fazing the already disturbed Barry. Brion's score also effectively conveys that sense of nervous adrenaline that accompanies spending time with a potential lover—it captures sonically that overwhelming feeling of love at first sight better than anything in Anderson's earlier films.

As production continued, Anderson modified his style in other ways. The casting of *Punch-Drunk Love* also reveals how he challenged himself to work against his usual instincts. There were few regulars returning—gone for the first time were Philip Baker Hall, John C. Reilly, and Melora Walters (all three of whom appeared in *Hard Eight*). Meanwhile, *Boogie Nights* and *Magnolia* staples like Ricky Jay, William H. Macy, Julianne Moore, Alfred Molina, and others were also absent. Guzman was the main holdover, while Hoffman joined only after Penn dropped out. Reilly was originally in talks to play one of the brothers who physically harass Barry, but both director and actor agreed his appearance might be a distraction. "He has this process of narrowing down the story," Reilly said in late 2002, "and at some point, I said, 'Paul, it's a love story. I might be distracting in this movie.'"[41] For being someone intensely loyal to his actors, Anderson embraced the challenge of working with mostly unfamiliar faces.

The filming schedule also revealed a new patience. As early as March 2001, Anderson, Sandler, and the rest of the crew were already off in Hawaii shooting scenes,[42] though the finished film would not appear at the Cannes Film Festival for another year. Anderson took so long shooting that the principal actors were contractually obligated to leave and complete other projects before returning. This no doubt led to Waxman's speculation that Anderson "raged around the set like the diva he was, shooting for months and months without much of a script." But it was as much the product of a director no longer committed to quickly shooting the script exactly as written. *Entertainment Weekly* reported then what otherwise went overlooked:

Filming proved a far more free-form venture [than the writing]. "He was very much experimenting," says Watson. "He said he wanted to do [the movie] like a musician lays down a track—he would do one line and then he'd go and he'd listen and come back and do another." The results of this painstaking process? First, scenes like the opener, which takes place at the crack of dawn, took days to shoot. Second, Anderson ran out of time. Up against a potential actors' strike, he lost his stars for months when Sandler had to shoot *Mr. Deeds* and

Watson departed for *Gosford Park*. "It was actually great for Paul," says Watson. "Because when we came back, his sense of experimenting was gone. He was on fire, knowing exactly what he wanted to do."[43]

Principal shooting didn't end until fall 2001.[44] Even by January of the following year, the project was still referred to in the press as "untitled."[45] However, that extra time to reflect on the project while collaborating with Brion and others may have been the best thing to happen for *Punch-Drunk Love* and its director. The end product was a movie that felt light and effortless in its careful execution.

"I DON'T LIKE MYSELF SOMETIMES"

Once completed, *Punch-Drunk Love* still had the difficult task of selling itself as both Adam Sandler movie and Paul Thomas Anderson film. "We had to treat this one gently," Sony distribution chief Jeff Blake noted. "We didn't want to deceive anyone with advertising. This isn't Adam like you're used to seeing him, but it's still a very accessible movie."[46] Added his boss, Tom Sherak, "It wasn't a role that you would normally see Adam Sandler in. . . . We've gone out of our way to say, 'This is a Paul Thomas Anderson movie that stars Emily Watson and Adam Sandler.' We're not selling it as an Adam Sandler vehicle."[47] As it turned out, Sandler didn't either. Although he worked the usual art-film circuits with Anderson (festivals, college tours, etc.) early on, Sandler resisted promotional appearances as the film moved closer to its theatrical release in late 2002. Perhaps he didn't want his persona to tarnish *Punch-Drunk Love*—or vice versa. Just as Cruise had largely shunned promotional appearances on behalf of *Magnolia* three years earlier, Anderson's work with a major Hollywood star was a complicated double-edged sword.

Yet Egan *is* a reincarnation of Happy Gilmore, uncomfortably so. Sandler began his career on *Saturday Night Live* in the mid-1990s but found considerable fame when he moved to films, making cult favorites such as *Happy Gilmore*, *Billy Madison*, and *The Waterboy* (1998). Sandler's performance in *Punch-Drunk Love* wasn't meant to be a stretch in the usual sense of the word. In each of his earlier roles, Sandler's funniest moments centered on breaking into uncontrollable fits of rage—whether punching Bob Barker in *Happy Gilmore* or tackling football players in *The Waterboy*. The actor told an interviewer in the summer of 2002 that "I never thought of this [role] as a departure"[48]—rather it was a part completely in keeping with the on-screen characters he had been playing for years. In another interview later, he added, "Departure suggests that I'm somehow moving on from something. I just did a movie with a guy [Anderson] who I think is an incredible filmmaker, and I played a role which I thought was a great part and one that would be a challenge for me to do."[49] The task for Sandler in *Punch-Drunk Love* rested in playing the same character he often played, but in a way that critiqued the easy laughs.

Meanwhile, much of his persona also derived from his musical skills, such as the famous "Chanukah Song." To a point, Sandler's early rise to fame was dependent as much on his albums as his films. He had produced four hugely successful albums that combined music with skit comedy—*They're All Going to Laugh at You* (1993), *What the Hell Happened to Me?* (1996), *What's Your Name?* (1997), and *Stan and Judy's Kid* (1999). In a particular fit of rage late in *Punch-Drunk Love*, Egan yells "What's your name?" over the phone to Trumbell—a direct reference to the title of his third album. The character of Egan and the film's larger musical style both pay homage to Sandler's persona.

Sandler's next film was a mainstream comedy appropriately called *Anger Management* (2003), featuring brief appearances by Reilly and Guzman. This follow-up included another persona often affiliated with irrational displays of rage, Jack Nicholson, and satirized what *Punch-Drunk Love* literalized—that Sandler's appeal is based on violent meltdowns. But *Anger Management* plays with Sandler's persona in a way more commonly associated with an auteur's work with an established star (such as Cruise in Kubrick's *Eyes Wide Shut*). The hook in this latter film is that Sandler was playing against type, as someone who's relatively stable but saddled with the much more psychotic Nicholson.

As *Punch-Drunk Love* debuted in fall 2002, a range of critics read Sandler's work as either a great performance *in spite of* his casting, or a great performance *in spite of* his previous roles. One gave Anderson all the credit for getting an un-Sandler-like performance out of the actor. The other thought the film suffered from the presence of an amateurish actor known primarily for playing overgrown children bursting out of an angry man's body. For example, *USA Today* critic Mike Clark, under the bold headline "Sandler Shatters the Mold," wrote in a positive review that the star was "no *Happy Gilmore*. For this Sandler we've never seen, thank the comic's first collaboration with a filmmaker of real stature, Paul Thomas Anderson. . . . Only the baggage Sandler carries from his dumbed-down farces will keep his performance from being recognized as one of the year's most defining."[50] In *The Orange County Register*, Barry Koltnow wrote more dismissively: "Adam Sandler is not funny when left to his own devices, or to the devices of his close friends, who write and direct most of his movies. They are devoid of talent, and their shortcomings expose Sandler as unfunny. However, in the competent hands of *Punch-Drunk Love* writer-director Paul Thomas Anderson, Sandler is able to shine."[51]

On the other extreme, some critics suggested that the performance needed a better actor for the film to work. "*Punch-Drunk Love* may have been billed as Adam Sandler's first attempt at a real performance," wrote the *Miami Herald*'s Rene Rodriguez, "but it was the film around him—a beautiful, swooning, 95-minute wisp celebrating the intoxication of being in love—that made the actor come off so well."[52] In a review that praised the movie but took exception with Sandler's presence, the Australian-based *Sun Times* noted that the actor's "outbursts of repressed rage are a play for sympathy, but they simply remind us of Sandler's former goofballs—passive-aggressive nice guys prone to throwing punches,"[53] suggesting that more serious actors wouldn't have undermined their own performance. *London Times* critic Barbara Ellen wrote that "Sandler has always had negative charisma, but here he flat-lines so badly you keep expecting paramedics to rush in and help him with his lines."[54]

Years later, critic Jim Emerson persisted: "I still would rather have been watching someone else [in the part]. And [*Punch-Drunk Love*] had Mary Lynn Rajskub [as Barry's main sister, Elizabeth]. She saves America every week on *24*, and she saved Sandler's behind in this movie."[55] Both evaluations—positive and negative—of the star baggage that Sandler carried with him missed a key point about *Punch-Drunk Love*: the whole movie really wouldn't make sense *without* Sandler's presence. Of course, many critics did recognize this metacommentary, particularly keeping in mind how Anderson as usual wrote the part for Sandler in the first place. Critics' opinions of *Punch-Drunk Love* often had as much to do with how they viewed Sandler in it as how it fit with Anderson's other films.

Critics often read the famous quote—"the art-house Adam Sandler film"—as implying that the star had been molded into an art-house formula (by an art-house director). Yet the movie is an exercise in Anderson's own reinvention of the preexisting genre assumptions in which the star thrived. *Punch-Drunk Love* works because of Sandler. The drooping presence, mumbling, weird swaying, inexplicable fits of anger—all create the impression of a man hopelessly insecure. As Roger Ebert wrote at the time:

In voice and mannerisms he is the same childlike, love-starved Adam Sandler we've seen in a series of dim comedies, but this film, by seeing him in a new light, encourages us to look again at those films. . . . The way to criticize a movie, [Jean-Luc] Godard famously said, is to make another movie. In that sense *Punch-Drunk Love* is film criticism. Paul Thomas Anderson says he loves Sandler's comedies—they cheer him up on lonely Saturday nights—but as the director of *Boogie Nights* and *Magnolia* he must have been able to sense something missing in them, some unexpressed need. The Sandler characters are almost oppressively nice, like needy puppies, and yet they conceal a masked hostility to society, a passive-aggressive need to go against the flow, a gift for offending others while in the very process of being ingratiating.[56]

Punch-Drunk Love is a Sandler comedy—but with the rage set at a distance, so that what was once offered as humor to some audiences is now not funny at all, and even quite disturbing. Similarly, Owen Gleiberman noted that "the Sandler we see is, in essence, the same Sandler we have come to know, to love, and (for some) to loathe, except that the movie isn't nudging us in the ribs to laugh at him. The camera hangs back, peering at Sandler inquiringly, inviting us to study him as if he were a shy creature at the zoo."[57] *Punch-Drunk Love* embraces his persona by taking a step back (it is not "funny" to be angry) thematically and formally.

When, for instance, Barry attends his sister's birthday party, the sequence is shot in a series of long takes (much like the scene with the phone-sex operator in his apartment later). He enters, greets his sisters, and walks through the kitchen. Then he walks into the dining room and greets a few more people. The camera slowly moves in on him as he does a slow burn for being constantly referred to as "gay boy" by his sisters. Finally, Barry smashes the sliding glass windows in a rage, with his family in the background. There is, for one, the remarkable staging of actors throughout the extended takes, made all the more remarkable when one considers that Sandler is one of the few professional actors in the sequence. The frame follows Sandler closely throughout the sequence—he is, as star, the centerpiece of the film. But right before his violent outburst, he suddenly exits left, out of the frame. Sandler's positioning in front of the family china set also effectively comments on Barry's fragile state—he is almost literally a "bull in a china shop."

4.13. Barry reenters the frame after he starts to smash the glass sliding doors. That Barry has always been the social outcast of the Egan clan is reflected by the fact that his portrait (screen right) is isolated from all the other family pictures on the far left of the frame.

Despite Sandler's being the center of the entire sequence, his initial burst of rage is offscreen. *Punch-Drunk Love* takes a step back—unlike in *Billy Madison* or *Happy Gilmore*, where the violence unfolds as an intended comedic spectacle. But here the film refuses to show the moment he physically snaps at being called "gay boy," because while Sandler's character is still an angry man-child, he's not so funny. "I don't like myself sometimes," Barry can barely say afterward (in another long take), before breaking into tears and again disappearing out of frame. This character isn't funny; he's pathetic. More to the point, Barry knows this. Sometimes, the film realigns with Barry because he's found his rhythm (his musical interludes with Lena but also his confrontations with thugs and the Mattress Man). Other times, we feel detached from him—uncomfortable because his behavior makes us uncomfortable. This discomfort, though, makes Barry more sympathetic.

SISTERS AND POSTPATRIARCHY

Where does Barry's unseemly anger stem from? In addition to a noticeable shift in tone, the glaring difference from earlier films is that there is suddenly no "father" (biological or surrogate) in *Punch-Drunk Love*. Family dynamics remain as important as ever, with Barry spending much of the film engaging with his obnoxious, verbally abusive sisters. As with Eddie's family in *Boogie Nights*, strong women emerge in the void created by the lack of an assertive masculine presence. Both Timothy Stanley and Julian Murphet have made a point to mention the glaring absence of a father figure in *Punch-Drunk Love* when compared to his other films. Each reading argues that the absence structures the entire narrative, giving thematic weight to Barry's unstable life.

Stanley and Murphet, respectively, embraced a "postpatriarchy" reading of *Punch-Drunk Love*. While it is problematic to argue that patriarchal power has dissipated in U.S. cultural and domestic spheres, Anderson's films often dramatize that claim. Stanley argued that Barry's gender performance, as he struggles to embody a strong masculine ideal, exists in a void where "men no longer hold patriarchal sway on a domestic level."[58] He further notes the general domination of Barry (and other men in the extended Egan family) by his sisters. When the audience is first introduced to Barry's family at the dinner get-together, his sisters dominate the conversation in the kitchen while the brothers-in-law hide quietly in the corner of the dining room. Meanwhile, the sisters' voices are heard throughout the house, even when we cannot see them.

Murphet repositions the dynamic of strong sisters and passive brothers as the result of "Anderson's own misogyny [which] is nowhere better realized than in this ghoulish tribe of identical-looking, copiously breeding, indelibly *familial* sisters."[59] For Murphet, this relationship is structured by the modern capitalist breakdown of an older agrarian patriarchal order, and more specifically, the "displacement of the father-obstacle" in Barry's life. Murphet suggests that the only "father" figure in *Punch-Drunk Love* is Trumbell, the head of the phone-sex business. As well as running its furniture-store front, he's in charge of the female operators and their multiple siblings. The back of the mattress store contains a maze of rooms in which Dean's employees not only work but also live.

Trumbell embodies the masculine authority that Barry must confront for resolution—just as Dirk (Mark Wahlberg) in *Boogie Nights*, Frank (Cruise) in *Magnolia*, H.W. (Russell Harvard) in *There Will Be Blood*, and Freddie (Joaquin Phoenix) in *The Master* must all confront the "father." Murphet provocatively argues that what sustains successful surrogate families in Anderson's films (where they are invariably more successful than biological families) is the presence of mutual financial interests. Trumbell's business, in that regard, echoes Jack's pornography operation in *Boogie Nights*, Earl Partridge and Jimmy Gator's quiz show in *Magnolia*, Daniel and H.W.'s

4.14. In a seemingly incidental shot of Barry answering the phone, we see a lens flare hovering in sync with the harmonium, Lance (Luis Guzman) continuing to test the breakability of one, and then two, "fungers" in the background, and the taped dollar bill on the left side of the screen foregrounding the centrality of monetary value to everything that occurs in the film.

business partnership in *There Will Be Blood*, and Lancaster Dodd's (Hoffman) cult in *The Master*.

Irrespective of the absent father question, there is no way around Barry's emotional predicament's being the product of oppressive female family members in *Punch-Drunk Love*. His sisters recall the irrationally angry mom in *Boogie Nights* or the hysterical Clementine in *Hard Eight*—in all three, the assertive female is seen as a source of family tension that threatens patriarchal stability (each time, they are contrasted with weaker, even silent, male partners). Lena echoes many of the passive women in *Magnolia* who peacefully coexist by avoiding any direct confrontation. Yet she also initiates the courtship by being the more aggressive one and dictates the terms of their relationship at the end.

A remarkable sequence early establishes Barry's problematic relationship with his sisters. While trying to sell prospective customers on his line of "fungers," he's constantly interrupted by calls coming from his seven siblings. This dramatizes the full-time tension between Barry's two primary occupations—his work and his family—while also providing a glimpse into the verbal abuse that Barry endures. One sister rudely hangs up on him after getting the information she needed, while another gives him grief for saying he didn't have time to "chat," and then calling him a "fucking phony." He becomes so flustered and distracted that, after briefly finding

4.15. At the end of a remarkable long take, Barry jumps at the sound of his approaching sister. His jittery reaction perfectly expresses how unstable he is physically and emotionally when surrounded by family.

solace with the harmonium, Barry slams face-first into his office's glass door—one of the film's few sight gags. Meanwhile, the uncomfortable relationship with his sisters becomes visualized when Elizabeth shows up at his work to talk him into meeting her friend (Lena). As she persists in hooking the two of them up, Barry sheepishly responds with weak excuses to avoid the party ("I need to renew my gym membership") and retreats to the corner of the warehouse. She follows him and berates him further for refusing to be more sociable.

This is also dramatized by the subsequent sequence at the dinner party, partially touched on above. Before Barry even enters the home, we hear the sisters chattering offscreen about a time in his youth when he angrily threw a hammer through the window after being called "gay boy." It's this same anecdote, when Lena repeats it on their first date, that sets Barry off to destroy the restroom. Leaning halfway in, Barry pivots back and forth in the front door entrance, hesitant to walk into the environment once he realizes the conversation is about him. When Barry finally enters, the camera pans with him as he steps into the kitchen, providing an overwhelming visual of several sisters turning at once to greet him. Even as they warmly embrace him, the sisters continue on with the "gay boy" conversation, while also asking him if he really *is* gay. When Barry finally works his way to the back of the kitchen, yet another sister startles him from behind. Meanwhile, this last sister finishes the "gay boy" conversation by noting that Barry had a hammer only because he was "building a doghouse"—where he symbolically spent his childhood (this whole sequence is shot in one continuous take from the moment Barry first hesitantly walks through the entrance).

He smashes windows, restaurant bathrooms, and office walls—often, but not only, provoked by his sisters' verbal abuse. The acts of physical violence are ineffectual outlets for venting frustration with his family and futile attempts at reasserting his masculinity through acts of aggression. Barry is an extremely flaccid physical presence most of the time, subjected to the taunts of "gay boy"—a homophobic slur that explicitly calls his masculinity into question. Barry is so passive regarding his masculinity that when asked point blank by his sister if he *is* gay, he responds, "I don't know." This mirrors another moment of masculine indecision shortly thereafter when Georgia asks him during phone sex if he has an erection—"*I don't know* what it's [his penis] doing." Both instances echo Barry's repeated use of the identical line throughout. Murphet reads Barry's violence as the inability to lash out at the (absent) Oedipal father, thus "the only things Barry can legitimately attack here are inanimate ones: plate glass windows, bathroom fixtures, etc."[60] The violence is at best a fleeting solution to certain circumstances, such as being bullied by the four brothers and Trumbell.

"I'M GOING TO DIVERSIFY . . ."

More than Buck in *Boogie Nights* or Donnie and Frank in *Magnolia*, Barry offers the most focused instance of the salesman's central narrative role in Anderson's films to date. Both benefiting from and marginalized by the commodity culture in which they are irreversibly tangled, salesmen embody the ambivalence toward capitalist-driven postmodern culture. Empowerment and alienation coexist when one's sense of self-worth is overtly defined by a ubiquitous relationship to commodities. This is especially explicit in a movie about a relatively successful small-business owner, Barry, who is nonetheless deeply unhappy with his life. A good U.S. capitalist, money is clearly important to Barry—he has the obligatory first dollar bill taped to his office window. His business does well enough, though he works out of another nondescript building that could be anywhere in America.

Barry has accumulated a decent amount of capital, but his life and apartment indicate that he doesn't spend or value much of it (he impulsively blows money on a flight to Hawaii). His Healthy Choice scam is more about the thrill of deception than accumulat-

4.16. This overlapping image of phone-sex ads and Healthy Choice coupons reiterates how, in Anderson's cinematic vision, sex is just another (unsatisfying) commodity to purchase.

ing the actual mileage, since he originally had no plans to travel. He tells Georgia that he intends to "diversify," which is ironic. Every aspect of Barry's existence suggests it's been inseparable from his work—there is no diversity in his existence outside the job. His lack of material fulfillment becomes another cause, as much as his sisters, for his feelings of inadequacy and loneliness, even while his business and its assumed revenue may be his sole day-to-day motivation to keep going.

The cultural logic of capitalism is particularly acute in *Punch-Drunk Love*. The film is focused on a generally unremarkable salesman as its main protagonist, with another salesman, the Mattress Man, as his main antagonist. The narrative often takes place inside an anonymous business warehouse and is driven by the personal repercussions of various financial transactions—buying pudding, commissioning the services of a phone-sex operator, and taking a trip to Hawaii. Healthy Choice and the phone sex are mutually reinforcing commodities—Barry consumes them both, but they fail to bring lasting pleasure or satisfaction into his life. This connection between sex and money is made explicit during a close-up of Barry's coffee table where their respective ads literally overlap. This two-shot reinforces the larger sense throughout *Hard Eight*, *Boogie Nights*, and *Magnolia* that, as Brian Goss noted, "market relations [are] a thinly veiled form of prostitution."[61]

Yet Barry's personal relationship with capitalist culture is a complicated one. When performing the role of salesman, Barry demonstrates effective social skills—a jarring contrast with his mumbling,

4.17. While the showering of rice may foreshadow the coming love in his life, the broken wedding "funger" also viscerally highlights the frivolity of the dumb product in which he's invested so much of his money and labor.

often violent, and otherwise ineffective interpersonal abilities. He maintains a clear economic intuition that manifests itself in his small-business achievements. His shrewd awareness of the importance of commodities to everyday life allows him to see the potential to exploit Healthy Choice products when no one else has. Despite his modest business success, the very object his company specializes in—novelty toilet plungers—indicates he symbolically exists on the unpleasant margins of society. Barry's products offer a spin on a vital, but uncelebrated, tool for dealing with an embarrassing bodily function, but with an emphasis on excess and frivolity. They foreground Barry's invisible role in culture while also mocking his ambitions. "Fungers" are a spectacularly pointless waste of money.

In Anderson's films, the greed and excess of capitalistic consumption often wreak havoc on individuals, but offer little alternative other than the consumption of more commodities. *Punch-Drunk Love*'s narrative establishes two strands of capitalism at odds with one another—Barry's modest, hard-working, transparent toilet-plunger business on one extreme and Dean Trumbell's shady, exploitative, and deceitful "furniture" store on the other. The film's ending implies that a kind of "responsible" capitalism is the only solution to its most indulgent, unregulated extremes. There is no space outside consumer culture in *Punch-Drunk Love*. Even its most utopian, richly affective moment of flight from the colorless consumerist world of Barry's life—the tour-de-force sequence involving his impulsive trip to see Lena in Hawaii—is the romanticized reenactment of one of America's most consistently commodified and media-intensified tourist activities. The only way out of Barry's drab world is even more conspicuous consumption (i.e., buying a ticket to Hawaii on a whim). In the end, his ultimate heterosexual union with Lena—ephemeral, problematic, and partially illusory—reinforces a larger cultural logic of capitalism that depends on the promotion and maintenance of a happy, *reproductive* workforce. The resolution to the love story is not only Lena and Barry's reconciliation. It also involves the idea that he can redeem the frequent-flyer mileage in order to follow her anywhere the job might take her—reinforcing the unending capitalist ritual of both production (work) and consumption (play).

In addition to reinforcing the very consumer culture that initially led to Barry's feelings of loneliness, the conclusion isn't unconditionally happy. While the passion that Barry and Lena may feel is real, much of the film suggests that the relationship isn't necessarily built to last. For one, Barry's physical anger issues haven't been addressed, and Lena can reach him (as in the Hawaii pillow talk scene) only by indulging his violent tendencies. Moreover, matters haven't been addressed with his sisters—if anything, they've gotten worse. In one sequence, just before Barry meets Lena in the Royal Hawaiian lobby, he finally stands up to his sister by cussing her out over the phone and bullying her into giving him Lena's location. Aside from being another way in which *Punch-Drunk Love* constantly disrupts its own textual rhythms, the horrifying display also suggests that the only solution to the Egan family dynamic is for Barry to be as verbally abusive as his sisters—hardly the foundation for a healthy relationship.

Moreover, Lena is a mysterious stalker with her own set of unresolved emotional issues (her divorce is mentioned but avoided). She sees Barry's picture and wants to meet him, following him secretly in grocery stores and showing up at his business, pretending to be in need of car repairs (giving no indication she's already friends with his sister). Lena always takes the first step in her relationship with Barry—prompting him to ask her out, asking him to come up and kiss her, etc. Barry replaces one controlling woman (his sister) with another who, not inconsequentially, is also his sister's good friend. *Punch-Drunk Love*'s depiction of the sisters doesn't suggest that Lena's aggressive attitude will necessarily be healthy for the passive Barry, especially if the next chapter of their lives involves him following her around for work. The power of their affec-

4.18. In one of *Punch-Drunk Love*'s most clever and subtle images, Lena (in her red dress) stalks Barry from a distance inside the grocery store, following him across several rows. Anderson's partner, Maya Rudolph, was reportedly Lena's stand-in during this shoot.

tion—like much of *Punch-Drunk Love*'s haunting beauty—is in the end how ephemeral it feels.

THE LIGHT LIFTING BETWEEN HEAVY WORKOUTS

Despite *Punch-Drunk Love*'s remarkable splendor, the film was yet another Anderson film that failed to find a major audience. "An open-ended oddity," reflected *London Times* critic Stephen Dalton a few years later, *Punch-Drunk Love* "was clearly a labour of love for both its director and star—although many audiences were baffled."[62] As with his other films, reviews were generally positive, but that did not translate to box-office numbers, even with a major star attached. Anderson's core international art-house demographic didn't abandon him. In the summer of 2002, Anderson won shared Best Director honors (along with South Korean director Im Kwon-taek for *Painted Fire*) at Cannes—where just two years earlier he'd been laughed at for suggesting that his next project would be collaborating with Sandler. As with the Golden Bear Award for *Magnolia*, it was an important but still minor footnote to another admirable film that struggled to find an audience beyond the proven bread-and-butter film festivals.

The beauty and difficulty of *Punch-Drunk Love* is that it never resolves the contradictions of its aesthetic and commercial status as an "art-house Adam Sandler film"—a perfect description but one that implies the film had no built-in audience. The final irony is that while many critics championed the film, neither Anderson's nor Sandler's core fan bases quickly warmed to *Punch-Drunk Love*.

USA Today summarized the dichotomy: "Adam Sandler makes movies that critics dislike and the mass audience loves. Writer/director Paul Thomas Anderson makes movies the critics love but the mass audience doesn't see."[63] *Variety* critic Todd McCarthy similarly noted *Punch-Drunk Love*'s "bizarre union of commercial Hollywood cinema at its most brainless and the indie world at its most intense . . . will no doubt be experienced very differently by the separate audiences who populate those respective realms."[64] While critics often appreciated how two starkly different talents collaborated in a remarkably unique film, they just as often saw it as a novelty for both, rather than a revolution in American cinema.

A generation of Anderson fans had begun to emerge by then—populist cinephiles discovering their passion for the grandiose excesses of *Boogie Nights* and *Magnolia* in their afterlives on DVD. Yet they didn't know what to make of such a sharp departure either. McCarthy's subsequent description proved particularly apt: "Anderson partisans could split [on *Punch-Drunk Love*] between those who revel in the thrill of his ongoing creative inventions and others who may find this to be light lifting between heavy workouts."[65] To this day, that assessment holds true, as the film boasts passionate cult followers who maintain that it is Anderson's most original and daring film. But there are just as many who pine for the fun times of *Boogie Nights*, the reassuring melodrama of *Magnolia*, or the stark, nihilistic power of his next film, *There Will Be Blood*—which justifiably brought Anderson the near-universal acclaim he'd been seeking for a decade. For the latter group, *Punch-Drunk Love* remains the little Adam Sandler movie that lacks the gravitas of his prior and subsequent work. But this dismissal overlooks the considerable aural and visual innovation, thematic ambivalence, and haunting ephemerality of Anderson's most experimental film. In retrospect, it was the patient and ambitious creativity of the truly idiosyncratic *Punch-Drunk Love*—not the final-cut status on *Magnolia*—that positioned Anderson as an American auteur.

that was one goddamn hell of a show.

"You feel like a bottom feeder at the bottom of this dark tunnel, chipping away at something that you're not quite sure is there and even if it is there, you're not quite sure what it's worth," he said. "I can completely relate to that fever and insanity that happens and takes over."

PAUL THOMAS ANDERSON, 2008[1]

CHAPTER 5

i have a competition in me

POLITICAL ALLEGORY, ARTISTIC COLLABORATION, AND NARRATIVES OF PERFECTION IN *THERE WILL BE BLOOD* (2007)

On the heels of *Magnolia*'s 1999 release, Anderson was asked by the *Guardian* whom he wanted to work with next. His first response was Adam Sandler, who would appear a couple years later in *Punch-Drunk Love* (2002). Anderson also mentioned Daniel Day-Lewis—saying, "He's just a powerhouse. All of his films are really solid."[2] Five years later, the two would work together on *There Will Be Blood* (2007), which suggested Anderson's status as one of the great American filmmakers. It was a potentially ephemeral ascendency—not unlike the premature attention garnered on the heels of *Boogie Nights* ten years earlier. The once-brash filmmaker had become more guarded in his interaction with the media while also projecting more self-reflection than he had after bursting loudly onto the international film scene in the late 1990s. Making *There Will Be Blood*, Anderson was surrounded by colleagues that he learned to respect and trust, while also accepting that his first creative instinct wasn't always necessarily the best one. On the 2007 film, he "worked with a production designer [Jack Fisk] and other people I've never worked with before," Anderson noted with newfound humility. "It's nerve-racking and exciting and you have to be more polite."[3] He was no longer the upstart who referred to himself

5.1. *There Will Be Blood* is the story of Daniel Plainview. The napkin over his head
symbolizes how he is a blank slate who remains a mystery even to the end.

as the cringe-worthy "hot young director" on the heels of *Magnolia*'s
appearance.

Collectively, the cast and crew of *There Will Be Blood* produced
one of the greatest American films of the decade. At the forefront
of that teamwork was Day-Lewis—and not simply because his
Oscar-winning performance as oil prospector Daniel Plainview is
the one aspect of *There Will Be Blood* most justifiably celebrated. Anderson collaborated with the actor on the project for years before
the film even started shooting in 2006. As early as 2004, Day-Lewis
had committed to playing the part of Plainview, which Anderson
wrote with the star in mind. They corresponded between Ireland
and the United States on brainstorming every aspect of Plainview—
his background as a silver miner, the tools he would use, his role in
the larger history of oil discovery in Southern California, and even
his voice, which the actor tried to perfect by listening to old audio
excerpts. Day-Lewis sampled "quite a lot of recordings, which Paul
managed to find for me, from the Dust Bowl years," he said, "some
from Oklahoma, some from Fond du Lac [Wisconsin], where Plainview came from. And I couldn't really find anything in those, except
maybe just a clue here and there."[4] Ultimately, Day-Lewis's inspiration came from another resource Anderson sent along to Ireland:
the work of John Huston, whose films (*The Treasure of the Sierra
Madre* [1948]) and performances (*Chinatown* [1974]) proved hugely
influential on the actor's approach to Plainview. Their extended
preparation dragged out further as the film struggled to find funding for a year—until Anderson's longtime agent, John Lesher, took

5.2. Plainview is most content alone—even with a coming storm. His physical positioning here recalls John's in the opening shot of *Hard Eight*. Yet whereas the drifter in Anderson's first film desires companionship, Plainview has little use for it.

over Paramount Classics and proceeded to commission *There Will Be Blood* as one of its projects.

The opening moments of *There Will Be Blood* lay bare the themes and contradictions of the film without uttering a word. After an imposing shot of the harsh California desert, we first see Plainview in a tunnel hacking away with relentless precision, determined to mine silver from the earth. This foreshadows his equal resolve in pursuit of oil later. We also see a man completely content with isolation, deep at the bottom of the shaft, more comfortable in the company of tools than with his fellow man. This seclusion is intensified as Plainview huddles alone by the fire, unfazed by either the wind or a coming thunderstorm.

We are also introduced to the sudden violence that repeatedly punctures an often eerily quiet film. Plainview uses dynamite to unearth the silver with only moments to spare; he stumbles from a faulty ladder, breaking his leg; he watches helplessly as his coworker is killed in an oil derrick accident. Throughout all this, the focus is squarely on a man who will remain an enigma. When he first stares blankly at his soon-to-be-adopted son, H.W., the image is a perfect expression of the ambiguity that underlies his feelings for the boy and that defines the audience's relationship to Plainview. The dialogue-free prologue closes with a touching shot of Plainview and the baby on a train. Yet it is nothing if not a ruse, in retrospect. The tender moment is drowned out by the voice-over of Daniel's manipulative, rehearsed sales pitch. We know nothing definitive except that Plainview is driven—a shattered leg while alone at the bottom of a mineshaft in the middle of the desert will not keep him from his goals.

Day-Lewis's total immersion into the earliest stages of this project reveals that he, too, was driven—something only intensified by his reputation as a method actor who prepares with meticulous detail. During an interview with Charlie Rose, the talk show host expressed admiration for his singular dedication, as he had during several interviews over the years. In attempt to discover Day-Lewis's personal motivations behind the professional, Rose asked him if he was "competing with perfection? Or with yourself?" "Well, not perfection," Day-Lewis replied with a laugh; "let's not be hasty."[5] Indeed, the idea of "perfection" is inherently unattainable. Whether creative, industrial, physical, or mental, it is a goal that motivates people to work harder than ever before but that can never be achieved. Yet the drive for perfection seems well suited to understanding how *There Will Be Blood* works aesthetically and narratively, as Day-Lewis's intense performance only begins to reveal.

There are several interlocking narratives of perfection involving the production history, cultural logic, and narrative structure of *There Will Be Blood*. One is Day-Lewis's legendary commitment: "Once drawn in" to the part, he said in 2007, "I have no option but to follow that path, and I really don't question why it is I need that at that particular moment, or why it needs me."[6] While resisting the idea that the actor was "always" in character, even between takes, Anderson nonetheless acknowledged that Day-Lewis had "a level of concentration that is unparalleled, that's really what it is. Somebody who's come to do one thing, and only one thing, to be Daniel Plain-

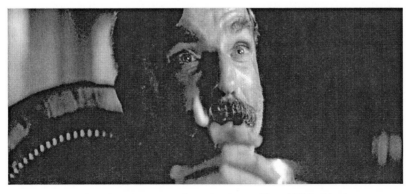

5.3. For all its thematic and visual ambition, *There Will Be Blood* depends upon Day-Lewis's method performance.

view, and indulge in that for three months."[7] The resulting performance reaffirmed Day-Lewis's extraordinary drive.

The star's professionalism is reflected in the film itself through Plainview's single-minded march towards perfection—the insatiable quest for money, land, resources, and complete domination. Plainview reflects Day-Lewis's persona in ways not unlike Sandler's Barry Egan or Tom Cruise's Frank T. J. Mackey comment on aspects of those personas. Although he has said in the past that he is often "hesitant" to discuss how much of himself he puts in a role "because I don't know,"[8] Day-Lewis recognizes the passion he shares with the character. "I suppose, if I had anything in common with Plainview," the actor observed, tongue somewhat in cheek, "it would be 'the fever' he has. With me, it just happens to be for my work—which is a kind of mining work, dark and sometimes unrewarding, but absolutely compelling."[9]

Highlighting the impossibility and danger of chasing perfection, Plainview's own destructive journey served as a critical metaphor, noted by critics at the time, for the worst excesses of global capitalism's drive toward monopolization. *There Will Be Blood* "feels like the first great American film of the twenty-first century," a Hollywood insider was quoted as saying after a sneak preview. The film "tackles all the big themes about America: blood, oil, religion,"[10] yet it is never reductive, simplistic, or didactic. *There Will Be Blood* resonated with audiences at the end of the eight-year reign of oilman turned born-again Christian U.S. President George W. Bush. Capitalism's mutually reinforcing partnership with Christianity is embodied in the tenuous relationship between Plainview and local preacher Eli Sunday (Paul Dano). In *There Will Be Blood*, evangelical Christianity is depicted as being just as corrupt, obsessive, and greedy as the oil industry. Yet the film's shockingly brutal finale posits that organized religion exists only as long as it serves big business's interests by producing a contented, distracted workforce.

Finally, there remains Anderson's own evolution as filmmaker—from headstrong writer-director of *Hard Eight*, to the industry's ordained auteur of *Boogie Nights* and *Magnolia*, to the more thoughtful filmmaker who quietly and slowly produced two of the best American films of the decade. *There Will Be Blood* was a powerful departure for Anderson. The wordlessness of the first twenty minutes is even more jarring when one considers that Anderson was a screenwriter whose career had been defined, at times, by a creatively unhealthy obsession with maintaining the integrity of his own dia-

5.4. The film's transparent allegory involves the mutually reinforcing but tenuous relationship between industry and religion, embodied in the dynamic between the preacher Sunday and the oilman Plainview.

logue. "I had a dream about making a movie that had no dialogue. Just music and pictures," Anderson said. "I got close with the first 20 minutes here."[11] The figurative rejection of his own written voice in *There Will Be Blood*'s opening spoke to a larger moment in his career—it revealed symbolically an increasing respect for other voices in the production process.

Much changed in the five years after *Punch-Drunk Love*. With the passing of a youthful confidence—one that sometimes spilled over into arrogance and thoughtlessness—came a more reflexive, patient maturity. "Cinematographers want to control things as much as we can," Anderson's longtime director of photography, Robert Elswit, observed in 2008, "but what I've learned from Paul is how much better it can be to let accidents happen [on set] rather than try to force everything to be a certain way."[12] By the time *There Will Be Blood* appeared in 2007, Anderson's own quest for cinematic perfection depended upon the collaboration with a range of extremely talented artists in front of and behind the camera. Anderson took more time with his own writing, ditching unworkable projects and taking on literary adaptations. As director, he incorporated ideas from Elswit, former Robert Altman editor Dylan Tichenor, composer Jonny Greenwood, and set designer Jack Fisk. The end result was his most impeccably constructed film to date. Anderson's own maturation is but one of several narratives reflecting the aesthetic and cultural implications of chasing perfection that accumulatively help to articulate the sheer brilliance of *There Will Be Blood*.

For the first time on the set of an Anderson film, it may have been

5.5. *There Will Be Blood*'s visual beauty results from a spirit of collaboration during production, including Robert Elswit's cinematography and Jack Fisk's set design.

the star, and not necessarily the headstrong director, whose commitment to artistic excellence drove the production—generating an energy and devotion that served as the model for everyone else to follow. Not everyone responded positively to Day-Lewis's intensity, though, as the first actor cast as Eli Sunday, Kel O'Neill, discovered. "Ideally, in a perfect world," Anderson said later, "everyone is doing what Daniel is doing—concentrating on doing their job. And that's what we were all doing. You could say that we were all in character the whole time."[13] That commitment also benefited from the experienced crew Anderson built over the course of a decade, starting with Elswit, who had perhaps better than anyone come to understand the director's distinctive working style, equal parts careful preparation and improvisation: "That's why we have the same crew over and over again—Paul has to work with people who are incredibly alert and aware on set. Everyone is truly a filmmaker."[14] With Day-Lewis, Anderson, and the rest of the cast and crew focused closely on the task at hand, the result was a film as thrillingly intense and focused as the circumstances under which it was made.

PLAINVIEW'S JOURNEY

There Will Be Blood is the story of a turn-of-the-century silver miner who discovers that his only real passion in life comes from searching for oil, buying all the accompanying land, and destroying all competition in the process. Plainview is arguably Anderson's most instantly iconic character. He's an often amusing and frequently horrifying misanthrope who possesses an uncanny knack for manipulation when it serves his purpose but otherwise has no use for people who don't fulfill a particular function. Plainview is a show-man, Day-Lewis said: "You know, he's got his snakebite remedy and he is going to sell that whatever way he can from town to town. And for a man that has lived in silence in holes in the ground for maybe years, he's now got to find a voice and a silver tongue that's got to convince people to turn their pockets inside out and invest in him as a man of irrefutable wisdom."[15]

We follow Plainview intensely, often silently, on his single-minded quest to attain untainted, uncompromised power over everything and everyone around him. Plainview's character is largely based on real-life oilman Edward Doheny (he was also the loose inspiration for Upton Sinclair's original novel, *Oil!*). He's also a collage of every other larger-than-life industrial figure from the period. "If you've heard one story about the oilmen of that time, you've heard them all," Anderson said. "So many of them were on the tail end of the wild, wild west, coming from silver mining."[16] Plainview's awkward social graces and animalistic tendencies reflect the irresoluble immersion of a nineteenth-century frontier man into the new domesticated culture of twentieth-century industry.

When we first meet Plainview, he is completely content to be alone. As his ambitions grow, he takes on more and more workers, though he never develops a personal friendship with any of them. As with Barry in *Punch-Drunk Love*, Plainview's only effective social skill—developed out of necessity—is that he is a highly persuasive salesman, conning people into selling their land. After one of his workers is killed in an accident that could have just as easily been

5.6. Like Barry in *Punch-Drunk Love*, Plainview's strongest social skill is the ability to communicate through a sales pitch, complete with (adopted) son as a prop for his "family" business.

him, Plainview inexplicably takes on the responsibilities of raising the man's orphaned son, H.W. When the film jumps years ahead, the audience begins to suspect that H.W. is largely a prop for Plainview, who is selling himself as a family man running a family business. When H.W. becomes deaf as a result of an oil explosion, the suddenly useless boy is cast aside from Plainview's plan, which now includes using his newfound "brother," Henry (Kevin J. O'Connor), as the visual support to his "family" business. When we discover later that the man claiming to be Henry is an imposter, it is the only time in Plainview's life we see the notoriously manipulative businessman genuinely thrown off by someone else's deception, which for him becomes the ultimate transgression.

As Plainview's power and influence grow, he comes into an unspoken business arrangement with the equally ambitious, singleminded, and cunning preacher Eli. Daniel recognizes him as a total fraud, one even more disingenuous and corrupt than he. Daniel is a man focused on life's materiality—the land, the tools, the hard physical labor, required for success. But Eli is simply an empty opportunist, a "false prophet," one who exploits weakness and inconsequence for quick monetary gain. "As far as Plainview is concerned," Day-Lewis reflected, "he recognizes the fraudulence of [Eli's] posture immediately. And I dare say to recognize that, you have to probably have a certain degree of self-hatred, so he probably knows that Eli has the measure of him too."[17] Eli is also a useful con man to the always business-savvy Plainview.

Thus, the two power-hungry businessmen maintain a mutually, but awkwardly, beneficial agreement for much of *There Will Be Blood*—as the town preacher, Eli keeps Daniel's workforce spiritually content and compliant, while Daniel's growing industry brings Eli more people, money, and power. Eli "loves to hear himself talk," Dano observed. "I think he gets off on it, actually. There's a lot of ego and power involved, and to have people in the palm of your hands, to have them worshipping you is a real rush for him."[18] By the end, Eli can satisfy his obsessive need for power—a bigger audience to preach to—only by embracing the "new" medium of radio (an interesting anticipation of *The Master*). Yet the film's shocking conclusion symbolically reinforces the notion that religion's power and influence exist only to the extent that they support big business's interests.

Although a uniquely allegorical figure, Plainview is also a powerful continuation of several characters and themes developed across

5.7. Unlike the respective ends of *Hard Eight*, *Boogie Nights*, and *Magnolia*, the father drunkenly and angrily turns the son away in *There Will Be Blood*.

Anderson's work. He is both a surrogate father and a salesman—essentially combining the two key traits that mark the protagonist of every one of Anderson's films to date. Although there's no evidence he changed his name, like Mackey or Diggler, Plainview is just as invested as they were in cutting ties with his past in the pursuit of material wealth. He is also, like Mackey and Egan, an angry, socially ill-adjusted man more invested in his business goals than in making meaningful connections with others. Yet despite the misanthropic contempt Plainview has for the world, Anderson is ever sympathetic to his despicable creation. "It's hard for me not to see Plainview as a little bit heroic," Anderson said; "he's enormously ambitious, and I can sympathize with his quest for survival, particularly during that time in the West."[19] The strength of Anderson's writing abilities is that he never loses sympathy for his characters—he never loses sight of how they see the world, even if he doesn't expect audiences to empathize with them at their worst.

Yet Plainview is also a powerful rejection of the more-sympathetic characters Anderson created in the past. Plainview's need for family is dictated by the demands of the sales pitch rather than the desire to feel loved. The film's ending is devastating not merely because of its swift, decisive violence. *There Will Be Blood* is such a final kick in the gut because, unlike in most every other Anderson film, the son is cruelly turned away when he attempts to reconcile with the father. Even in *Punch-Drunk Love* the resolution is fleetingly optimistic. In *There Will Be Blood*, however, the ending fulfills not only its title but also the full extent of Plainview's destructive legacy.

A lot of time passed between *Punch-Drunk Love* and *There Will Be Blood*. The five-year wait was easily the longest to that point in his career (since matched by the long gestation of *The Master*). After the underwhelming reception of *Magnolia* and *Punch-Drunk Love*, Anderson had another uphill battle to reestablish his industry reputation, which had been sliding since the promise of *Boogie Nights*. Some viewed Anderson's long layoff between projects as a sign that the once-hotshot director's brief moment of fame had passed. In 2007, critic Christopher Goodwin was not optimistic about the director's maturation. Anderson was struggling, he wrote, to find his "creative mojo," adding that

Anderson's most recent movie was the disappointing *Punch-Drunk Love*, in 2002, which made just $18m in the USA. His next film, *There Will Be Blood*, about the turn-of-the-century oil business, won't be released until the end of the year. That's a five-year gap for a film-maker who should be at full throttle.[20]

Ironically, Goodwin would be one of many to lavish great praise on *There Will Be Blood* when it was released months later. In retrospect, the delay affirmed the more deliberate use of creative energy. The postponement on *There Will Be Blood* was partially due to Anderson's own creative process. After finally deciding on a project, the research and writing involved in completing the script required a long-term commitment. The other factor was that *There Will Be Blood* struggled to find the money needed to make it. The lack of funding also reflected how little demand existed then for the next Anderson film.

The era of the maverick director so celebrated in the days of *Boogie Nights* was long gone by 2006. Even *Punch-Drunk Love* supporters, impressed by the director's creative reinvention, would have been hard-pressed to argue with confidence that it necessarily signaled a long-term shift in the filmmaker's career. It was during this period that Sharon Waxman wrote *Rebels on the Backlot*—an often critical take on what the celebrated 1990s maverick directors ultimately accomplished. In addition to painting a consistently unflattering image of Anderson during the days of *Hard Eight*, *Boogie Nights*, and *Magnolia*, Waxman concludes that his career ran off the rails due to his overindulgent working style—most recently demonstrated, according to her, by the endless months it took to finish *Punch-Drunk Love*. In a review of Waxman's book, meanwhile, *Vari-*

ety critic Steven Zeitchik added further commentary. Neither Anderson nor fellow 1990s Hollywood "rebels" David Fincher, David O. Russell, and Spike Jonze, he argued in 2006, had "gone on to the kind of meteoric and biz-changing success predicted for them"[21] a decade earlier.

Goodwin concurred with Waxman and Zeitchik on the state of Anderson's career. "Nearly a decade later," he wrote, ". . . it's clear that most of the directors Waxman was extolling have lost their way and have not produced anything like the important work done by the previous great generation of American *auteurs* in the 1970s."[22] Meanwhile, even as word leaked out on his next project, *There Will Be Blood*, skepticism remained. When commenting on the news of Anderson's forthcoming adaptation of Sinclair's novel, the *New Yorker*'s David Denby derisively observed that "with luck, the title will be changed again."[23] In 2006, Anderson faced a crucial crossroads as one of several directors who had yet to prove that long-term critical support had been earned.

Yet the freedom and reflection offered by that hiatus (and lack of spotlight) was one of many admirable qualities Anderson acquired as he moved into another phase of his career. As each project has taken more time to produce (though not always as the result of artistic deliberation) the result has been more provocative, more thoughtful films. Gone too is the unrelenting stubbornness of the young writer of *Sydney*, who insisted that every word of his script get on the screen as soon as possible, without interference. However, Anderson hadn't become any less persistent in his ambitions—on the contrary, the drive for cinematic perfection only intensified with time. In contrast, this quest was structured by the belief that open-minded collaboration with trusted friends is more fruitful than a narrow (often vulgar) resolve based on one's own egotistical aspirations.

COMPANIONS

While waiting for *There Will Be Blood* to find funding, Anderson went off to the Fitzgerald Theater in St. Paul, Minnesota, in the summer of 2005. There, he served as backup director to his longtime friend and mentor, Altman, helping him shoot what would prove to be his final film—an adaptation of the Garrison Keillor's popular public radio program, *A Prairie Home Companion* (2006). By then, Anderson had been friends with Altman for nearly a decade—"but," he said, "I had gotten to know him particularly well in the last three or four

5.8. Anderson with Robert Altman on the set of *A Prairie Home Companion* in 2005.

years."[24] Anderson had privately screened *Punch-Drunk Love* for Altman, hoping the elder director would be pleasantly surprised by the film's unlikely musical reference to *Popeye* (1981). Watching Altman work up close further revealed the importance of improvisation and collaboration.

Broadcast every Saturday evening since the 1970s, *A Prairie Home Companion* is a folksy two-hour variety show, hosted by Keillor, which features light comedy skits and musical acts. For the film version, Keillor wrote the adaptation and starred as himself (along with many of the program's regular contributors). As with every Altman film, though, much of the dialogue was improvised on set. To fill out the cast, Altman brought back old regulars like Lily Tomlin while also attracting a host of other major stars for the rich ensemble—Kevin Kline, Tommy Lee Jones, Woody Harrelson, Virginia Madsen, and Meryl Streep. Anderson's old friend, John C. Reilly, and his partner, *Saturday Night Live* star Maya Rudolph (who was several months pregnant with Anderson's first child during the shoot), also had small parts in the movie.

On the set of *A Prairie Home Companion*, Anderson was not assigned any day-to-day tasks per se. Rather, he was there to serve as the standby director, an insurance-mandated requirement that he be ready to take over in case the 80-plus-year-old Altman died midway through. It wasn't the first time for such an arrangement—Stephen Frears had served in an identical capacity during the earlier shooting of *Gosford Park* (2001). Anderson did not pass up the chance to take what could have been perceived as a passive task: "Any hesitation? None. None at all, because I knew he wasn't going to die."[25] Frears and Anderson were "being very generous, I think," Altman said then, "to take their time to support my project."[26] In addition to assisting his friend, Anderson also got a rare opportunity to quietly observe how other filmmakers worked.

A Prairie Home Companion is a soft-spoken but deeply moving depiction of a night in the life of a typical broadcast, while also capturing a pastiche historical image of mid-twentieth-century populist media culture (equal parts country music and film noir). The only major change was to set *A Prairie Home Companion* on the fictional night of the program's last broadcast, after an unnamed corporation from Texas purchases the show and decides to shut it down for the sake of profit (in real life, the show was still running as of 2012). In classic Altman fashion, there isn't much plot—the camera meanders around the Fitzgerald Theater capturing conversations, wandering actors, musical acts, and other performances as they come and go. It's not a direct adaptation of the program's content, as most of the film reflexively explores its fictional backstage life. *A Prairie Home Companion* captures ephemeral moments of whimsy—on and off the stage—as they pass.

Ultimately, the influence on Anderson had less to do with how Altman constructed his distinctive cinematic look—the long takes, the zooms, the overlapping dialogue—and more to do with Altman's on-set demeanor. The influence, Anderson said later, wasn't "the films themselves. It's him and the way in which he *made* films."[27] On the set of *A Prairie Home Companion*, Altman conceded a healthy amount of artistic liberty to his cast and crew, trusting that the professionals around him would do their jobs. From that chaotic work environment emerge fleeting moments of artistic beauty. Anderson later observed:

[Altman] would give things time to settle, to rise or to fall, and watching him do that was a great lesson in patience. Because at the end of the day, he invited everybody in to work on this film, but he ended up getting exactly what he wanted, and everyone else felt that they had been part of it, because they had.[28]

Kline, meanwhile, phrased Altman's style differently: "it's trust [in cast and crew]. It's a willingness not to control, to let things happen that you didn't plan."[29] Anderson took away a renewed appreciation

5.9. The last movie scene Altman ever shot—Guy Noir playing a piano while the "Prairie Home" sets are taken down around him. The mise-en-scène is taken from *Yankee Doodle Dandy* (1942).

for the collaborative spirit in which the legendary auteur worked. The cast and crew, Anderson said years later, "really made the film with Bob. How he did that was a lesson to me."[30] Altman understood the importance of surrounding oneself with the best talent and trusting their instincts.

Shooting *A Prairie Home Companion* went relatively quickly, and the experience was intensely emotional for the cast and crew. Nearly everyone involved recognized that it might prove to be Altman's last film. This realization came into particular relief at the very end of shooting. On the last day of production, the cast and crew shot the second-to-last scene in the film—Guy Noir (Kline's character) playing a piano, while the Fitzgerald Theater was being taken apart all around him (the scene itself was an homage to the 1942 Michael Curtiz film *Yankee Doodle Dandy*). Anderson recalled the experience:

[Altman] had a Starbucks coffee in his hand and his coat was zipped up because it was cold in there and he had his glasses on. He was staring at the monitor and he just looked really sad that it was ending. I think we only did the shot twice. I remember sitting there thinking, "Fuck, do it again, do it . . . do more, do more." I wanted to do more—not 'cause it wasn't good, but I wanted to keep shooting.[31]

Principal photography wrapped ahead of schedule in September 2005.[32] A professional to the end, Altman finished production when the work was done and did not draw it out just to prolong the experience of making a movie. In March 2006, Altman finally received an Oscar, not for the film, but an Honorary Lifetime Achievement Award. Later, *A Prairie Home Companion* opened in the summer of 2006 to mild business and favorable, if underwhelming, reviews— but it wasn't trying to be a masterpiece. Rather, Altman's last film was a much more small-scale meditation on something that largely went unsaid.

Like the original radio program, *A Prairie Home Companion* was a melancholic, nostalgic affair. But what Altman and Keillor managed to draw out in the adaptation process was the *specter of death*, the fear of mortality that underlies most forms of nostalgia. On the surface, *A Prairie Home Companion* is harmless, light entertainment—but beneath lies something more tragic. Allegorically, it is about the passing of the radio medium and of the era in which it was a dominant form of mass communication—a motif established by the film's unforgettable first image of the radio tower looking out over a calm rural Midwestern night. More subtly, *A Prairie Home Companion* also comments on the death of the film medium along with its director, as it is the only movie Altman ever shot on high-definition video.

In the story, the theater is quietly stalked by an angel of death (Madsen) who appears periodically to serve as a companion guiding characters on their journeys to the next life. When she ambiguously appears again at the very end of the film, it is unclear for whom she has come. But symbolically the angel has come for Altman himself—particularly as she walks straight into the camera. Shortly before his death, Altman looked back on *A Prairie Home Companion*:

I didn't get it until we got to the end. I mean, if at any time in the shooting of this, someone had said, "What is this about?" I could not have said, "This is about death." Now, in retrospect, I can say this is about death because everyone is avoiding saying that. But that's what it's about.[33]

In stark contrast to the barely suppressed contempt beneath the cool, detached surfaces of classics such as *M*A*S*H* (1970), *Nashville* (1975), or *The Player* (1992), the melancholic nature of *A Prairie Home Companion* revealed a quiet resignation to the inevitability of time's passing. The movie presents a final elegiac acceptance of death, rather than angry, or just ironic, resistance to it. A month after the film's release, Altman passed away. One of the last things he

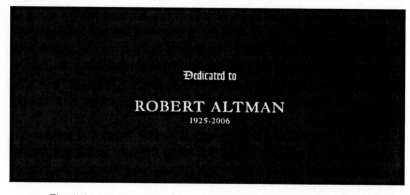

5.10. The dedication to Altman comes at the end of *There Will be Blood*'s credits.

said to Anderson was "I think this film [*There Will Be Blood*] is something different for you."[34] Anderson, who was well into production by then, dedicated the film to his old mentor.

ON KUBRICK

The dedication was heartfelt and fitting, given Altman's immeasurable impact personally and professionally. But in one regard, it was deeply ironic. With the making of *There Will Be Blood*, Anderson was not as inspired by Altman's sensibility as he'd been with *Boogie Nights* and especially *Magnolia*. *There Will Be Blood* reflected the influence of a very different filmmaker—the ultimate cinematic perfectionist, Stanley Kubrick, whom he had briefly met on the set of *Eyes Wide Shut* a decade earlier. "Kubrick had a really small crew," Anderson noted at the time. "'I asked him, 'Do you always work with so few people?' He gave me this look and said, 'Why? How many people do you need?' I felt like such a Hollywood asshole.'"[35] By the time of *There Will Be Blood*, Anderson was more comfortable, like Kubrick, working with smaller crews. Elswit "occasionally had to dismiss crewmembers who couldn't grasp the director's freewheeling approach to filmmaking."[36]

Whereas the respective styles of Scorsese and Altman dominated earlier films, Kubrick's sensibility felt particularly powerful in Anderson's fifth film. "In its reach and intensity, and most of all its masterful visual eloquence," film critic Ryan Gilbey wrote at the time, "*There Will Be Blood* is the best Kubrick film that Kubrick never made."[37] In earlier films, Anderson's work directly referenced Kubrick through visual and aural clues (such as Mackey's introduction in *Magnolia*). But it wasn't until this latest film that the connection between the two felt particularly acute. Elswit remembered that, while shooting *There Will Be Blood*, "Paul kept marveling at how Kubrick did things."[38] When visualizing the film's musical score later, Anderson talked with composer Greenwood "about how *The Shining* had lots of [Polish composer Krzysztof] Penderecki in it."[39]

As such, there is a clear stylistic debt to the late auteur in *There Will Be Blood*. We have extended close-ups on Day-Lewis's expressionless face, not unlike the countless blank stares that populate Kubrick's films. We're also invited to long narrative sequences of inconsequence and isolation, disrupted suddenly by bursts of shocking violence. The rather liberal adaptation of an original literary source was a common Kubrick process, much to the chagrin of his writing collaborators. More specifically, Anderson's insistence on using natural light during several sequences (such as the derrick explosion) recalls the legendary candle lighting on *Barry Lyndon* (1975). The dialogue-free opening echoes the wordless prologue of *2001: A Space Odyssey*. Moreover, the final sequence, also bounding with visual references to the sci-fi classic, was intended to evoke the harsh, bright look of a Kubrick movie. "Paul wanted to paint the walls white and turn [the bowling alley] into a white cube, like something out of *A Clockwork Orange*," recalled Elswit.[40]

The strongest Kubrick influence, however, is *The Shining* (1980). Like that horror classic, *There Will Be Blood* is a story of isolation, of a man pitted against the indifference of nature only to discover his greatest adversity is encroaching insanity—which is the direct result of professional obsessions and disintegrating family ties. Plainview and *The Shining*'s Jack Torrance are both larger-than-

5.11. Anderson's Kubrickian insistence on natural lighting during the burning derrick scene meant using blowtorches just off camera to light the actors' faces.

5.12. The brightly lit bowling alley, according to Elswit, was influenced in part by the mise-en-scène of *A Clockwork Orange*, while its long, narrow symmetry and red stripes evoke memories of the blood-soaked elevator corridor in *The Shining*.

life monsters who eventually turn on their respective sons. As Julian Murphet noted, both benefit from over-the-top performances. A shot of Plainview hacking away at the insides of a mine echoes the shot of Jack and his axe outside the family's bathroom. The barren wilderness of *There Will Be Blood*'s first shot recalls an identical opening to *The Shining*, just as Greenwood's score evokes memories of both Wendy Carlos's eerie compositions and Kubrick's effective repurposing of classical music. Greenwood even "talked about *The Shining* with P. T. Anderson and how Kubrick had avoided the clichés of using romantic film music."[41] Finally, the deep red stripes along the wall of the bowling alley evoke *The Shining*'s overflowing elevator and blood-soaked hallway.

But aside from the rather transparent, if no less powerful, textual allusions to Kubrick, there is also the equally important production aspect. Since bursting onto the scene in the late 1990s with a prolific string of ambitious but uneven films, Anderson had become more reclusive and more deliberate in his filmmaking over the last decade. Like Kubrick, Anderson tended to reuse many of the same actors in his early films, often making the same type of movie. Just as *Magnolia* and *Boogie Nights* were multicharacter Valley epics, *Killer's Kiss* (1955) and *The Killing* (1956) were noirs taken from the larger trend in 1950s American cinema. In the span of three years (1996–1999), Anderson made three films—*Hard Eight*, *Boogie Nights*, and *Magnolia*. That's the same total number of movies that he has made in the dozen years since then (including *The Master*). And, as promising as his early work was, *Punch-Drunk Love* and *There Will Be Blood* are arguably better than anything that came before them. Kubrick's early production was similarly prolific but erratic in quality—*Fear and Desire* (1953), *Killer's Kiss*, and *The Killing*. It was only with *Paths of Glory* (1958), *Lolita* (1960), and *Dr. Strangelove* (1964) that Kubrick began to produce a string of masterpieces that cemented his auteur status—one he maintained by becoming increasingly methodical about the projects he picked and the manner in which he went about making them.

After that initial phase, both Kubrick and Anderson became more interested in challenging themselves to tackle different projects featuring largely new casts. Both accumulated a small but tightly knit crew of trusted production members along the way. On *There Will Be Blood*, this includes Elswit and Tichenor, both of whom have been with the filmmaker for nearly his entire career (Tichenor quit halfway through postproduction on *Punch-Drunk Love*). While neither returned for *The Master*, Anderson's sixth film featured the same editor as *Punch-Drunk Love* (Leslie Jones), as well as the same composer, set designer, and casting director from *There Will Be Blood*. Meanwhile, Mark Bridges, the film's costume designer, has the rare distinction of being one of the few to work on every Anderson film through *The Master*, dating back to *Hard Eight*. Anderson's remarkable work in the last decade reflects a Kubrickian work ethic that emphasizes patience, thorough research, and absolute focus in the pursuit of one's own definition of cinematic perfection. This paid off handsomely on no less a Kubrickian homage than *There Will Be Blood*. In a final twist, meanwhile, Anderson even used Kubrick's very own 65mm camera to shoot *The Master*.

SLASHING AWAY

Even before *Punch-Drunk Love* was completed, Anderson had Sinclair's *Oil!* in mind for a possible project. The idea began as early as 2001, though he didn't begin serious work on adapting the novel until two years later. While Anderson was on a trip to the United Kingdom, the filmmaker saw the cover for *Oil!* in a Heathrow Airport bookstore, which immediately made him homesick for his beloved California. Given the book's setting and central dynamic, Anderson was unsurprisingly hooked. He recalled that *Oil!* was

so visually exciting, just this boy and his father driving, driving, driving, talking about the roads [reminiscent of *Hard Eight*'s opening]. And then there's this fantastic moment where the father gets pulled over for a speeding ticket and he pays the cop twice. He says "I'm going to pay you now, and I'm also gonna pay you for the way back." And I thought what a cool character. It was irresistible not to figure out more about him.[42]

The autobiographical appeal ran deeper than just its California setting and father-son story. *Oil!* made Anderson look at his home state in a new way. "Being from California . . . , not that far from the oil fields of Bakersfield," Anderson recalled, there was also "the kind of curiosity about what the hell is this stuff [crude oil]? And how do they get it out of the ground?"[43] Instead of focusing on the perpetual present of Los Angeles's endless suburban sprawl and entertainment industries, Sinclair's *Oil!* forced Anderson to rethink the state and its industrial origins, setting in motion a project that required more historical research than any other film he had made.

Oil! appealed to Anderson, but the idea of literary adaptation proved to be a bigger challenge to him than he had encountered on previous projects. As a result, Anderson took several years on the script, a task made all the more daunting by trying to adapt such a massive historically and politically loaded novel (even if the final version ultimately retained very little of the original material). Embracing the challenge itself was telling of Anderson's maturation, as for the first time he managed to work within the confines—however loosely—of someone else's story. A decade earlier, by contrast, he had tried unsuccessfully to adapt Russell Banks's novel *Rule of the Bone* (1995) for filmmaker Jonathan Demme. "I didn't do a very good job," he said years later. "I didn't really know what I was doing in general, let alone how to adapt a book."[44] On *Rule of the Bone*, Anderson claimed the primary mistake he made was in trying to put everything that Banks had written into the script, instead of focusing on the main story arc and building from there.

Initially, Anderson made the same mistake with *Oil!* He was composing an ambitious script that followed the book more closely by approaching the subject as an epic battle involving two rival families (shades of *Magnolia*'s scope). Anderson sensed that he was on familiar ground—an epic that was focused not only on large families but on fathers and sons in particular. The screenwriter "was trying to write a movie about fighting families," he recalled later, "and however it ends up taking this path, there it is. There [were] brothers fighting, we have some brothers fighting and everything, but at the center of it, yeah, this father and son."[45] This approach clearly was not working—in part because Anderson was revisiting older tendencies to put too much in, but also because he was struggling to find a new creative voice. "I was frustrated by the things I was writing" then, Anderson said, "and had gotten sick of my own voice."[46] As a result, he stripped the story back down to the relationship between a father and son—a narrative focused more closely, as *Punch-Drunk Love* had been, on developing one primary character and storyline in greater depth. The once-indulgent storyteller was liberated: "it was such a great feeling," he said, "cutting things out, slashing away."[47]

To work past his writer's block and find that core, Anderson threw himself into returning to the book and more or less adapting the first part directly into a screenplay, with little focus on his own personal ideas for a grander narrative. Anderson just "sort of transcribe[d] the book to see how it looked."[48] Rather than decide what the film would be about, he began to consciously concede control to Sinclair: "it was thrilling to transcribe someone else's words and look at them on the page," he said; "it was like having a great collaborator sitting over your shoulder."[49] The perseverance paid off, even as the story began veering sharply in the second half from its literary origins: "it's like you've written enough," he said, "and there's enough good scenes in a row that there's a point of no return."[50] Meanwhile, *Oil!* was not the script's only literary influence. On the relationship between Eli's and Daniel's respective "brothers," Anderson admitted later that "it's Cain and Abel stuff. *East of Eden* has been for years my favourite book. The connection isn't planned out but it appears and if you're lucky you grab hold of it."[51]

Anderson recognized the familiar thematic limitations of the story he was writing—namely, the core story of a father's relationship with his son: "I remember writing a scene from the book with a 9-year-old boy and his father. And I thought, I'm not writing this again. I'm not writing that. I don't want to do that . . . But yeah, there you go, whatever happens, happens."[52] As the story evolved, however, the father/son relationship went in a radically different direction for a filmmaker who usually elevated the importance of strong father figures in a man's life. The entire script was also rewritten to reflect, as Anderson envisioned it, the core story of Plainview's obsessive quest for land and oil and the challenge posed by the preacher Eli.

"THERE COULDN'T BE A BETTER TIME
TO MAKE A MOVIE OUT OF *OIL!*"

More troubling for Anderson than repeating himself with stories about fathers, however, were the political implications involved in taking on a book about the mutually beneficial rises of the oil and religion industries in twentieth-century America—especially given Sinclair's socialist leanings, which framed oil's ruthless rise to power as an indictment of capitalism's inhuman tendencies. "I was thinking that we'd better be very careful not to do too much of [the political allegory]," Anderson said later. "We should approach the film as a horror film and a boxing match first. You know you're walking into a film about an independent oilman and a guy that runs a church."[53] The political critique was already implied in *There Will Be Blood*'s often brutal, even nihilistic, narrative focusing on the battle of wills between two generally unsympathetic protagonists in Plainview and Eli. Anderson's reservations had more to with derailing the film's dramatic momentum. "The risks that you run" with such a transparently political concept, he recalled, "are big, long speeches that would help in paralleling or allegoricalizing, if that's a word."[54] This would kill the film's narrative energy and reduce characters to one-dimensional archetypes rather than flesh-and-blood people in whom audiences could become invested.

By 2007, the subject of oil and religion in America was a timely topic. Cultural critic Lennart Sjöberg wrote that "nobody who sees it today can avoid associating it with the enormous importance of oil in the current global economy and the great wealth it produces."[55] This was embodied in particular in the figure of then–U.S. President George W. Bush (whose father, former president George H. W. Bush, shares initials with Plainview's adopted son). Born in Connecticut and raised in Houston, the younger Bush saw himself as a Texas frontier man and returned to the Lone Star state after Harvard business school and worked in the oil industry. Later in life, Bush also embraced the Christian faith in order to overcome his alcoholism. As he moved full-time into politics in the 1990s, Bush proudly flaunted his evangelical underpinnings to win over religious voters, particularly middle-class and poor voters.

Bush remained a fiscal conservative interested primarily in protecting the wealth of America's economic elite. By 2001, Bush had successfully ridden that marriage of social and fiscal conservatism to the presidency, after which he began implementing policies that decimated America's economy for the benefit of the rich. He sponsored massive tax cuts that gutted the nation's resources, relaxed government regulations on business practices, and allowed oil prices to soar without oversight. Much of the nation's economic trouble was blamed on the September 11 attacks and the subsequent military invasions of Afghanistan and Iraq, but many policies were in place before then. The "war on terror" only embedded those policies further. With U.S. military forces going to the Middle East, private American companies increased profits by providing supplies for war, while U.S. energy companies gained increased access to foreign oil fields and transport routes. Bush's Wall Street allies benefited enormously from his decision to go to war in Iraq—a devastatingly arbitrary move.

When *There Will Be Blood* premiered, *Vanity Fair* observed that "with its price tickling $100 a barrel at press time, and the U.S. allegedly not waging war for it all over the Middle East, there couldn't be a better time to make a movie out of *Oil!*, Upton Sinclair's muckraking 1927 novel about the petroleum industry—except for maybe pretty much any other time over the last 80 years."[56] Murphet articulated *There Will Be Blood*'s symbolism more sharply:

Obviously, in straightforward political terms, *There Will Be Blood* is meant as an allegory, offered explicitly as a cinematic redaction of Halliburton's America: petrochemical capital and evangelical religion ruling the land with unchecked abandon. If the allegory is loose and not perfectly joined (there is, after all, no fundamental social incompatibility between oil money and millenarian baptism; quite to the contrary, despite what the film ends by suggesting), then that is all the better for the resilience of the model, and in no way negates the underlying mesh of allegorical gears within the 'lived experience' of Bush's America, where it is impossible not to feel the adequacy of the textual figures to their worldly referents.[57]

As important as oil money was the more contentious issue of faith. Often, the "war on terror" was painted, by extremists on both sides, as a religious war—an epic battle between Christianity and Islam. America's transparently Christian leader did little to defuse such inflammatory rhetoric, repeatedly making references to how God wanted him to be president. By 2006, with the Iraq war at a standstill and the U.S. domestic economy headed toward ruin, the American public began to turn on Bush and the Republican Congress as the destructive alliance Bush had successfully exploited for half a decade became increasingly apparent. Bush presided over a partic-

5.13. Religion is depicted as being as extreme as the oil industry. Here too Eli seems to cast out the camera itself from the church, rejecting any powerful (mediated) presence that might challenge his control and influence within his house of worship.

ularly acute moment in American history where the flames of faith (the conservative delusion of a war on Christianity, domestic and abroad) were being fanned in support of economic gains (increased oil availability overseas and profits at home).

Thus, a film about the alliance between a greedy oilman and an equally ambitious preacher unsurprisingly triggered discussion about America's political and economic state. In an especially observant comment, Denby suggested that, when looking over *There Will Be Blood*'s vast rural landscape, "the thrown-together buildings look scraggly and unkempt, the homesteaders are modest, stubborn, and reticent, but, in their undreamed-of future, Wal-Mart is on the way."[58] In *There Will Be Blood*, the rural poor are taken over by an outside industry that promises jobs and civic engagement but that is interested only in exploiting a desperate workforce, eradicating all business competition, and maximizing profits for itself even at the expense of worker safety. Anderson was repeatedly asked by critics and reporters about this obvious historical context for *There Will Be Blood*, and always had largely the same answer:

I'm no dummy. I'm living in 2007. But that said, I would feel completely out of place making a political film that tackled something straight on. We really approached it like a battle between two families: attack it as Battle Royale and dress it up as a horror film.[59]

A focused storyteller first, Anderson refused to concede the film to the long reach of its palpable political allegory, even though audiences often read the film as such regardless. "One doubts that Anderson would wish his film to be regarded as a straight allegory for current issues arising around blood, oil and old-time religions," Hannah McGill wrote in *Sight & Sound*:

still, the final scenes of a raging, crippled Plainview, couched in luxury but devoid of all compassion, offer a grim image of the ultimate wages of rapacious greed. Like *Chinatown* (1974), *There Will Be Blood* directly connects personal corruption and cruelty with the exploitation of the earth's basic resources—and acknowledges the irony that only by some combination of the three do industries, cities and nations prosper.[60]

Even Anderson ultimately could not completely dismiss the timely political implications of *There Will Be Blood*: "I remember thinking [at first] how exciting it was that I was in a venue about the history of California. But by the end of it, (even though) it's there to a certain extent, it's not about [the history] at all."[61] Anderson generally avoided speculating on what *There Will Be Blood* was "supposed" to mean, preferring to focus on the construction of the narrative's dramatic arcs.

For Steve Sailer, *There Will Be Blood*'s ultimate ambivalence towards history was the main problem. The film was disappointing precisely because it failed to mount an explicit political critique that rose above anything other than the watered-down politics of the personal. The *American Conservative* columnist saw *There Will Be Blood* as a disappointingly hollow film more interested in stylized cinematic flare than political engagement: "the strangely apolitical *There Will Be Blood*," Sailer criticized, "turns out to be just another movie about movies."[62] Much of this came back to the issue of adaptation. The film's political disengagement was significantly rooted in Anderson's lack of fidelity to the original source material. Sailer also felt that *There Will Be Blood* missed an opportunity to stay closer to Doheny's sordid personal history, which included not only oil profits but also private scandals such as his son's unsolved murder-suicide in the very mansion in which the film was shot.

Approaching the (a)political content from a different perspective, Murphet's issue came back to the liberties it took with Sinclair's socialist beliefs. *Oil!* critiqued American capitalism in the 1920s as a counterpoint to the Revolution in Russia, one of many historical events the film ignores. Moreover, Anderson's film—as with most Hollywood movies—reduces political struggle to the symbolic personal story of a father's relationship to his son, thus marginalizing the larger social and historical struggles against the dehumanizing effects of capitalism at the dawn of the twentieth century. In "PT Anderson's Dilemma," Murphet argues that Anderson's representation of patriarchy structures the "family" as a commercial corporate structure rather than a biological or surrogate one. Anderson's work, he wrote, "demands that we shift the locus of 'authenticity' away from the 'legal fiction' of biological paternity, and towards the 'commercial fiction' of patriarchal-corporate subjectivity."[63] A successful, functional family is held together by mutually defined commercial interests—be it Jack Horner's film production "family" in *Boogie Nights*, Earl Partridge's TV game show "family" in *Magnolia*, or Dean Trumbell's Mattress Man "family" in *Punch-Drunk Love*.

For Murphet, this dynamic becomes most explicitly realized in *There Will Be Blood*, where the construction of the Plainview "family"—a man, his adopted son, and later his imposter "brother" —is structured entirely around the business interest of Daniel's emergent oil dynasty. By shifting the emphasis of capitalism's critique, through adaptation, from the political (socialist revolutions, labor struggles) to the personal (Plainview's lack of social and parenting skills), Anderson undermined the story's explicit political power:

Even if the prevailing liberal wisdom, that Hollywood—even 'independent' Hollywood—can never cease from prattling, is that Sinclair's political 'utopianism' was not only incompatible with the American 'family myth,' but moreover complicit with the full savage history of Stalinism, nevertheless there remains more to admire in a book that places its wager on a genuine political event, than a film that turns its back on it and consigns it to a weak political unconscious.[64]

Yet an advantage that *There Will Be Blood* had was the timing of its release. In 2007, the "genuine political event" of Soviet Revolution in Sinclair's book became displaced by the event of the "war on terror," which audiences repeatedly identified in the film. Sjöberg argued in contrast that:

Sinclair's socialist and anticapitalist attitude is well conveyed by the movie. Of course, others view the successful capitalist as an entrepreneur who is the basis of economic progress and welfare for all. However, the type of person represented by Plainview is impossible to see in a positive light; this is probably why the story is so powerful and persuasive.[65]

There Will Be Blood doesn't ultimately navigate irreconcilable political ideologies regarding the cultural impact of capitalism (as embodied in Plainview), primarily because the ending is so unapologetically definitive in its presentation of him. The symbolic figure of capitalism in the film has no positive personal characteristics that could be read allegorically as virtues of capitalism itself.

Reading the effectiveness of *There Will Be Blood*'s politics rests on seeing Plainview as a metaphor for capitalism. On a primitive level, "Plainview's ideology," Deanna Boyd McQuillan and Matthew McQuillan argue, "is reminiscent of the social Darwinistic theories prominent at the time that purported the benefits of the culling of the weak from society."[66] Social Darwinism is at the heart of capitalism's basest financial instincts, destroying the economically weak for the sake of the strong (i.e., the most business-savvy). Plainview evokes memories of "the 'robber baron' view of the capitalist [which] was common when Sinclair wrote his book, and it still is," Sjöberg argued; "historical examples such as Henry Ford come to mind."[67] Over the twentieth century, capitalism moved toward faceless corporations that enjoy the legal rights of any citizen through the doctrine of corporate personhood. The idea of the robber baron humanizes the destructive greed of capitalism at a time when such avaricious behavior hides behind anonymous buildings and corporate logos. Plainview embodies the single-minded desire of big business to streamline industrial output, maximize profit, and minimize economic risk with no regard for the interests of the disposable worker or the community.

PLAINVIEW

Even well written, Plainview would not work as a convincing character without a great performance that could find the humanity within an inhuman monster. "When I met [Plainview] in the form of Paul's script," Day-Lewis recalled, he liked that the character appeared to be "an entirely honest examination of a life to me."[68] Having written the part with the actor in mind, "I probably wouldn't have shot the movie," Anderson said later, "if Daniel Day-Lewis had turned me down."[69] Yet, Day-Lewis joked, "It's probably easy for him to say [he wouldn't have made it] now. My feeling is that he probably wrote it partly with me in mind, but I think he didn't chain himself to the idea of one actor to the exclusion of any other. But he certainly didn't need to sell it to me."[70] Indeed, Anderson admitted that:

I didn't want to grab on to the thought and keep thinking this is who I am writing it for, because I didn't know Daniel. I didn't want to make presumptions about him. . . . But that said, it kept coming and coming and coming, that the only man for the job would be Daniel if he decided he would want to do it.[71]

According to JoAnne Sellar, they "approached [Day-Lewis] when the script was about three-quarters done."[72] It turned out Day-Lewis was already a fan. "We had a mutual friend who had let me know how Daniel felt about *Punch-Drunk Love* [which featured *The Boxer* costar Emily Watson] . . . ," Anderson said, "so I was armed with that to give me a boost of confidence."[73] For Day-Lewis, the process was simpler: "Paul asked me," the notoriously project-shy star said later, "and that's all it took."[74] By 2004, Day-Lewis had committed to the project.

Once devoted, the actor throws himself into his part; Day-Lewis is notoriously selective because he takes the work involved so seriously. In the two decades since first bursting onto the international film scene with his Oscar-winning turn in *My Left Foot* (1989), the actor has made only ten films. On *There Will Be Blood*, he reflected: "For me, from beginning to end, it was about 3 years of my life invested in telling this story, so it had to be something I felt a pretty compelling need to be involved in."[75] Day-Lewis's reputation as a perfectionist has been overstated at times, yet the evidence is overwhelming. For his role as Christy Brown, who suffers from cerebral palsy in *My Left Foot*, he reportedly never left a wheelchair for months, doing every task possible, including writing and painting, with his left foot. On *In the Name of the Father* (1993), Day-Lewis spent time in prison to research the part of a man wrongly imprisoned. For the legendary part of Hawkeye, a white adopted Native American trapper, in *Last of the Mohicans* (1992), he built a canoe and hunted animals with a handmade knife. On *The Boxer* (1997), Day-Lewis trained for months as a boxer; while on *Gangs of New York* (2002), he worked in a butcher's shop and learned to throw giant chopping knives to prepare for his part as Bill the Butcher.

Day-Lewis prepares on an intensely physical level and does not necessarily follow other method routines such as understanding psychologically where someone like Plainview comes from. "You begin with nothing," he said. "You reduce yourself as far as possible to the state of an empty vessel, which may or may not fill with something that's going to be useful to you."[76] Like his character, Day-Lewis threw himself solely into the *material* labor of the project, with less consideration for the deeper motivation of the person he was playing. When asked about the source of Plainview's desires, Day-Lewis responded honestly: "I don't know where it came from. I don't want to know. It seemed to come from probably a very unconscious place, but there seemed to be great truth in it, in the outrageous trajectory of that man's life. I can't explain it. And I still feel the same way about it."[77] Ultimately, Day-Lewis's method deemphasized "knowing" the character in favor of what it "feels" like to *be* the character—the process of consciously reflecting on the character's motives becomes secondary.

Anderson suggested that Day-Lewis begin researching Huston, who became the primary influence for his performance. In addition to passing along documentaries about the classic filmmaker, Anderson also sent a copy of his most famous film, *The Treasure of the Sierra Madre*. A story about the California gold rush and the depths to which greed can drive a man in search of material wealth, Huston's classic was a clear influence on *There Will Be Blood*. Anderson did not shy away from his affection: "It's my favorite movie,"[78] he told the *New York Times* in 2007. As Plainview descends deeper and deeper into murderous madness, driven by his lust for wealth and control, we see in his mad eyes the same rage that eventually drove Fred C. Dobbs (Humphrey Bogart) on a destructive rampage to a tragic end. In describing the simple power of *The Treasure of the Sierra Madre*, Anderson told *Variety*:

It was the economy with which that story is told, but at the same time it's very meaty. They just give you the steak; there's no sides, there's no mashed potatoes, there's no greens. And that was it more than anything—that classic storytelling which I've always tried to do but I've never felt like I've succeeded. Maybe my natural instincts don't lead me there.[79]

Unlike Anderson's aurally and visually flashy predecessors, *There Will Be Blood* is told within carefully controlled moments of excess. Yet Anderson's film departs from Huston's in one crucial respect. In *The Treasure of the Sierra Madre*, the guilty must pay for their crimes, in classic Hollywood fashion, while the good are saved. But in *There Will Be Blood*, Plainview emerges untouched, even perversely triumphant.

Equally important was Huston's memorable performance as the thoroughly evil land developer Noah Cross in Roman Polanski's retro-noir *Chinatown* (1974), another classic of the 1970s New Hollywood that proved hugely influential—like the films of Scorsese, Altman, and Kubrick. *Chinatown* is the story of private eye Jake Gittes (Jack Nicholson), who investigates an affair and then the murder of a local politician in 1930s Los Angeles. The story was partially inspired by a real-life politician, William Mulholland, who obtained water for Los Angeles residents by building its famous aqueducts. Once again, the setting was key for Anderson. "*Chinatown* is so ingrained," he told *Sight & Sound* in 2008, "when I first saw it I knew everything they were talking about, very directly. That [the San Fernando Valley] was where I grew up."[80] Gittes discovers that the root of the conspiracy involves Cross's plan to trick the voters of Los Angeles into approving a new water delivery system that will turn his worthless desert land into highly desirable suburban property.

There Will Be Blood was a symbolic prequel to the classic retronoir. Within their overlapping historical timelines, Cross and Plainview are more or less the same age, living in the same location. Both are remnants of California's frontier past, and both are deeply influential but reclusive civic figures who have amassed an immeasurable fortune by exploiting local workers, resources, and the barren

5.14. Plainview's violent descent into madness over the land's resources recalls
Fred Dobbs's similar journey in Huston's *Treasure of the Sierra Madre*.

5.15. Day-Lewis's physical performance was partially modeled on Huston's work as Noah Cross in *Chinatown*—another fictional character with historical similarities to Plainview.

California desert for decades. Both are positioned, with knowing irony, as ambitious industrialists whose respective visions more or less shaped the society that surrounds them. They are also sociopaths—ruthless misanthropes—capable of the worst possible transgressions imaginable against their fellow man, including horrific crimes against their own children. In the end both men survive, while the consequences of their actions are suffered by the less powerful around them. When Plainview speaks, he also speaks as Cross.

THERE WILL (EVENTUALLY) BE BLOOD

With Anderson's script ready after years of writing, and a major star attached, shooting on *There Will Be Blood* was originally set for summer 2005. However, the start date was delayed for another year, and in the meantime Anderson went off to Minnesota to help on *A Prairie Home Companion*. Anderson's longtime agent John Lesher attempted to set up independent financing, but without luck. The prospective budget for Anderson's ambitious historical epic scared interested parties away—particularly at a time when the director's moment as a promising up-and-comer had long since passed. In contrast to the standoffish approach he took toward Rysher and New Line a decade earlier, Anderson was more reflective: "the first time we tried to get the money for [*There Will Be Blood*]," he admitted in retrospect, "we didn't really know what we were doing . . . there were so many variables about how you shoot down a mine shaft and building the derrick and where we would shoot and all this sort of stuff."[81] Rather than disparage prospective financiers for rejecting the project, the director admitted: "in all fairness to those places that said 'no, get out of here,' . . . we did need to go back to the drawing board. We needed more time to research it, get it all sorted."[82]

Day-Lewis remained so committed to doing *There Will Be Blood* sooner or later that he refused other roles in the meantime, waiting for the opening to finally participate in Anderson's film. Meanwhile, the friendship between director and actor strengthened. In early 2005, Anderson helped out by moderating a postscreening discussion at the Los Angeles County Museum of Art with the actor and his wife, director Rebecca Miller, for her film *The Ballad of Jack and Rose* (2005). "Anderson led the discussion with fanlike enthusiasm," reported *Variety* at the time, "often following their answers with a dreamy 'I really liked that.'"[83] *The Ballad of Jack and Rose* also called Anderson's attention to Paul Dano, who was later cast in the small role of Paul Sunday and eventually took on the larger role of brother Eli when the original actor (O'Neill) was dropped after a few weeks' shooting.

The time off while waiting for funding allowed Anderson and Day-Lewis to continue working on the character, while the director and crew researched how to actually build and shoot the oil derrick sets. Part of the research was cinematic, as Elswit recalled: "An enormous amount of footage was shot back then. We watched all these old-time guys working on wooden rigs, and we could see what early rotary or cable-tool rigs looked like."[84] With the historical research underway, Anderson became excited at the visual possibilities:

You get giddy looking at all those amazing photos, getting a real sense of how people lived their lives. There's so much history in the oil areas around Bakersfield—they're filled with the grandsons of oil workers and lots of folklore. So we did an incredible amount of research and I got to be a student again and that was a thrill.[85]

Anderson and the rest of the production crew, including Fisk, used the extra time to make several trips to do additional research on oil derricks at the West Kern Oil Museum outside Bakersfield, which boasts an original 106-foot derrick on display. While Anderson kept a low profile at the museum (no one there claimed to recognize him), Fisk devoured all the relevant materials he could. "They came in one day and said they wanted to make a movie and wanted to build a

5.16. To research the time period, filmmakers watched old industrial films about oil in California during the early twentieth century.

derrick," said museum volunteer Bob Foreman.[86] Fisk purchased the blueprint of a 1914 oil derrick in the gift shop, using it as the model for the eighty-foot version in the film. The reproduction took four weeks to build and was destroyed in one night for the film's memorable oil-explosion sequence. Such attention to historical detail just scratched the surface of Fisk's work as production designer—a key part of the film's powerfully gritty, minimalist aesthetic. "In my opinion," said Elswit, who won an Oscar for *There Will Be Blood*'s cinematography, Fisk's "production design was *the* great contribution to the film."[87] Although Fisk did not win an Academy Award (despite being nominated), he was recognized by his peers when he won the award for Excellence in Production Design for a Period Feature Film at the Twelfth Annual Art Directors Guild Awards.

In addition to concerns over the film's production budget, prospective financiers also had reservations about *There Will Be Blood*'s dark subject matter, muted tone, and lack of female roles (eliminating the possibility of a love story such as Hollywood often privileges). "They took one look at the film," Day-Lewis recalled, "and said 'no' . . . they said 'no, no, no.'"[88] The lack of female characters in *There Will Be Blood* is conspicuous, and revives the specter of misogyny that often haunts Anderson's films. Anderson didn't know quite how to address it:

I remember feeling, 'there's no girls in this movie.' But the truth is that there were no women in the oil fields, at least not when they were prospecting. There were whores in the bars but there were no families. I used to joke, 'We had a love story in the film but Paramount Vantage test-screened it and they wanted us to take it out.' That would have been the sin—to tack a romance on top of the movie.[89]

Anderson's claim that there were historically no women in the oil fields raised more questions than answers. His focus on historical accuracy and resistance to a superficial, formulaic love story was creatively admirable. He also argued later that his critique of the oil industry in the film stemmed from the "negative thoughts about what he called the 'boys network' of business today."[90] But the absence of women in *There Will Be Blood* still brings up the troubling question of what meaningful role women play in Anderson's body of work; this film no more answers it than others.

Articulations of gender in *There Will Be Blood* play out through an unrelenting emphasis on ambiguously defined images of masculinity. The two main characters, Plainview and Eli, are asexual and quite possibly homosexual. Neither man pursues a relationship, sexually or otherwise, with a woman. Eli betrays a possibly lustful affection for Bandy's grandson late in the film. Plainview is uninterested in sex, even expressing disgust at the lusting behavior of his fake brother. In the original script, Plainview admitted to Henry that he was impotent in the course of explaining why H.W. was not his biological son. In the exchange, Daniel follows up his own admission that his penis "doesn't work" by asking Henry if his does. In *There Will Be Blood*, Plainview's admission could be read historically as a code for more than just physical dysfunction. At the beginning of the twentieth century, Angus McLaren wrote in *Impotence: A Cultural History*, "impotence was frequently taken as a symptom of homosexuality."[91] The final version of *There Will Be Blood*, though, avoids the overt homophobia of Anderson's previous films by ignoring the subject entirely. Plainview puts all his mental and bodily energies into the quest for oil.

The project began to find traction in January 2006 as a joint collaboration between Miramax—the former indie king that Anderson was finally working with after all these years—and Paramount Vantage (still called "Paramount Classics" then). Lesher, Anderson's longtime agent, had taken over as president of Vantage, the specialty films division. The studio venture allowed Anderson a greater budget than he would have had independently—between $20[92] and $25[93] million—but that still wasn't close to the starting projected budget for *Magnolia* a decade earlier. "We did it on an incredibly small amount of money," producer Sellar said, "though it was more than the average for an art film. The studios didn't think it had the scope of a major picture."[94] The budget quickly ballooned after shooting finally got underway, eventually reaching as high as $45 million[95] (with Lesher in charge, Paramount Vantage largely went along with the indulgences). This is a number that would be critically, if not quite financially, offset by the time *There Will Be Blood* hit theaters a year later.

Principal photography began in May 2006. After years of prep work, actual shooting started roughly. Anderson recalled that "we were cooped up in the starting gate [while waiting so long for funding], and the second the starting gate opened, we fell flat on our faces with all of this energy. We had the most horrendous beginning of a film, for two weeks, just completely off of the mark."[96] Day-Lewis's intensity was part of the issue. The cast and crew tried to determine if his intentionally larger-than-life take on Plainview was translating well to film, or if the actor was overdoing it. This concern was highlighted when they realized the actor cast as Eli wasn't going to work opposite Day-Lewis's intense demeanor, causing him to be replaced by Dano. Everyone avoided discussing the subject later, but, as the *New York Times* noted, "there are reports that the first actor suffered from intimidation [from working with Day-Lewis]. 'It just wasn't the right fit,' Anderson explained diplomatically."[97] Anderson "wants to see things unfold on the set," added Elswit, "and if something isn't working, he's willing to stop in his tracks and start all over again. So there's a constant recharging and renewal of creative energy."[98]

Dano's dedication matched the legendarily intense star. Already cast as Paul, Dano now played a dual role that made the brothers identical twins in a way the script never indicated. The combustible dynamic between Dano and Day-Lewis would provide a thrilling cinematic experience, but that didn't translate to a warm personal relationship during the shoot. While he was working with Day-Lewis, Dano admitted, "we weren't too chummy,"[99] as both actors buried themselves in their respective roles. Anderson, meanwhile, stayed out of the way: "it reminds me of the Will Rogers line 'Never miss a good chance to shut up.' Sometimes standing out of the way is the best direction of all."[100] Anderson deferred throughout his career to performers' routines, which paid off especially well in the chemistry between Dano and Day-Lewis. Embracing a unique environment of trust, they'd take turns slapping and punching each other in the face without restraint, for instance. "They had the benefit of working together before [on *Ballad*]," Anderson observed, "so Paul knew what to expect, and Daniel gave Paul respect, underneath all of it. That said, they kept their distance from each other"[101] when the cameras weren't rolling.

For the first time, Anderson stepped outside the comfort of the American West to shoot a film elsewhere—although the decision was more practical than artistic. The true setting of Bakersfield was never an option. "We scouted all over California looking for a California that doesn't exist anymore," Sellar noted. "There's always a Burger King or a Starbucks or a freeway in the way. You can't get away from it. We couldn't have a 360 (degree) view."[102] This wasn't a problem for just California, as Elswit noted: "There aren't many spots in America where you can stand on top of a hill and see absolutely nothing in all directions."[103] *There Will Be Blood*'s crew ended up in the barren middle of West Texas, near where their eventual Oscar competition, the Coen brothers' *No Country for Old Men*, was also being shot (and the set of the legendary oil film *Giant* [1955]).

The crew built a 500-acre set outside Marfa, including a small town, an oil derrick, a worker's camp, and Eli's church. "Everything you see on the film was built [around the existing train line]," Sellar said. "There was nothing there; it was just an empty piece of land."[104] Meanwhile, Fisk's construction focused on historical accuracy rather than visual efficiency. "We were working from research material of what a derrick and the town looked like," Anderson said, "and we never made allowances for what a camera might do."[105] The conditions resulted in a less overtly stylized film, as there was very limited advanced storyboarding. Anderson reflected that "it's one of the nice things about shooting in a desert location: You're just struggling for survival, because it's hot, it's fucking dusty, and you don't have time to think."[106] Nor was anyone preoccupied by outside issues on the isolated set. "You felt you were going back in time," Sellar said. "There were no distractions, and we were totally in the movie. When we did come back to L.A., it was a culture shock because you got so used to living in that environment."[107]

Day-Lewis relished the setting, which allowed him to focus on the role for which he'd long been preparing. "It was one huge playground," he noted, "in which we merrily played with a group of, you know, like-minded people for a period of time."[108] Day-Lewis's dedication was reflected in his on-screen performance. "It's difficult to imagine him emerging between takes as just an actor playing a part," observed *Variety*'s Todd McCarthy in a review of *There Will Be Blood*.[109] It would be a stretch to say Day-Lewis never broke character during production, but not by much. He was occasionally spotted jogging in heavy sweat suits around Marfa, keeping fit during those rare times when he wasn't needed on set.[110] *Newsweek* critic and longtime Anderson supporter David Ansen was granted a rare visit to the set in 2006. When he interviewed Day-Lewis, Ansen observed that the actor was polite and gracious but retained "the deliberate, semi-aristocratic voice he's devised for the role and refuses to relinquish,"[111] even between takes.

The filmmakers filled both extra and key parts with locals. Anderson wanted unknown faces to reflect the unfamiliarity of a story set in the turn of the century. Casting director Cassandra Kulukundis drove a rental car around to find people who fit a frontier look: "people were starving on the land. They were 35 but looked 55."[112] The most remarkable find was the young Dillon Freasier to play H.W. He was discovered at school in nearby Fort Davis. Anderson originally balked at writing the young character for exactly this reason: it "can be difficult to find an actor who's 10 years old who's going to be required to do all this stuff."[113] Kulukundis added, "I had gone on a search for a child who was more interested in the outdoors, not [one who] watched TV and Game Boy."[114] Ironically, securing Freasier proved to be harder than signing Day-Lewis. His parents had never heard of Day-Lewis or Anderson, and they weren't particularly seduced by the call of Hollywood. They rented *Gangs of New York* to learn more about the actor and were horrified by the prospect of Dillon working with Bill the Butcher. "The producers were panicked, but they found a solution," reported Ansen. "A DVD of *The Age of Innocence* was rushed over to the Freasier household. [And] Dillon got the job."[115]

On set, Anderson continued working with longtime collaborator Elswit, who had shot every Anderson film to that point since the low-budget indie days of *Hard Eight* a decade earlier. The cinematographer knew Anderson's demanding but open-minded habits perhaps better than anyone. This includes not only his on-set demeanor but technical preferences as well. Anderson remains fond of shooting on old-fashioned 35mm film in an increasingly digital age, experimenting with innovative camera tricks like reusing an old 43mm Pathé camera once employed on *Magnolia* (and the "Fast as You Can" music video), and avoiding postproduction digital touchup as much as possible. Anderson clearly had an especially trusting partnership with Elswit, to whom he openly admits conceding control at times:

Bob and I disagree just as often as we agree, but the relationship wouldn't be as good if we agreed on everything. Sometimes I'll sit right over his shoulder and all he'll want me to do is go away. At other times, we have a great time sitting together and coming up with ideas. Or, sometimes, I'll get distracted and he'll put something together that's really lovely.[116]

The impressive visual style on *There Will Be Blood* is as indebted to Elswit as to the director. His work was so key that later he was one of the few participants to take home an Oscar for his contribution, despite the film's numerous nominations. *There Will Be Blood*'s stark visual look oscillates between brightly lit day shots of the vast California (Texas) desert and pitch-black nights, often lit only by the natural glow of fire (flamethrowers were used to light the actors' reaction shots to the exploding oil well). Both day and night reflected the barrenness of Plainview's soul and naked ambition.

POSTPRODUCTION

Principal photography wrapped in the fall of 2006. As he began putting together a rough cut, Anderson commissioned guitarist Jonny Greenwood, from the legendary rock band Radiohead, to score *There Will Be Blood*—another collaboration with a professional pop musician (like Aimee Mann or Jon Brion) with little formal film music background. Unknown to Greenwood at the time, "Anderson had edited parts of my piece 'Popcorn Superhet Receiver' to [*There Will Be Blood*] and liked the way it fitted. So he asked if I would be interested in adding more new music."[117] First meeting Greenwood while Radiohead was putting together the album *In Rainbows* (2007), Anderson, as usual, was passionately insistent. The director "just attacked me with his daunting enthusiasm and a kind of mad certainty that I'd do okay," Greenwood recalled.[118] To convince the would-be composer, Anderson showed him an early cut. Afterward, Greenwood "kind of bounded across the room. He said, 'I just have to write music to this story. That is all I have to do, right?' And [Anderson] thought, 'Yeah, if that is what you think you have to do.'"[119]

While the classically trained Greenwood had never done a feature score before, he'd composed music for Simon Pummell's documentary *Bodysong* (2003) and did occasional work for the British Broadcasting Corporation (BBC). As he began to envision how to make the sounds he wanted with *There Will Be Blood*, Greenwood followed the ideal of period authenticity established by Anderson, Fisk, Elswit, and others. The composer set "constraints such as only using instruments from the period. I wanted to write music that sounded as if something had gone slightly wrong with it, and even the quartet pieces would have small hesitations written into them, to suggest something dark happening among what is ordinarily a comforting sound."[120] One such instrument was the ondes Martenot, a device invented in the 1920s. "To me it's the first and last time that someone has taken electricity and in a very pure sense made a musical instrument with it," Greenwood said. ". . . It's magical and it's not jarringly modern, despite using electricity. It ties with the story in that sense, with things becoming gradually mechanized."[121]

Even the supportive Anderson was thrown off by some of the earliest compositions: "Greenwood was sending me score pieces [from the UK]. I was like 'What?' But ultimately you have a day, maybe two days, to get out of yourself and see what another person was thinking."[122] Although Greenwood brought Radiohead's distinctive experimentation to many of the haunting sounds, he was more influenced by classic twentieth-century French composers like Olivier Messiaen, Claude Debussy, and Maurice Ravel. As in the early days of his working relationship with Day-Lewis, Anderson was separated from Greenwood by the Atlantic for much of the process, which worked for the better creatively. Anderson "could never over-direct [someone so far away], which is a really good feeling," the director stated, "because, you know, best to let him to his own devices and gentle suggestions here and there. And that's kind of how it worked."[123]

Anderson was taking the same mindset into the editing room. "I don't miss scenes at all the way that I used to miss them when I was younger making a film," Anderson admitted; "it's actually quite fun to get rid of them now."[124] Such an attitude was a stark contrast from the headstrong days of *Hard Eight*, *Boogie Nights*, and *Magnolia*, when Anderson often refused to touch a single frame once he was done with a first cut that largely followed the original script. Even Anderson conceded in 2008 that "I certainly wish I could take 15 or 20 minutes out of" *Magnolia*.[125] For *There Will Be Blood*, Anderson patched things up with longtime editor Tichenor, who had quit in the middle of *Punch-Drunk Love*. Their relationship was based on a longer history of trust. In 2005, Tichenor recalled an anecdote:

On *Magnolia*, I put a sequence together, a very emotional section of the movie. Paul sat down on the couch to watch it and I literally couldn't press the play button. Paul understood that I had put something of myself into it and that I was understandably nervous. That's one of the reasons I respect Paul as much as I do. He understands the contribution.[126]

Together, Anderson and Tichenor worked through the hours of footage, often shot on the fly in the Texas summer. It took a lot of work, Anderson noted, "to get the pacing right, the rhythm of it. . . . we kind of knew the parts that we didn't like, or that we wanted to work on. Speaking for me and Dylan, we knew the parts that we wanted to work out, that we weren't happy with."[127] Despite the lengthy two-and-a-half-hour running time, *There Will Be Blood* is cut together by a real economy of storytelling—the editing, especially in the silent opening, subtly but quickly moves the story from moment to moment with little flourish, establishing Plainview's character, his misanthropy, and his ambitions.

"THIS MOVIE WAS BUILT TO GET TO THE BOWLING ALLEY"

As the film's title suggests, one scene never in doubt in the editing room was the shocking finale inside Plainview's mansion, though it took a lot of time to perfect. The ending turned out to be the hardest part, according to Anderson: "Getting the ending just right. We really did lots of work on that to make it the best it could be. Just making up our minds was hard."[128] In *There Will Be Blood*'s outrageous ending, the now-elderly oilman banishes his adopted son for declaring that he wants to start a business for himself (which makes him, to Plainview, a competitor). He's then greeted by a desperate Eli,

5.17. Doheny's real-life mansion in Beverly Hills was the location for Plainview's fictional one, further solidifying the parallels between the two. The basement used to serve as a soundstage for American Film Institute filmmaking students, including Elswit—giving the film's violent finale an ironic metatextual layer, since Elswit learned his craft while shooting student footage in the exact same physical location.

who lost money in the stock market. Plainview first mocks and humiliates the preacher and then impulsively beats him to death with a bowling pin. "From the very beginning, when we started cutting the film," Anderson said, "we knew we were heading to the bowling alley. It wasn't like 'Yeah, we originally had this other ending, but Paramount asked us if we could do something kind of crazy and outlandish instead.' This movie was built to get to the bowling alley."[129] In retrospect, this fit the movie's larger arc. Plainview was always determined to be completely alone—obliterating all competition (such as the Standard Oil man whose throat he'd once promised to slit) and killing senselessly if the occasion presented itself (as with the quick execution of his brother's imposter). On a first viewing, though, it's hard to see the stark brutality and thematic clarity of it all coming.

The 1927 sequence begins with perfect irony—as isolated as he'd been in the very beginning, Plainview is now locked up in the mansion he always sought, fulfilling his dream of being completely removed from the world. Yet he does little except re-create the wilderness all over again, firing his rifle at stuffed animals as though still a hunter surviving off the earth. The large jump in time, the cavernous spaces, the old man awaiting death, all evoke memories of *2001: A Space Odyssey*. In the opening of *There Will Be Blood*, Plainview's first big accomplishment was signing his name proudly to the silver

5.18. The first image of Plainview's signature announced his triumphant
financial emergence from the dark depths of a silver mine . . .

5.19. . . . while the last image of it becomes an ironic commentary on the emptiness
of his success and of his physical removal from the world itself. Plainview is
reduced in function to signing his name. This is also an homage to the end of
Kubrick's *Barry Lyndon*, where the once-proud title character is reduced to
little more than a name on a form that his ex-wife apathetically signs.

assay deed. Yet by the end of the film, he is now nothing *but* a signature, reduced to signing checks while his life drains away in this giant, cavernous mansion.

In one of the clearest indictments of capitalism's greedy excesses,
Plainview has found no lasting satisfaction after a lifetime of intensive labor and immense material wealth, while all human connection slowly fades away. He is everything he aspired to be yet remains restless, looking for a way to reengage the competition that
defined his life. Day-Lewis observed that

Those guys [like Doheny. . .] thought they knew what they were after, which is the vast mansion on the Pacific Coast. By the time they had accumulated enough wealth to build that pyramid for themselves, the work was actually an end in itself. The fever was the thing that they lived for.[130]

Anderson's narratives have often been defined by a son's successful search for a father. When the adult H.W. returns, the filmmaker's previous body of work leads us to anticipate the reconciliation of father and son. Whether Sydney and John in *Hard Eight*, Jack and Dirk in *Boogie Nights*, or Frank and Earl in *Magnolia*, father figures had always reunited in the end with their children to claim some amount of peace, however ephemeral. But in this film, that quest is turned grotesquely on its head.

Instead, *There Will Be Blood* ends with the first of two violent partings, even more shocking for the way it departs from that au-teurist expectation. "Plainview releases [H.W. . . .]," Day-Lewis ob-served, and "he does it in the cruelest and most destructive way."[131] Part of the father's rejection is rooted in the emotional hollowness at Plainview's core. Equally important is his need to reclaim a goal in life, a purpose for going on, by identifying his son as an indus-try rival. Plainview's eyes light up—as though he is alive again—at the very moment he realizes, joyfully, that the man he raised is now a competitor. This leads to a very brief, but devastatingly ef-fective, flashback. We see Plainview playing with his adolescent son in the oil fields, decades earlier, before he wickedly pushes him away in order to walk back to his derrick. The impact of Plainview's choices are brought into particular relief when the film cuts back to

5.20. The film's brief but devastating flashback: the last image of a man abandoning his son to attend to his business.

a shot of the old man, hunched over, drunkenly stumbling down the stairs, as though his existence has been left in ruins by the abandonment of his son. This quiet flashback is far more shattering than the touching image of Plainview and baby H.W. in the train because we finally appreciate the illusion of warmth at the heart of their relationship. Daniel's only true passion is his own greed.

Plainview's disavowal of his only child, after which he passes out in a drunken stupor, at first implies he has been left in the end a defeated, broken man in the absence of fatherly duties or any human contact whatsoever. Yet the return of Eli gives Plainview the opening he craves to end on a violently triumphant note. With H.W. gone, Plainview has only the preacher left as that last bit of "competition" to remove. Yet Plainview toys with him at first, finally relishing the opportunity to expose Eli as the false prophet he has always believed the preacher to be. Day-Lewis's performance is absurdly over the top and out of place with the rest of the film. However, the kick into performative overdrive makes sense as Plainview's mocking emulation of the exaggerated phony sermons he's heard Eli give countless times (and which he demands the preacher give again in renouncing his faith for cash).

Plainview taunts him with the idea that his brother Paul was really the chosen one—the person smart enough to take advantage of the situation and get out while things were good. This idea of two people serendipitously taking separate paths serves as a bookend to the film's opening, where it could just as easily have been H.W.'s biological father, and not Plainview, to survive the oil-well accident and go on to be the pioneering entrepreneur. For all their accomplishments, Plainview, H.W., and Eli are also still very much beholden to

5.21. Plainview in the gutter, literally.

5.22. The film's iconic final shot. The visual parallel between the remnants of Plainview's unfinished meal and Eli's corpse suggests that the murder is simply another mess for the butler to clean up.

the effects of random chance so common to many Anderson films. But Plainview is certainly the one who most emphatically resists it.

He begins comically chasing Eli around the bowling alley, chucking pins at him. As the scene escalates to a moment of inexplicable rage, similar to when he shot the fake brother, Plainview impulsively clubs the defenseless preacher to death, pummeling him repeatedly with the bowling pin (just as the ape pounds away in the beginning of 2001). When the butler arrives, an exhausted Plainview, too worn out to even turn around, merely says "I'm finished." He's finally outrun his limitations, having committed a heinous crime that he might not get away with. Yet considering he says it to his butler, the line "I'm finished" just as easily indicates this is another mess to clean up, no different from dirty dinner dishes. Like Noah Cross, Plainview is too powerful to be punished. As Day-Lewis speculated, Plainview "makes the last final gesture of separation from the world."[132]

"I'M FINISHED"

Although it wasn't a huge financial success, *There Will Be Blood* would become Anderson's most well-received film yet. With *There Will Be Blood* finally finished, buzz on the film slowly but steadily built in media and cinephile circles. When looking for the opportunity to premiere the film, Anderson avoided the prestigious Cannes, Toronto, and New York Festivals—the niche markets that over the years had been traditionally supportive. Instead, *There Will Be Blood* made a surprise debut in the fall of 2007 at the Fantastic

Fest film festival at the fan favorite Alamo Drafthouse in Austin, Texas—which specializes in showcasing horror and science-fiction fare rather than would-be Oscar contenders. The choice was typical of the open-minded nature and understated confidence that produced such a strong film in the first place. In regard to his choice of premiere venue, Anderson stayed true to his initial conviction that *There Will Be Blood* was—like its kindred spirit, *The Shining*—a horror film at heart.

With initial reports favorably comparing it "to *Citizen Kane* and *The Treasure of the Sierra Madre*,"[133] *There Will Be Blood* circulated through advanced showings in late 2007. The buzz culminated with a limited Christmas release in New York and Los Angeles that netted "one of the best recent per-location averages" of any film.[134] In January 2008, the film went wider every week, steadily doing business throughout domestic movie theaters as word of mouth spread. After the Oscar nominations were announced in early February, its box office jumped 225% in one month.[135] *There Will Be Blood* would be Anderson's highest-grossing film thus far (not a high bar to cross), boosted further by its success during the 2008 awards season.

The Berlin Festival again recognized Anderson's work, awarding *There Will Be Blood* the Silver Bear, while the International Federation of Film Critics picked the film for the FIPRESCI Grand Prix. The film also netted awards for Best Picture and Best Director with the Los Angeles Film Critics Association. The shining moment came in late February 2008 when *There Will Be Blood* was warmly received by the Academy Awards—the triumph that Anderson had been chasing since the days of *Boogie Nights* and *Magnolia*. *There Will Be Blood* achieved Oscar success in part because it wasn't rushing to be an "Oscar" picture—in design or execution—in the way that his 1990s epics had been a decade earlier. In addition to nods for Best Picture, Best Director, and Best Adapted Screenplay, *There Will Be Blood* also received nominations for Best Actor (Day-Lewis), Cinematography (Elswit), Editing (Tichenor), Art Direction (Fisk and Jim Erickson), and Sound Editing (Matthew Wood). Oscars ultimately went to Day-Lewis and Elswit. Dano wasn't recognized; nor was Greenwood, whose score was judged to contain too much previously recorded material (such as work on *Bodysong*) to be eligible. In keeping with *There Will Be Blood*'s collective attitude, Anderson was appropriately humble. The nominations were, he told *Variety*, "a testament to the cast and crew, who I am deeply grateful to, for their talent and collaboration."[136] The big winner was the Coen brothers' equally deserving *No Country for Old Men*—a rare moment in Oscar history when two darkly nihilistic visions dominated.

Over time, *There Will Be Blood*'s reputation strengthened. By one measurement, the film appeared most often on various "Best Films of the Decade" lists, beating out *Eternal Sunshine of the Spotless Mind* (2004).[137] *Rolling Stone*'s Peter Travers added: "Two years after first seeing *There Will Be Blood*, I am convinced that Paul Thomas Anderson's profound portrait of an American primitive—take that, *Citizen Kane*—deserves pride of place among the decade's finest."[138] He added that Anderson was *the* filmmaker to watch in the years to come. "Towards the end of the decade," argued *The Guardian*'s Peter Bradshaw,

director Paul Thomas Anderson unburdened himself of this strange and disquieting masterpiece, a mesmeric and utterly distinctive movie . . . The film was of a higher order of intelligence and innovation than anything he had attempted before, and anything else in noughties Hollywood.[139]

Critics' respective reactions at the end of the decade were typical of a larger consensus—*There Will Be Blood* was one of the best American films of the decade, due both to its technical and artistic achievements and the ways in which it spoke to larger historical issues of the time. It was a cinematic masterpiece both artistic and timely. The film's continually strong critical reception as the decade came to a close suggested that *There Will Be Blood* had transcended being "just" a movie allegorically about religion and oil in George W. Bush's America. While Anderson's critical success in the past—even at its best (*Boogie Nights*)—was fleeting, *There Will Be Blood*'s longevity suggests that the ambitious filmmaker's reputation may finally be on firmer ground.

In the human condition, people were always projecting themselves from one
moment in time to another, engaged in the endless quest for immortality
and immutability, arriving at something permanent . . . If anything gave
coherence to the cultural and social patterns of the postwar era, it was
the way in which phenomena as diverse as the "organizational man,"
the fight against McCarthyism, or the quest for meaning in suburbia
were in some way related to the existential dilemma of finding a way to
create meaning in the face of forces over which one had no control.

WILLIAM CHAFE, *THE UNFINISHED JOURNEY: AMERICA SINCE WORLD WAR II*

afterword

ON *THE MASTER*

In September 2012, after a few months of sneak previews and
festival appearances, Paul Thomas Anderson's latest film, *The
Master*, opened wide in American theaters. Shot on 70mm, the
movie presented a glorious, even defiant, celebration of film in the
age of digital cinema. Befitting that technical distinction, *The Master* was also an ambitious historical reflection on media, celebrity,
and consumerism from the second half of the twentieth century.
Meanwhile, *Blossoms and Blood*, which had spanned three years of
research and writing in the aftermath of *There Will Be Blood* (2007),
had been more or less completed just two months prior to *The Master's* much-hyped and long-awaited appearance. It is difficult to reflect on the critical and cultural impact of a movie a mere couple
of weeks after its debut, so this final section will be a brief reflection—without the benefit of much hindsight—on some of the ways
in which this new film fits thematically with his five earlier films,
as well as how it may also suggest a departure. The flip side is that
no doubt some of these ideas will feel more familiar to readers than
others by the time this book is actually in print. The goal of this
afterword is not to exhaust the possibilities of what could be said
about *The Master*, which on a first pass appears as rich for analysis
as much of Anderson's previous work. Rather, my aim is merely to

offer a few tentative thoughts on how this film reflects ideas raised elsewhere in the book. Anderson's latest articulates a vision of postmodern America consistent with what was previously explored in other chapters. Supporting this assertion is the modest scope of the following pages.

POSTWAR EXISTENTIALISM

As a larger analytical framework, *The Master* subtly presents a throwback to Anderson's earlier meditations on the thematic role of serendipity and random chance that Jeffrey Sconce, for example, argued characterized the "smart film" in postmodern American culture. Like *Magnolia* (1999), which deals with the issue most explicitly, and to a lesser extent *Boogie Nights* (1997) and *Punch-Drunk Love* (2002), *The Master* is quietly consumed by the existential question that has often driven characters in Anderson's overall body of work: *what does it all mean?* The people and surrogate families at the heart of *The Master* are structured around this same quest for meaning. And the fact that these particular relationships cannot hold may suggest a shifting thematic sensibility. Part of this latest film's subtle beauty is the way in which it resists transparently announcing or dramatizing this potentially tiresome thematic dilemma. Unlike those earlier films, which presented such quests for meaning as the by-product of growing up adrift in the mass-media-saturated, commodity-driven hollowness of contemporary Southern California, *The Master* situates this same dilemma within its own historical origins—the cultural anxieties of post–World War II America—while also ultimately resisting easy solutions, be they allusions to the Bible and the research of Charles Fort (*Magnolia*) or the reassuring power of heterosexual union (*Punch-Drunk Love*). Perhaps the biggest revelation of *The Master* is its seemingly conscious resistance to *believing* in anything.

What is immediately striking about *The Master* is how explicitly the film historicizes the rise of a new cultural sensibility in American society in the direct wake of World War II. Indeed, "wakes"—particularly, a ship's wake on the high seas—are a dominant motif throughout *The Master*. A time of tremendous postwar economic prosperity, this period was also marked by anxieties and fears regarding the fallout from global conflict such as the unresolved horror of the Holocaust and the continuing fear of atomic destruction and Communist infiltration during the emergence of the Cold War. World War II called into doubt the power of scientific understanding and rational applications of logic to elevate society into a higher state of enlightenment, which was a key foundation to discourses of modernity. The assembly-line efficiency of Taylorist modes of mass production at the start of the century quietly gave way to the efficiency of concentration-camp labor and atomic weapons in the service of mass destruction. After the war, then, a dualistic American mindset emerged: the sense that modernist discourses of logic and science were, at the very least, open to manipulation—and at the very worst, as arbitrary and empty as any other mode of understanding.

This specific historical contradiction is embodied in the relationship between *The Master*'s two central characters: Lancaster Dodd (Philip Seymour Hoffman) and Freddie Quell (Joaquin Phoenix). Their awkward dynamic symbolizes the historical tensions between rationality and irrationality, order and chaos, control and excess, modernity and postmodernity. Dodd is an author and celebrity founder of the Cause, a cult that thrives after the war by promising to free people from their past traumas. The comparison of Dodd to Eli (Paul Dano) from *There Will Be Blood* appears clear enough—both men are religious charlatans who build massive empires on the backs of a blindly following flock. While Eli embodies the ambitions of prewar evangelism, Dodd represents the renewed promises of postwar New Age mysticism. His financial success speaks to the long-term hollowness of an illusory postwar economic prosperity. Yet more subtly, Dodd also evokes echoes of *Magnolia*'s Frank T. J. Mackey (Tom Cruise)—both are, above all, white-noise celebrity *salesmen* in the post–World War II media age, and both sell glorified and lucrative self-help programs based in part on the personal ideal of forgetting one's past. Certainly, the extratextual dimensions of Cruise's persona in relation to Scientology and L. Ron Hubbard, who forms the loose but undeniable inspiration for Dodd, strengthens this connection all the more. At the same time, it is easy to overstate the connection between that particular controversial movement and *The Master*'s historical reinterpretation. Anderson's film ultimately feels like a broader indictment of postwar America's need for personal reassurance in the face of inherent moral ambiguity, rather than just a simplistic criticism of one particular facet of that period.

Dodd's authority lies unmistakably in his careful command of language—verbal and written words—all the more because of the tenuous thought and lack of substance behind them. At one point, Dodd's son confesses to Freddie what is abundantly clear but otherwise goes unstated—namely, that Dodd's speeches, and the grander ideas behind them, are generally made up on the fly (and often while he is inebriated—the only meaningful connection he has to Freddie). But it would not be accurate to say that Dodd lies. Instead, his words draw from the Deleuzian idea of *nonsense* (or the simulacrum)—they are neither true nor false but rather draw their power from the effect they have on his audience, who willingly find in them the personal affirmation they seek. Indeed, Dodd even says to Freddie at one point in a "processing" session—the Cause's name for therapy—that it doesn't matter whether Freddie says something true or false—only that he say something, anything, as a means to initiate an exchange.

This is where the main character of Freddie becomes central. Whereas Dodd and his Cause symbolize the deeply rooted need for meaning in the terrifying meaninglessness of a postwar world, Freddie in the end embodies America's (still) unresolved demons— the psychological fallout from that war, the continuing need to solve issues through violence, the constant tendency towards self-destruction, and the unapologetic shift toward excess. We first see Freddie tracking down ingredients for moonshine ("torpedo juice") at the exact same moment we hear Harry S. Truman declare that peace is now at hand. This brilliant juxtaposition highlights how dealing with the ramifications of World War II was only just beginning, while also playing on the different forms of destruction at work in the film. A rare moment of self-awareness for Freddie comes relatively early in the movie when he admits to fearing how "inconsequential" his life is, though the unspoken idea is that everyone else's existence is similarly insignificant. Thus, in the end, Freddie must be left behind by the Cause, just as the problems he represents must be pushed aside for America to reinvent itself in the wake of World War II.

As with Dodd, Freddie has a clear affinity with a character from *There Will Be Blood*: Daniel Plainview (Daniel Day-Lewis). They are both irredeemably violent and purely physical visions of nihilism reacting impulsively to the world around them. Including *Punch-Drunk Love*, Anderson's last three movies have all closely followed, to the point of discomfort, male protagonists with unresolved anger management problems. They represent the worst of American impulses—Plainview reflects the inherent indulgences of capitalist greed, while Freddie speaks to the insatiable tendency toward war. Like Plainview, the asocial Freddie retreats to alcoholism to alleviate his inability to deal with the people around him. And, as with the earlier protagonist, Freddie is a man curiously with neither a clearly defined past nor much in the way of a deeper interiority—their identities are both right there on the surface. Yet whereas Plainview is focused and motivated by the need for absolute control over everything and everyone, Freddie is ultimately unmoored, hopelessly adrift—a fitting metaphor for the moral uncertainty of his time. What grounds him in the end is only the basest of human/animal needs—the self-preservation of sexual desire, the one thing constantly driving him.

Indeed, our first image of Freddie is that of a *caged animal*, sitting on a military transport ship—his wild eyes darting about restlessly. A fascinatingly unredeemed beast at the lowest rung of human behavior, he is kept in check only by the confines of military institutions and the larger "cause" of victory in Pacific combat. At the end of war, Freddie is cut adrift and eventually gives up one boat (the naval ship) for another (Dodd's luxury cruiser); he gives up one cause (war) for another (a postwar cult). Of course, boats are a key motif in the film, as well as in the history of Scientology. But in *The Master*, their connotation is inverted—they symbolize the arbitrary causes that Freddie joins throughout the voyage of life, maintaining the illusion of order and purpose in the midst of a vast, empty horizon. There are no fixed points (truths) in life—only endless drifting relative to agreed-upon coordinates. This notion of random spatial and symbolic positions is likewise echoed in Dodd's bizarre motorcycle game of "pick a point" in the middle of the desert, where any sense of specific locations becomes completely arbitrary. The myth at the core of *The Master* is that we believe that it is the bike or the boat—the mythologies and institutions in which we invest our whole lives—that is the reality, and not the great chaotic and unknowable vastness beyond—the ocean/desert/frontier.

"MEMORIES ARE NOT INVITED"

More than any Anderson film to date, there is a clear fascination with temporality in *The Master*—one that, like existentialism, grows out of the particular historical context re-created on-screen. Postmodern science fiction was often obsessed with the idea of *time travel*, which is a significant component to the Cause's form of therapy in the film. The theoretical fascination with this plot device was how it exposed a deeper impulse regarding postwar America's relationship to history—that it was more about the present's romanticization of an idealized past than about an uglier, more complex series of events that becomes left behind. A rare Anderson flashback here gives us Freddie as he recalls visiting Doris (Madisen Beaty) right after the war—his character's only real tender moment and one that may be, like other moments in the movie, largely a dream or fantasy. Very early in the film, Freddie explicitly refers to this memory as "nostalgia."

Abandoning the (wartime) past becomes an explicit theme by the end. Late in *The Master*, Dodd snaps at one of his supporters for questioning his ideas—a common occurrence throughout the film that highlights just how tenuous his celebrity pseudointellectual façade really is. When Helen (Laura Dern) points out that he has changed a key word in his second book from "recall" to "imagine" during the processing sessions, Dodd thoughtlessly suggests that the change is based on "new data." His explanation lays bare the film's critique of the cult's pseudoscience, since the idea of any genuinely quantifiable data by that point is complete gibberish. Just as important is how the shift from remembering the past to imagining it cuts to the heart of postwar America's desire to forget the past in favor of a nostalgic reinvention of time—repeatedly hinted at by Dodd's obsession with the idea of a true past that has been repressed through several lifetimes.

"A CAPTAIN NEVER ABANDONS HIS SHIP"

The medium of film—both still photography and the cinema—is also a key idea throughout the movie. Before he joins Dodd's crew, Freddie works a series of odd jobs after the war. His most substantial work involves shooting portraits in a local department store—a perfect symbol of twentieth century capitalist consumption, consumer convenience, and material waste. On one level, the appeal of such a position is that it grants him access to photo processing chemicals that help fulfill his constant need for homemade alcoholic concoctions. Yet Freddie's interest in photography also demands closer attention. This extravagant setting contrasts sharply with the mise-en-scène of the migrant labor camp to which he flees after fighting with one of his customers (W. Earl Brown). Certainly, Freddie's hostility toward the man is partly about a deeper resistance to accepting his expected patriarchal position as husband and father, made explicit by his annoyance that the photograph is for the customer's wife. Similarly, this scene immediately follows a single shot of him asleep at home with his department store coworker and girlfriend, Martha (Amy Ferguson)—the only time we see Freddie in a traditional domestic space (which is obviously unappealing to him). Her baby bump foregrounds the social pressure he feels to settle down.

During World War II, the power of film becomes increasingly highlighted and scrutinized—both in its ability to actively distort reality and manipulate audiences (such as government propaganda films being produced on all sides of the conflict) and in its inability to fully capture the scope and horror of the war (as explored, for instance, in Alain Resnais's cinematic meditations in the 1950s on the Holocaust and Hiroshima). Freddie's relative command of photography reflects a belief that the (fixed) image has replaced a (chaotic) reality. Does he also finally snap at the man in the department store because he knows the image will not match the reality? Perhaps he is even disgusted by the way in which the man's posing highlights a prosperous postwar America's need to reinvent itself. Postwar America comes to embrace, through film and television, the image's ability to create a new reality—a distinctive vision of individualism, prosperity, domesticity, and consumerism in suburbia. It's this same mediated ideal that continues to haunt Anderson's other aimless characters in *Boogie Nights*, *Magnolia*, and *Punch-Drunk Love*—those still wandering adrift in Southern California at the dawn of the new millennium.

The relationship between cinema's social role and the opportunity to start over manifests itself in *The Master* in other ways as well. Freddie and Dodd's son-in-law both handout flyers for the Cause and attempt to sell passersby on the chance to alleviate their pain while standing outside a movie theater. In this shot, the Cause becomes equated with movies as a way for people to forget the past. The idea of rebirth and the cinema is also played upon by Freddie's wartime sweetheart, Doris, who gives up waiting for him to return and finally weds another man, thus taking on the married name "Doris Day," just like the movie star. She symbolizes America's desire to forget the war by explicitly immersing itself in a newfound prosperity dominated and shaped by quickly expanding media industries. This connection to the cinema is intensified when *The Master* immediately follows the "Doris Day" scene by cutting to Freddie in a movie theater, where he dreams of receiving a call from Dodd.

Most prominently, Dodd's emergent celebrity—in which Freddie's photography plays a role—late in the film is centered on deserts and other motifs of the Western genre. Dodd poses for pictures on a ranch set deep in the wilderness, evoking the frontier mythology so key to the nostalgic popularity of that genre during the 1950s. The (imagined) possibilities of the frontier spoke to abstract postwar American ideals of renewed freedom and opportunity—that the United States (like the phoenix) could be reborn in the same desert where Dodd's work is buried. But it also spoke to the more tangible appeals of an emergent suburban expansion during this time of cheaper automobiles and a new highway culture. The desire to escape the congestion and challenges of the city in favor of starting over again in the country is brought forth when at one point Peggy (Amy Adams) angrily lashes out at the vices of New York City.

"A MASTER . . . ANY MASTER . . ."

Anchoring this postwar existential search for meaning is again Anderson's fondness for surrogate families—as the members of Dodd's Cause echo Jack Horner's (Burt Reynolds) porn company in *Boogie Nights* or Sydney (Philip Baker Hall), John (John C. Reilly), and Clementine (Gwyneth Paltrow) in *Hard Eight* (1996). Yet increasingly the need for companionship across Anderson's body of work seems rooted less in a desire for familial affection and more in the sense that it is difficult to go through life with neither purpose nor alliances of some kind. Hence, Dodd's central request to Freddie in the end: "if you figure out a way to live without a master . . . any master . . . be sure to let the rest of us know, for you would be the first in the history of the world." Among other possibilities, it suggests that the existential crisis after the war would invariably give way to another focus—that America could not live adrift forever. But it also suggests that our personal connection to the people with whom we choose to surround ourselves is perhaps dominated by more cynical impulses than Anderson's earlier films sought to believe.

As in *There Will Be Blood*, the surrogate family ultimately becomes a source of distrust and disintegration. Indeed, a second look reveals considerable similarities between the endings of that film and of *The Master*—even if Anderson's most recent and quietly subdued work lacks the overt audacity and shocking violence of the former. Although the ambiguous relationship between Freddie and Dodd is ultimately more complicated than a simple father-son dynamic, Dodd clearly presents himself as the patriarchal authority of the Cause's family, while Freddie's behavior constantly evokes a reckless child in need of discipline and guidance. In both *There Will Be Blood* and *The Master*, the surrogate son returns to a father now buried deep within the recesses (and excesses) of the empire he spent his career building. In both cases, the relationship between the two of them is now beyond repair, and all that is left is an awkward, even damning, goodbye that raises as many new questions as it answers. In both cases, the father extravagantly serenades the son through melodic repetition—Plainview's "bastard in a basket" gets replaced by Dodd's softer but equally contemptuous phrase for Freddie, "slow boat to China."

The latter song foregrounds the implicit homoeroticism between the two men, but it also taunts Freddie for his lack of a long-term commitment to the Cause, as the arduous "slow boat" refers both to the larger motifs of boats and metaphoric journeys throughout the film and to the multiple reincarnated lives across trillions of years that the Cause members believe in. One big difference in this final parallel to *There Will Be Blood* is that the dynamic between the two is ultimately inverted—in *The Master*, it's the son who coldly turns away the father's need for affection, rather than the reverse. The charismatic Dodd ironically needs Freddie more than the veteran loner needs Dodd, because Dodd has no friends whatsoever (a comparable situation, meanwhile, doesn't faze the similarly isolated Plainview). Over the first two decades of Anderson's career, his body of work has expressed increasing disdain—or at least distrust—for that need for human companionship his early films once so sincerely and passionately championed.

Of course another, perhaps more significant, difference from *There Will Be Blood* is the presence of Peggy Dodd, Dodd's quietly manipulative and controlling wife. At one point, she completely dominates Dodd sexually—a powerful scene on its own that also proves an ironic counterpoint to his unofficial title as the "master" in charge. It is implied by the end of the film that Peggy—not her husband—is the real force behind the Cause, with her husband as little more than the public façade needed to fit the expectations of a patriarchal society. Although she is ultimately one of Anderson's more intriguingly ambiguous female characters, she nonetheless fits pretty clearly within a long line of dominant—and thus destructive—female family members in Anderson's films: Eddie's irrationally angry mom in *Boogie Nights*, Barry's verbally abusive sisters in *Punch-Drunk Love*, and even Clementine in *Hard Eight*. In all these films, the dominant female's control over the weaker men in their lives is presented as at least part of the problem for the male protagonists. While Clementine is hardly a dominant figure in that film, she is an assertive female character whose bad choices disrupt the close bond between John and Sydney. And, just as the mom in *Boogie Nights* destroys Dirk's family, Peggy ultimately drives the final wedge between Freddie and Dodd. If Peggy is a more interesting and complicated character than those other problematic women in Anderson's body of work, it is only because her deeper motivations, as well as the full extent of her relationship to Dodd, are more carefully explored.

"DO YOUR PAST FAILURES BOTHER YOU?"

In the end, *The Master* has no easy resolution because Freddie has found no meaningful course in life; he is increasingly disillusioned by an arbitrary Cause that he most likely never really believed in. The ambiguity of the narrative's final act in the end reflects a significant strand of the larger nihilism that pervaded postwar America. Many Americans symbolically embraced the likes of the Cause, in all its manifestations—not just Scientology, but more broadly the (arbitrary) narratives of reassurance necessary to maintaining one's sanity in the chaotic aftermath of a war that raised deeply disturbing—and ultimately unanswered—questions about man's inherent capacity for self-destruction and the essential meaninglessness of the world. These lingering doubts find embodiment in Freddie, who becomes a symbol of postwar America's unredeemed sins.

This brief afterword has been a tentative attempt to extend some of the major themes discussed throughout *Blossoms and Blood* into the shadow of Anderson's most recent and, in many ways, most mature film. *The Master* fits thematically within his larger ambivalent vision of a postmodern American media culture and may even bring the pop-leftist historicity therein full circle. Beyond that narrow investment, however, *The Master* will continue to inspire provocative discussion and profound insights that go unnoticed, or unacknowledged, here. By the time the reader arrives at the end of this book, it may likely be the case that Anderson has made yet another film. Such a hypothetical situation is not a concern, of course, as the joy in understanding the power of cinema lies precisely in the awareness that new opportunities to do so are never exhausted.

notes

INTRODUCTION

1. Susan Jeffords, *Hard Bodies: Hollywood Masculinity in the Reagan Era* (New Brunswick, NJ: Rutgers University Press, 1993).

2. Stanley, "Punch-Drunk Masculinity," *The Journal of Men's Studies* 14.2 (Spring 2006), pp. 235–242.

3. Murphet, "P. T. Anderson's Dilemma: The Limits of Surrogate Paternity," *Sydney Studies* 34 (2008), pp. 63–85.

4. As quoted in Waxman, *Rebels on the Backlot: Six Maverick Directors and How They Conquered the Hollywood Studio System* (New York: Harper, 2005), p. 86.

5. Waxman, p. 85.

6. Richard Dyer, *Heavenly Bodies: Film Stars and Society*, 2nd ed. (New York: Routledge, 2004), p. 5.

7. Dyer, p. 6.

8. As quoted in Konow, "PTA Meeting: An Interview with Paul Thomas Anderson," *Creative Screenwriting* 7.1 (January–February 2000), p. 48.

9. Newman, *Indie: An American Film Culture* (New York: Columbia University Press, 2011), pp. 156–157.

10. Fredric Jameson, *Postmodernism, or, The Cultural Logic of Late Capitalism* (Durham, NC: Duke University Press, 1991), p. 22.

11. Jameson, p. 19.

12. Goss, "'Things Like This Don't Just Happen': Ideology and Paul Thomas Anderson's *Hard Eight*, *Boogie Nights*, and *Magnolia*," *Journal of Communication Inquiry* 26.2 (April 2002), p. 172.

13. Sconce, "Irony, Nihilism and the New American 'Smart' Film," *Screen* 43.4 (Winter 2002), p. 351.

14. Sconce, p. 358.

15. Sconce, p. 363.

16. Crous, "Paul Thomas Anderson: Tracking Through a Fantastic Reality." *Senses of Cinema* 45 (Nov. 2007), http://www.sensesofcinema.com/2007/feature-articles/paul-thomas-anderson/.

17. Harmon, "Ordered Chaos: Three Films by Paul Thomas Anderson," *Image: A Journal of Arts and Religion* 27 (Summer 2000), http://imagejournal.org/page/journal/articles/issue-27/harmon-essay.

18. Scanlan, "Combustion: An Essay on the Value of Gambling," *Gambling: Who Wins? Who Loses?* ed. Gerda Reith (New York: Prometheus, 2003), pp. 348–354.

19. Sconce, p. 363.

20. Richardson, "The Secret History of Paul Thomas Anderson," *Esquire* (Oct. 2008), http://www.esquire.com/features/75-most-influential/paul

-thomas-anderson-1008. Unlike most popular material out there, Richardson's research provides a lot of new and valuable information about Anderson's past, even if it does seem excessive in its attempts to deconstruct the "fairy tale" of Anderson's life story.

21. Mim Udovitch, "It Went Down Like This on the Set of *Boogie Nights*," *Esquire* (October 1997), p. 110.

22. Sconce, p. 364.

23. As quoted in "Bloody and Unbowed," *Irish Times* (15 Feb. 2008), n.p.

24. Pizzello, "Blood for Oil," *American Cinematographer* (Jan. 2008), http://www.theasc.com/ac_magazine/January2008/ThereWillBeBlood/page1.php.

25. My emphasis. Jameson, p. 284.

26. Lehman, "*Boogie Nights*: Will the Real Dirk Diggler Please Stand Up?," *Jump Cut* 42 (December 1998), http://www.ejumpcut.org/archive/onlinessays/JC42folder/BoogieNights.html.

27. Sickels, "1970s Disco Daze: Paul Thomas Anderson and the Last Golden Age of Irresponsibility," *Journal of Popular Culture* (2002), pp. 49–60.

28. Dillman, "Twelve Characters in Search of a Televisual Text: *Magnolia* Masquerading as Soap Opera," *Journal of Popular Film and Television* 33.3 (Fall 2005), pp. 142–150; and Fischer, "Theory into Practice: En-Gendering Narrative in *Magnolia*," *Screening Genders*, ed. Krin Gabbard and William Luhr (New Brunswick, NJ: Rutgers University Press, 2008), pp. 29–46.

29. Price, "Color, the Formless, and Cinematic Eros," *Framework* 47.1 (2006), pp. 22–35; and MacDowell, "Notes on Quirky," *Movie: A Journal of Film Criticism* 1 (2010), http://www2.warwick.ac.uk/fac/arts/film/movie/contents/notes_on_quirky.pdf.

30. King, "*Punch Drunk Love*: The Budding of an Auteur," *Senses of Cinema* 35 (April–June 2005), http://archive.sensesofcinema.com/contents/05/35/pt_anderson.html.

CHAPTER 1

1. Newman, "Characterization in American Independent Cinema" (PhD Thesis: University of Wisconsin–Madison, 2006), p. 202.

2. In the documentary *Magnolia Video Diary* (2000), we see Anderson showing Sidney Lumet's *Network* to the crew of *Magnolia* as a template for the look and feel of his Los Angeles epic.

3. Newman, "Characterization," p. 201.

4. As quoted in Mim Udovitch, "The Epic Obsessions of Paul Thomas Anderson," *Rolling Stone* (3 Feb. 2000), http://ezproxy.msu.edu/login?url=http://search.proquest.com/docview/220171809?accountid=12598.

5. Richardson, "The Secret History of Paul Thomas Anderson." *Esquire* (Oct. 2008), http://www.esquire.com/features/75-most-influential/paul-thomas-anderson-1008.

6. Mottram, *The Sundance Kids: How the Mavericks Took Back Hollywood* (New York: Faber and Faber, 2006), p. 129.

7. Richardson.

8. McKenna, "An Interview with: Paul Thomas Anderson," *Creative Screenwriting* (1998), p. 24.

9. Vary, "Paul Thomas Anderson, *Hard Eight*," *Daily Variety* (19 Jan. 2006), p. B3.

10. Mottram, *Sundance Kids*, p. 129.

11. As quoted in Udovitch, "Epic Obsessions."

12. Newman, "Characterization," p. 202.

13. Mottram, *Sundance Kids*, p. 145.

14. Waxman, *Rebels on the Backlot: Six Maverick Directors and How They Conquered the Hollywood Studio System* (New York: Harper, 2005), p. 89.

15. As quoted in Mottram, *Sundance Kids*, p. 145.

16. Waxman, p. 83.

17. As quoted in Waxman, p. 88.

18. Waxman, p. 89.

19. As quoted in Waxman, p. 89.

20. As quoted in Udovitch.

21. Waxman, p. 90.

22. As quoted in Waxman, p. 90.

23. As quoted in Waxman, p. 91.

24. Mottram, *Sundance Kids*, p. 107.

25. D'Aries and Hirsch, "'Saint' Sydney: Atonement and Moral Inversion in *Hard Eight*," *The Philosophy of Neo-Noir*, ed. Mark T. Conard (Lexington: University Press of Kentucky, 2007), p. 95.

26. D'Aries and Hirsch, p. 95.

27. D'Aries and Hirsch, p. 91.

28. D'Aries and Hirsch, p. 100.

29. Harmon, "Ordered Chaos: Three Films by Paul Thomas Anderson," *Image: A Journal of Arts and Religion* 27 (Summer 2000), http://imagejournal.org/page/journal/articles/issue-27/harmon-essay.

30. Scanlan, "Combustion: An Essay on the Value of Gambling." *Gambling: Who Wins? Who Loses?* ed. Gerda Reith (New York: Prometheus, 2003), p. 351.

31. Harmon.

32. Harmon.

CHAPTER 2

1. Gorfinkel, "The Future of Anachronisms: Todd Haynes and the Magnificent Andersons," *Cinephilia: Movies, Love, Memory*, ed. Marijke de Valck and Malte Hagener (Amsterdam: Amsterdam University Press, 2005), p. 162.

2. Ryan Gilbey, "A Simple Little Movie?," *The Sunday Times* (2 Feb. 2003), p. 14.

3. Gorfinkel, p. 162.

4. Gorfinkel, p. 153.

5. Konow, "PTA Meeting: An Interview with Paul Thomas Anderson," *Creative Screenwriting* 7.1 (January–February 2000), p. 52.

6. Udovitch, "It Went Down Like This on the Set of *Boogie Nights*," *Esquire* (Oct. 1997), p. 110.

7. Mim Udovitch, "It Went Down Like This," p. 109.

8. Waxman, *Rebels on the Backlot: Six Maverick Directors and How They Conquered the Hollywood Studio System* (New York: Harper, 2005), p. 85.

9. As quoted in Vary, "Paul Thomas Anderson, *Hard Eight*," *Daily Variety* (19 Jan. 2006), p. B3.

10. Konow, p. 50.

11. Konow, p. 50.

12. Mottram, *The Sundance Kids: How the Mavericks Took Back Hollywood* (New York: Faber and Faber, 2006), p. 187.

13. As quoted in McKenna, "An Interview with: Paul Thomas Anderson," *Creative Screenwriting* (1998), p. 25.

14. Mottram, *Sundance Kids*, p. 187.

15. Kauffmann, "The Rake's Progress," *New Republic* (10 Nov. 1997), p. 32.

16. Mottram, *Sundance Kids*, p. 145.

17. Waxman, p. 119.

18. Waxman, p. 122.

19. Waxman, pp. 120–21.

20. Waxman, p. 121.

21. Konow, p. 52.

22. As quoted in Waxman, p. 122.

23. Konow, p. 52.

24. Waxman, p. 169.

25. Waxman, p. 170.

26. As quoted in Waxman, p. 121.

27. Tincknell, "The Soundtrack Movie, Nostalgia and Consumption," *Film's Musical Moments*, ed. Ian Conrich and Estella Tincknell (Edinburgh: Edinburgh University Press, 2007), p. 133.

28. Tait, "That 70s Sequence: Remembering the Bad Old Days in Summer of Sam," *Cinephile* 5.2 (Summer 2009), pp. 17–23.

29. Ritter, "Spectacle at the Disco: *Boogie Nights*, Soundtrack, and the New American Musical," *Journal of Popular Film and Television* 28.4 (Winter 2001), p. 167.

30. Ritter, p. 167.

31. Tincknell, p. 143.

32. Tincknell, p. 135.

33. Tincknell, p. 141.

34. Doherty, "*Boogie Nights*," *Cineaste* (April 1998), p. 40.

35. Gorfinkel, p. 153.

36. Gorfinkel, p. 161.

37. Sickels, "1970s Disco Daze: Paul Thomas Anderson and the Last Golden Age of Irresponsibility," *Journal of Popular Culture* (2002), p. 49.

38. Sickels, p. 55.

39. Simmons, "*Boogie* Opera: Eddie, Douzi and Artistic Convention," *Journal of Popular Culture* 33.4 (Spring 2000), pp. 116–117.

40. Sickels, p. 57.

41. Sickels, pp. 55–56.

42. Sickels, p. 50.

43. Glass, "After the Phallus," *American Imago* 58.2 (Summer 2001), p. 546.

44. Glass, p. 547.

45. Addelston, "Doing the Full Monty with Dirk and Jane: Using the Phallus to Validate Marginalized Masculinities," *Journal of Men's Studies* 7.3 (Spring 1999), p. 337.

46. Addelston, p. 337.

47. Sickels, p. 50.

48. Waxman, p. 173.

49. Lehman, "*Boogie Nights*: Will the Real Dirk Diggler Please Stand Up?," *Jump Cut* 42 (Dec. 1998), http://www.ejumpcut.org/archive/onlinessays/JC42folder/BoogieNights.html.

50. Zuromskis, "Prurient Pictures and Popular Film: The Crisis of Pornographic Representation," *The Velvet Light Trap* 59 (2007), p. 9.

51. Zuromskis, p. 9.

52. Waxman, p. 117.

53. As quoted in Waxman, p. 165.

54. Waxman, p. 166.

55. "TK-421" was the name of one of the storm troopers assigned to guard the spaceship *Millennium Falcon* while it was docked on the *Death Star*.

56. Waxman, p. 122.

57. Konow, pp. 50–51.

58. Molina was a last-minute replacement for another actor. When Anderson called, Molina asked, "'Well what's the part?' And [Anderson] said: 'It's a coked-up drug dealer on a shotgun rampage.' I went: 'Nice. Never done that before.'"—as quoted in Ed Potton, "If The Tentacles Fit," *The London Times* (20 Nov. 2004), p. 4.

59. My emphasis. Chin and Qualls, "To Market, To Market," *PAJ: A Journal of Performance and Art* 20.1 (Jan. 1998), p. 38.

60. Waxman, p. 173.

61. Chin and Qualls, p. 39.

CHAPTER 3

1. Sarris et al., "The Next Scorsese," *Esquire* (March 2000), p. 217.

2. Mim Udovitch, "It Went Down Like This on the Set of *Boogie Nights*," *Esquire* (October 1997), pp. 108–111.

3. As quoted in Hirschberg, "His Way," *New York Times Magazine* (19 December 1999), p. 52.

4. Anderson, "Introduction," *Magnolia: The Shooting Script* (New York: Newmarket Press, 2000), p. vii.

5. As quoted in Waxman, *Rebels on the Backlot: Six Maverick Directors and How They Conquered the Hollywood Studio System* (New York: Harper, 2005), p. 193.

6. As quoted in Waxman, p. 123.

7. As quoted in Konow, "PTA Meeting: An Interview with Paul Thomas Anderson," *Creative Screenwriting* 7.1 (January–February 2000), p. 48.

8. As quoted in Konow, p. 48.

9. As quoted in Chuck Stephens, "Interview with Paul Thomas Anderson," *Magnolia: The Shooting Script* (New York: Newmarket Press, 2000), p. 200.

10. As quoted in Udovitch, "The Epic Obsessions of Paul Thomas Anderson," *Rolling Stone* (3 Feb. 2000), http://ezproxy.msu.edu/login?url=http://search.proquest.com/docview/220171809?accountid=12598.

11. As quoted in Udovitch, "Epic Obsessions."

12. As quoted in Waxman, p. 252.

13. As quoted in Stephens, p. 197.

14. Udovitch, "Epic Obsessions."

15. Anderson, "Introduction," p. vii.

16. Hirschberg, "His Way," p. 52.

17. As quoted in Konow, p. 47.

18. Anderson, "Introduction," p. vii.

19. Anderson, "Introduction," p. viii.

20. Anderson, "Introduction," p. viii.

21. Fischer, "Theory into Practice: En-Gendering Narrative in *Magnolia*," *Screening Genders*, ed. Krin Gabbard and William Luhr (New Brunswick, NJ: Rutgers University Press, 2008), p. 43.

22. Anderson, "Introduction," p. viii.

23. As quoted in Stephens, "Interview," p. 198.

24. As quoted in Stephens, "Interview," p. 197.

25. As quoted in Konow, p. 47.

26. As quoted in Ed Pilkington, "Tell the Story! Tell The Story!," *The Guardian* (2 Jan. 2008), http://www.guardian.co.uk/culture/2008/jan/04/awardsandprizes.

27. As quoted in Waxman, p. 286.

28. As quoted in Waxman, p. 286.

29. Waxman, p. 287. De Luca's exact words reportedly were "fuck you, buddy."

30. As quoted in Waxman, p. 285.

31. Susan Faludi, "It's 'Thelma & Louise' for Guys," *Newsweek* (October 25, 1999), p. 89.

32. Sconce, "Irony, Nihilism, and the New American 'Smart' Film," *Screen* 43.4 (Winter 2002), p. 358.

33. Sconce, p. 358.

34. Sconce, p. 363.

35. Hirschberg, "His Way," p. 52.

36. Dillman, "Twelve Characters in Search of a Televisual Text: *Magnolia* Masquerading as Soap Opera," *Journal of Popular Film and Television* 33.3 (Fall 2005), p. 145.

37. Dillman, p. 146.

38. Fischer, p. 32.

39. Fischer, p. 30.

40. Fischer, p. 31.

41. Fischer, p. 33.

42. Peberdy, "From Wimps to Wild Men: Bipolar Masculinity and the Paradoxical Performances of Tom Cruise," *Men and Masculinities* (Feb. 2010), p. 6.

43. Peberdy, p. 3.

44. Peberdy, p. 3.

45. Peberdy, p. 14.

46. Peberdy, p. 15.

47. Fischer, p. 37.

48. Hsu, "Racial Privacy, the L.A. Ensemble Film, and Paul Haggis's *Crash*," *Film Criticism* (2006), p. 11.

49. Fuchs, "Interview with Paul Thomas Anderson," *PopMatters* (1999), http://www.popmatters.com/pm/feature/anderson-paulthomas/.

50. The documentary, which provides a fascinating glimpse into the production of the film, is available on *Magnolia*'s various home media releases on DVD and Blu-Ray. It was directed by Mark Rance, Anderson's friend and the one in charge of creating special features for New Line's DVD releases.

CHAPTER 4

1. King, "*Punch Drunk Love*: The Budding of an Auteur," *Senses of Cinema* 35 (April–June 2005), http://sensesofcinema.com/2005/feature-articles/pt _anderson/.

2. As quoted in Roger Ebert, "Review: *Punch-Drunk Love*," *Chicago Sun Times* (18 Oct. 2002), http://rogerebert.suntimes.com/apps/pbcs.dll/article ?AID=/20021018/REVIEWS/210180308/1023.

3. As quoted in Ryan Gilbey, "A Simple Little Movie?," *The Sunday Times* (2 Feb. 2003), p. 14.

4. As quoted in Gilbey, "A Simple Little Movie?," p. 14.

5. Gilbey, "A Simple Little Movie?," p. 14.

6. Mark Kawar, "Adam Sandler Movie Gives Big Boost to ConAgra's Healthy Choice Brand," *Omaha World-Herald* (15 Nov. 2002), n.p.

7. As quoted in Penelope Cross, "Disarmed & Dangerous—Flicks," *The Daily Telegraph* (2 April 2010), p. S47.

8. As quoted in Gilbey, "A Simple Little Movie?," p. 14

9. As quoted in Gilbey, "A Simple Little Movie?," p. 14.

10. Lawrie Masterson, "Camera Shy," *Sunday Herald Sun* (30 March 2003), p. 92.

11. As quoted in Gilbey, "A Simple Little Movie?," p. 14.

12. Mottram, *The Sundance Kids: How the Mavericks Took Back Hollywood* (New York: Faber and Faber, 2006), p. 353.

13. Waxman, *Rebels on the Backlot: Six Maverick Directors and How They Conquered the Hollywood Studio System* (New York: Harper, 2005), p. 336.

14. Michael Fleming, "Cage, Mostow team for pic," *Daily Variety* (28 Sept. 2000), p. 14.

15. Jenny Eliscu, "Fiona Apple," *Rolling Stone* (6 Oct. 2005), pp. 64–66.

16. Charles Lyons, "Rebels without a Pause," *Variety* (11 Sept. 2000), p. 1.

17. Charles Lyons, "Why Did They Nuke-A De Luca?," *Variety* (22 Jan. 2001), p. 1.

18. Charles Lyons, "Evolution comes to Roth's Revolution," *Variety* (15 Jan. 2001), p. 9.

19. David Bloom, "The Grapes of Roth: A First Harvest," *Variety* (21 Jan. 2002), p. 7.

20. Michael Fleming, "Anderson Project Beckons Sandler," *Daily Variety* (10 Nov. 2000), p. 1.

21. "Magnolia Maniac," *The Guardian* (10 March 2000), http://www.guardian.co.uk/film/2000/mar/10/culture.features.

22. My emphasis. Udovitch, "The Epic Obsessions of Paul Thomas Anderson," *Rolling Stone* (3 Feb. 2000), http://ezproxy.msu.edu/login?url=http://search.proquest.com/docview/220171809?accountid=12598.

23. Fleming, p. 14.

24. Claude Brodesser, "Hoffman eyes 'Seagull,'" *Daily Variety* (8 Dec. 2000), p. 68.

25. Robert Koehler, "Hi-Lo Country," *Variety* (16 July 2001), p. 33.

26. Kenneth A. Woods, "Thinking Outside the Boxes," *Electronic Musician* 18.7 (June 2002), p. 42.

27. Charles Lyons, "Revolution Tide Rises," *Daily Variety* (12 Jan. 2001), p. 1.

28. Richard Dyer, *Only Entertainment* (New York: Routledge, 1992), p. 18.

29. Price, "Color, the Formless, and Cinematic Eros," *Framework* 47.1 (2006), p. 23.

30. Price, p. 24.

31. Price, p. 24.

32. Price, p. 24.

33. My emphasis. King.

34. Mottram, *Sundance Kids*, p. 356.

35. As quoted in "Jon Brion," *Daily Variety* (6 Jan. 2003), p. A12.

36. As quoted in "Jon Brion," p. A12.

37. King.

38. "Jon Brion," p. A18.

39. Woods, p. 43.

40. Mottram, *Sundance Kids*, p. 356.

41. As quoted in Steve Daly, "The Reilly Factor," *Entertainment Weekly* (15 Nov. 2002), p. 76.

42. Tim Ryan, "For Hush-hush Roth Plot, Proof in Pudding Coupon," *Daily Variety* (19 March 2001), p. 5. Interestingly, this article also stated that Sandler's character was going to be "the owner of a failing phone-sex business"—which was either bad intel on the part of the reporter's sources or the result of a very early draft. Given the premise of *Boogie Nights*, the latter is not impossible, though unlikely.

43. As quoted in *"Punch-Drunk Love," Entertainment Weekly* (23 Aug. 2002), p. 99.

44. Michael Fleming, "Sandler Takes Look at 'Management,'" *Daily Variety* (3 Dec. 2001), p. 9.

45. David Bloom, p. 7

46. As quoted in Scott Bowles, *"Punch-Drunk* Has Giddy Goal," *USA Today* (21 Oct. 2002), p. 5D.

47. As quoted in Thom Geier, Brian M. Raftery, and Gillian Flynn, "Stretch Marks," *Entertainment Weekly* (25 Oct. 2002), p. 8.

48. As quoted in Jacobson Harlan and Bear Liza, "Making the Scene at the Cannes Film Fest," *USA Today* (20 May 2002), p. 4D.

49. As quoted in Cross, p. S47.

50. Clark, "Sandler Shatters the Mold in *Punch-Drunk Love,*" *USA Today* (11 Oct. 2002), p. 1E.

51. Koltnow, "An Able Adam and a Hirsute Salma," *Orange County Register* (28 Oct. 2002), no pag.

52. Rene Rodriguez, *"Blood* Is the Latest Eccentric Masterpiece from Quirky Filmmaker," *Miami Herald* (11 Jan. 2008), n.p.

53. "Sandler KO's Moron Role," *The Sunday Times* (Perth) (30 March 2002), no pag.

54. Ellen, "A Fine Romance, with No Passion," *The London Times* (6 Feb. 2003), p. 13.

55. Emerson, "Revulsion," *Jim Emerson's Scanners* (14 March 2007), http://blogs.suntimes.com/scanners/2007/03/revulsion.html.

56. Ebert.

57. Owen Gleiberman, "Adam Antsy," *Entertainment Weekly* (18 Oct. 2002), p. 87.

58. Stanley, "Punch Drunk Masculinity," *The Journal of Men's Studies* 14.2 (Spring 2006), p. 236.

59. Murphet, "P. T. Anderson's Dilemma: The Limits of Surrogate Paternity," *Sydney Studies* 34 (2008), p. 72.

60. Murphet, p. 72.

61. Goss, "'Things Like This Don't Just Happen': Ideology and Paul Thomas Anderson's *Hard Eight*, *Boogie Nights*, and *Magnolia*," *Journal of Communication Inquiry* 26.2 (April 2002), p. 172.

62. Stephen Dalton, "Film Choice," *London Times* (16 Feb. 2005), p. 23.

63. Andy Seiler, "A Brigade of Films Charges in this Fall," *USA Today* (6 Sept. 2002), p. 11D.

64. McCarthy, *"Punch-Drunk Love,"* *Variety* (27 May 2002), p. 23.

65. McCarthy, p. 23.

CHAPTER 5

1. "Paul Thomas Anderson Strikes Cinematic Oil," *MSNBC* (2 Jan. 2008), http://today.msnbc.msn.com/id/22477614/ns/today-entertainment/.

2. "Magnolia Maniac," *The Guardian* (10 March 2000), http://www.guardian.co.uk/film/2000/mar/10/culture.features.

3. As quoted in Willman, "The Music (*There Will Be Blood*)," p. 59.

4. In Charlie Rose, "The Paul Thomas Anderson and Daniel Day-Lewis Interview," *Charlie Rose Show* (21 Dec. 2007).

5. In Rose.

6. As quoted in Christopher Goodwin, "Blood, Oil, Tears and Sweat," *Sunday Times* (25 Nov. 2007), p. 4.

7. As quoted in Josh Modell, "Paul Thomas Anderson," *A.V. Club* (2 Jan. 2008), http://www.avclub.com/articles/paul-thomas-anderson,2120/.

8. In Rose.

9. Goodwin, "Blood, Oil, Tears and Sweat," p. 4.

10. Anonymous industry source after screening at Writers Guild of America, as quoted in Goodwin, p. 4.

11. As quoted in Willman, "The Music (*There Will Be Blood*)," p. 59.

12. As quoted in Pizzello, "*Blood* for Oil," *American Cinematographer* (January 2008), http://www.theasc.com/ac_magazine/January2008/ThereWillBeBlood/page1.php.

13. As quoted in Modell.

14. As quoted in Pizzello, "*Blood* for Oil."

15. In Rose.

16. As quoted in Walter, "How Big is Your Steeple?" *Sight & Sound* (Feb. 2008), p. 33.

17. In Rose.

18. As quoted in Tapley, "Paul Dano," *Dailey Variety* (7 Dec. 2007), p. 20.

19. As quoted in Pizzello, "*Blood* for Oil."

20. Christopher Goodwin, "Where Are Their Heads At?," *The Sunday Times* (6 May 2007), p. 8.

21. Steven Zeitchik, "'Rebels' without a Backlot," *Variety* (11 Sept. 2006), p. 7.

22. Goodwin, p. 8.

23. David Denby, "Uppie Redux?" *New Yorker* (28 Aug. 2006), p. 70.

24. As quoted in Modell.

25. As quoted in Mitchell Zuckoff, *Robert Altman: The Oral Biography* (New York: Alfred A. Knopf, 2009), p. 487.

26. As quoted in Claire Sutherland, "Retire? I'd Be Bored to Death," *The Daily Telegraph* (5 Oct. 2006), p. 03B.

27. As quoted in Zuckoff, p. 488.

28. As quoted in Modell.

29. As quoted in Zuckoff, p. 489.

30. As quoted in Modell.

31. As quoted in Zuckoff, p. 492.

32. "Arts," *The Australian* (17 Sept. 2005), p. 16.

33. As quoted in Zuckoff, p. 493.

34. "Paul Thomas Anderson Strikes Cinematic Oil," http://today.msnbc .msn.com/id/22477614/ns/today-entertainment/.

35. As quoted in Benjamin Svetkey, "Behind the Scenes of *Eyes Wide Shut*," *Entertainment Weekly* (23 July 1999), http://www.ew.com/ew/article/0,,272431 _3,00.html.

36. Pizzello, "*Blood* for Oil."

37. Gilbey, "Power, corruption and lies," *New Statesman* (11 Feb. 2008), p. 45.

38. As quoted in Pizzello, "*Blood* for Oil."

39. As quoted in Willman, "The Music (*There Will Be Blood*)," p. 59.

40. As quoted in Pizzello, "*Blood* for Oil."

41. As quoted in Bell, "Jonny Greenwood," *Sight & Sound* 18.2 (Feb. 2008), p. 34.

42. As quoted in Rene Rodriguez, "*Blood* is the Latest Eccentric Masterpiece from Quirky Filmmaker," *Miami Herald* (11 Jan. 2008), n.p.

43. In Rose.

44. As quoted in Modell.

45. In Rose.

46. As quoted in Goodwin, "Blood, Oil, Tears and Sweat," p. 4.

47. As quoted in Ed Pilkington, "Tell the Story! Tell The Story!," *The Guard-*

ian (2 Jan. 2008), http://www.guardian.co.uk/culture/2008/jan/04/awards andprizes.

48. As quoted in Goodwin, "Blood, Oil, Tears and Sweat," p. 4.

49. As quoted in Rodriguez, n.p.

50. As quoted in Anthony Kaufman, "Paul Thomas Anderson," *Daily Variety* (5 Dec. 2007), p. A2.

51. As quoted in Walter, p. 33.

52. In Rose.

53. As quoted in Modell.

54. As quoted in Modell.

55. Lennart Sjöberg, "Personality, Situation, or Interaction?" *PsycCRITIQUES* 53.31 (2008), n.p.

56. Handy, "Striking Oil, Striking *Blood*," *Vanity Fair* (January 2008), p. 42.

57. Murphet, "P. T. Anderson's Dilemma: The Limits of Surrogate Paternity," *Sydney Studies* 34 (2008), p. 78.

58. Denby, "Hard Life," *New Yorker* (17 Dec. 2007), p. 106.

59. As quoted in Walter, p. 33. Interestingly, Anderson said something very similar about being "no dummy" when asked a similar question by *The Guardian*; see Pilkington.

60. McGill, "*There Will Be Blood*," *Sight & Sound* 18.2 (Feb. 2008), p. 83.

61. As quoted in Weisman, "*There Will Be Blood*," *Daily Variety* (17 Dec. 2007), p. A6.

62. Steven Sailer, "The Oilman Bowls Alone," *American Conservative* (28 Jan. 2008), p. 27.

63. Murphet, p. 68.

64. Murphet, p. 84.

65. Sjöberg, n.p.

66. McQuillan and McQuillan, "Review of *There Will Be Blood*," *Journal of Feminist Family Therapy* 20.3 (2008), p. 273.

67. Sjöberg, n.p.

68. In Rose.

69. As quoted in Ansen, "Making a Killing in Oil," *Newsweek* (17 Dec. 2007), p. 74.

70. As quoted in "Bloody and Unbowed," *Irish Times* (15 Feb. 2008), n.p.

71. In Rose.

72. As quoted in Goodwin, "Blood, Oil, Tears and Sweat," p. 4.

73. As quoted in Modell.

74. As quoted in Freydkin, "Day-Lewis Has Recognition in His 'Blood,'" *USA Today* (11 Dec. 2007), p. 2D.

75. As quoted in Goodwin, "Blood, Oil, Tears and Sweat," p. 4.

76. As quoted in Melissa Block and Robert Siegel, "In *Blood*, Day-Lewis Revisits His Darker Side," *All Things Considered* (26 Dec. 2007).

77. In Rose.

78. As quoted in Lynn Hirschberg, "The New Frontier's Man," *The New*

York Times (11 Nov. 2007), http://www.nytimes.com/2007/11/11/magazine /11daylewis-t2.html?_r=2&pagewanted=all.

79. As quoted in Chang, "Directors Shoot Down Convention," *Daily Variety* (18 Dec. 2007), p. 25.

80. As quoted in Walter, p. 33.

81. In Rose.

82. In Rose.

83. "'Ballad' Reception Rosy," *Daily Variety* (10 March 2005), p. 11.

84. As quoted in Pizzello, *"Blood* for Oil."

85. As quoted in Shellie Branco, "Kern's Past Helped Fuel New Film: Filmmakers Looked to Oil Rush, Wooden Derrick for *There Will Be Blood,"* *Bakersfield Californian* (12 Jan. 2008), n.p.

86. As quoted in Branco.

87. As quoted in Pizzello, *"Blood* for Oil."

88. In Rose.

89. As quoted in Walter, p. 33.

90. As quoted in "Paul Thomas Anderson Strikes Cinematic Oil."

91. Angus McLaren, *Impotence: A Cultural History* (Chicago: University of Chicago Press, 2007), p. 161.

92. Fleming and Mohr, "Miramax, Par draw 'Blood,'" *Daily Variety* (18 Jan. 2006), p. 9.

93. "Paramount, Miramax Team for Anderson's 'Oil!' Take," *Hollywood Reporter—International Edition* (24 Jan. 2006), p. 47.

94. As quoted in Goodwin, "Blood, Oil, Tears and Sweat," p. 4.

95. Patrick Goldstein and James Rainey, "Paramount's Vantage Now Disadvantaged," *The Los Angeles Times* (25 July 2008), http://latimesblogs.latimes .com/the_big_picture/2008/07/paramounts-vant.html.

96. As quoted in Modell.

97. As quoted in Hirschberg, "The New Frontier's Man."

98. As quoted in Pizzello, *"Blood* for Oil."

99. As quoted in Freydkin, p. 2D.

100. As quoted in Ansen, "How to Make A Star Follow Directions," *Newsweek* (2 July 2007), p. 72.

101. As quoted in Modell.

102. Kit, *"Blood* Transition Not in Vain," *Hollywood Reporter—International Edition* (4 Jan. 2008), n.p.

103. As quoted in Pizzello, *"Blood* for Oil."

104. Kit, n.p.

105. As quoted in Anthony Kaufman, "Paul Thomas Anderson," p. A2.

106. As quoted in Anthony Kaufman, "Paul Thomas Anderson," p. A2.

107. Kit, n.p.

108. In Rose.

109. McCarthy, "'Blood' Runs Deep," *Variety* (5 Nov. 2007), p. 41.

110. Kelly, "Crude Truth," *Texas Monthly* (Dec. 2007), p. 68.

111. Ansen, "Making a Killing in Oil," p. 74.

112. Pincus-Roth, "Casting Directors Grope with Groups," *Daily Variety* (30 Nov. 2007), p. A1.

113. In Rose.

114. Pincus-Roth, p. A1.

115. Ansen, "Making a Killing in Oil," p. 74.

116. As quoted in Pizzello, "*Blood* for Oil."

117. As quoted in Bell, p. 34.

118. As quoted in David Mermelstein, "This Year's Models," *Daily Variety* (12 Dec. 2007), p. A4.

119. In Rose.

120. As quoted in Bell, p. 34.

121. As quoted in Bell, p. 34.

122. As quoted in Modell.

123. In Rose.

124. "Paul Thomas Anderson Strikes Cinematic Oil."

125. "Paul Thomas Anderson Strikes Cinematic Oil."

126. As quoted in Debra Kaufman, "Pieces of Dylan Tichenor," *Film & Video* (1 Dec. 2005), http://www.studiodaily.com/filmandvideo/technique /craft/f/finishing/5716.html.

127. As quoted in Modell.

128. As quoted in Weisman, "*There Will Be Blood*," p. A6.

129. As quoted in Rodriguez, n.p.

130. In Rose.

131. In Rose.

132. In Rose.

133. Michael Dwyer, "Day-Lewis Epic Gets the Blood Up," *Irish Times* (5 Oct. 2007), n.p.

134. McClintock and McNary, "B.O. a River of *Blood*," *Daily Variety* (28 Dec. 2007), p. 1.

135. Pamela McClintock, "Oscar Casts Glow," *Daily Variety* (22 Feb. 2008), p. 1.

136. As quoted in Anthony Kaufman, "Paul Thomas Anderson," p. A2.

137. "*There Will Be Blood* Wins Decade," *Gawker* (18 Dec. 2009), http:// gawker.com/5428998/there-will-be-blood-wins-the-decade. *Gawker* did an extensive, if unscientific, study of numerous "Top Ten" lists posted online. It reported that *There Will Be Blood* had appeared on more lists total than any other film from the decade.

138. Pete Travers, "50 Best Movies of the Decade," *Rolling Stone* (24 Dec. 2009), p. 66.

139. Peter Bradshaw, "Best films of the noughties No 1: *There Will Be Blood*," *The Guardian* (1 Jan. 2010), http://www.guardian.co.uk/film/filmblog/2010 /jan/01/best-films-noughties-there-will-be-blood.

select bibliography

BOOKS

Allon, Yoram, Del Cullen, and Hannah Patterson, eds. *Contemporary North American Film Directors*. London: Wallflower, 2002.

Anderson, Paul Thomas. *Boogie Nights: Screenplay*. New York: Faber & Faber, 2000.

———. *Magnolia: The Shooting Script*. New York: Newmarket Press, 2000.

———. *Punch-Drunk Love: The Shooting Script*. New York: Newmarket Press, 2002.

Berra, John. *Declarations of Independence: American Cinema and the Partiality of Independent Production*. Chicago: Intellect/University of Chicago Press, 2008.

Biskind, Peter. *Down and Dirty Pictures: Miramax, Sundance, and the Rise of Independent Film*. New York: Simon and Schuster, 2004.

Bruzzi, Stella. *Bringing Up Daddy: Fatherhood and Masculinity in Postwar Hollywood*. London: BFI, 2008.

Chafe, William. *The Unfinished Journey: America since World War II*. 6th ed. New York: Oxford University Press, 2007.

Hanson, Peter. *The Cinema of Generation X: A Critical Study of Films and Directors*. Jefferson, NC: McFarland, 2002.

Hillier, Jim. *American Independent Cinema: A Sight and Sound Reader*. London: BFI, 2008.

Hulmund, Chris, and Justin Wyatt. *Contemporary American Independent Film: From the Margins to the Mainstream*. New York: Routledge, 2004.

King, Geoff. *American Independent Cinema*. Bloomington: Indiana University Press, 2005.

Levy, Emmanuel. *Cinema of Outsiders: The Rise of American Independent Cinema*. New York: New York University Press, 2001.

Mottram, James. *The Sundance Kids: How the Mavericks Took Back Hollywood*. New York: Faber and Faber, 2006.

Newman, Michael. *Characterization in American Independent Cinema*. PhD Thesis: University of Wisconsin–Madison, 2006.

———. *Indie: An American Film Culture*. New York: Columbia University Press, 2011.

Perkins, Claire. *American Smart Cinema*. Edinburgh: University of Edinburgh Press, 2011.

Reay, Pauline. *Music in Film: Soundtracks and Synergy*. London: Wallflower, 2004.

Root, Colin. *Paul Thomas Anderson: From Hard Eight to Punch-Drunk Love*. Saarbrücken, Germany: Lambert Academic Publishing, 2009.

Thompson, David, ed. *Altman on Altman*. Foreword by Paul Thomas Anderson. New York: Faber & Faber, 2006.

Waxman, Sharon. *Rebels on the Backlot: Six Maverick Directors and How They Conquered the Hollywood Studio System*. New York: Harper, 2005.

Zuckoff, Mitchell. *Robert Altman: The Oral Biography*. New York: Alfred A. Knopf, 2009.

INTERVIEWS

Ansen, David. "How to Make a Star Follow Directions." *Newsweek* (2 July 2007): 72.

Figgis, Mike. "Paul Thomas Anderson." *Projections* (1999): 28–37. Reprinted in *Projection 10: Hollywood Film-makers on Film-making*, ed. Figgis. London: Faber & Faber, 1999.

Fuchs, Cynthia. "Interview with Paul Thomas Anderson." *PopMatters* (1999): http://www.popmatters.com/pm/feature/anderson-paulthomas/.

Konow, David. "PTA Meeting: An Interview with Paul Thomas Anderson." *Creative Screenwriting* 7.1 (Jan.–Feb. 2000): 46–53.

McKenna, Kristine. "An Interview with: Paul Thomas Anderson." *Creative Screenwriting* (1998): 24–25.

Pilkington, Ed. "Tell the Story! Tell The Story!" *The Guardian* (2 Jan. 2008): http://www.guardian.co.uk/culture/2008/jan/04/awardsandprizes.

Ponsoldt, James. "GIANT Ambition." *Filmmaker: The Magazine of Independent Film* (Winter 2008): 40–45, 107.

Udovitch, Mim. "It Went Down Like This on the Set of *Boogie Nights*." *Esquire* (Oct. 1997): 108–111.

Walter, Ben. "How Big Is Your Steeple?" *Sight & Sound* (Feb. 2008): 33.

Willman, Chris. "Mann Crazy." *Entertainment Weekly* (7 Jan. 2000): 67.

SCHOLARLY (PEER-REVIEWED) ARTICLES

Addelston, Judi. "Doing the Full Monty with Dirk and Jane: Using the Phallus to Validate Marginalized Masculinities." *Journal of Men's Studies* 7.3 (Spring 1999): 337–352.

"Biography: Anderson, Paul Thomas." *Contemporary Authors* (New York: Thomson Gale, 2007).

Bruns, John. "The Polyphonic Film." *New Review of Film and Television Studies* 6.2 (Aug. 2008): 189–212.

Cate, Andrew C. "'New' Hollywood Narratives: An Analysis on *Boogie Nights* and *Magnolia*." *Honors Project Overview* Paper 23 2009: http://digitalcommons.ric.edu/honors_projects/23/.

Chin, Daryl, and Larry Qualls. "To Market, To Market." *PAJ: A Journal of Performance and Art* 20.1 (Jan. 1998): 38–43.

Clyburn, Scott. "*There Will Be Blood.*" *Journal of Religion and Film* 12.2 (Oct. 2008): 16.

Crawford, Sarah. "The New Romantic Violence: A Consideration of *Punch-Drunk Love.*" *Film Journal* 1.4 (2002): http://www.thefilmjournal.com/issue4/romanticviolence.html.

Crous, André. "Paul Thomas Anderson: Tracking through a Fantastic Reality." *Senses of Cinema* 45 (Nov. 2007): http://www.sensesofcinema.com/2007/feature-articles/paul-thomas-anderson/.

D'Aries, Donald R., and Foster Hirsch. "'Saint' Sydney: Atonement and Moral Inversion in *Hard Eight.*" *The Philosophy of Neo-Noir*, ed. Mark T. Conrad (Lexington: University Press Kentucky, 2007): 91–100.

DeGiglio-Bellemare, Mario. "*Magnolia* and the Signs of the Times: A Theological Reflection." *Journal of Religion and Film* 4.2 (Oct. 2000): http://www.unomaha.edu/jrf/magnolia.htm.

Dillman, Joanne Clarke. "Twelve Characters in Search of a Televisual Text: *Magnolia* Masquerading as Soap Opera." *Journal of Popular Film and Television* 33.3 (Fall 2005): 142–150.

Ecksel, Robert. "*There Will Be Blood.*" *Bright Lights Film Journal* (May 2008): 60.

Fischer, Lucy. "Theory into Practice: En-Gendering Narrative in *Magnolia.*" *Screening Genders*, ed. Krin Gabbard and William Luhr (New Brunswick, NJ: Rutgers University Press, 2008): 29–46.

Fuller, Glen. "*Punch Drunk Love*: A Post-Romance Romance." *M/C: A Journal of Media and Culture* (June 2007): http://journal.media-culture.org.au/0706/03-fuller.php.

Glass, Loren. "After the Phallus." *American Imago* 58.2 (Summer 2001): 545–566.

Gorfinkel, Elena. "The Future of Anachronisms: Todd Haynes and the Magnificent Andersons." *Cinephilia: Movies, Love, and Memory*, ed. Marijke de Valck and Malte Hagener (Amsterdam: Amsterdam University Press, 2005): 153–168.

Goss, Brian Michael. "'Things Like This Don't Just Happen': Ideology and Paul Thomas Anderson's *Hard Eight, Boogie Nights*, and *Magnolia.*" *Journal of Communication Inquiry* 26.2 (April 2002): 171–192.

Harmon, A. G. "Ordered Chaos: Three Films by Paul Thomas Anderson." *Image: A Journal of Arts and Religion* 27 (Summer 2000): http://imagejournal.org/page/journal/articles/issue-27/harmon-essay.

Hawskley, Theodora. "But It Did Happen: Sound as Deep Narrative in P. T. Anderson's *Magnolia* (1999)." *Journal of Religion and Film* 13.2 (Oct. 2009): http://www.unomaha.edu/jrf/vol13.no2/Hawksley_Magnolia.html.

Heyraud, Joyce King. "A Review of *There Will Be Blood.*" *Psychological Perspectives* 51.1 (Jan. 2008): 179–80.

Hsu, Hsuan L. "Racial Privacy, the LA Ensemble Film and Paul Haggis' *Crash*." *Film Criticism* (2006): 1–25.

Ivakhiv, Adrian. "Stirring the Geopolitical Unconscious: Towards a Jamesonian Ecocriticism." *New Formations* 64 (Spring 2008): 98–109.

Karlyn, Kathleen Rowe. "Too Close for Comfort: *American Beauty* and the Incest Motif." *Cinema Journal* 44.1 (Fall 2004): 69–93.

Kerins, Mark. "Narration in the Cinema of Digital Sound." *The Velvet Light Trap* 58 (Fall 2006): 41–54.

King, Cubie. "*Punch Drunk Love*: The Budding of an Auteur." *Senses of Cinema* 35 (April–June 2005): http://sensesofcinema.com/2005/feature-articles /pt_anderson/.

Kleinhans, Chuck. "The Change from Film to Video Pornography: Implications for Analysis." *Pornography: Film and Culture*, ed. Peter Lehman (New Brunswick: Rutgers University Press, 2006): 154–167.

Lehman, Peter. "*Boogie Nights*: Will the Real Dirk Diggler Please Stand Up?" *Jump Cut* 42 (Dec. 1998): http://www.ejumpcut.org/archive/onlinessays/JC 42folder/BoogieNights.html.

———. "Crying over the Melodramatic Penis: Melodrama and Male Nudity in Films of the 90s." *Masculinity: Bodies, Movies, Culture*, ed. Lehman (New York: Routledge, 2001): 25–41.

MacDowell, James. "Notes on Quirky." *Movie: A Journal of Film Criticism* 1 (2010): http://www2.warwick.ac.uk/fac/arts/film/movie/contents/notes _on_quirky.pdf.

McQuillan, Deanne Boyd, and Matthew McQuillan. "Review of *There Will Be Blood*." *Journal of Feminist Family Therapy* 20.3 (Aug. 2008): 271–273.

Murphet, Julian. "P. T. Anderson's Dilemma: The Limits of Surrogate Paternity." *Sydney Studies* 34 (2008): 63–85.

Naremore, James. "Films of the Year: 2007." *Film Quarterly* 61.4 (Summer 2008): 48–61.

Nochimson, Martha P. "New York Film Festival 2002." *Film-Philosophy* 6.37 (2002).

Peberdy, Donna. "From Wimps to Wild Men: Bipolar Masculinity and the Paradoxical Performances of Tom Cruise." *Men and Masculinities* (Feb. 2010): 1–24.

Price, Brian. "Color, the Formless, and Cinematic Eros." *Framework* 47.1 (2006): 22–35.

Prout, Ryan, and Jonathan Murray. "Film Reviews." *Film International* 6.3 (2008): 84–87.

Ramsey, David. "Paul Thomas Anderson and the Postmodern Cinema of American Civil Society." Paper presented at Southern Political Science Association, Jan. 2008.

Ritter, Kelly. "Spectacle at the Disco: *Boogie Nights*, Soundtrack, and the New American Musical." *Journal of Popular Film and Television* 28.4 (Winter 2001): 166–175.

Salt, Barry. "The Shape of 1999: The Stylistics of American Movies at the End of the Century." *New Review of Film and Television Studies* 2.1 (May 2004): 61–85.

Scanlan, John. "Combustion: An Essay on the Value of Gambling." *Gambling: Who Wins? Who Loses?*, ed. Gerda Reith (New York: Prometheus, 2003): 348–354.

Sconce, Jeffrey. "Irony, Nihilism, and the New American 'Smart' Film." *Screen* 43.4 (Winter 2002): 349–369.

Sewell, Matthew. "Short Takes: Cinematography (*Magnolia*)." *Bright Lights Film Journal* 73 (Aug. 2011): http://www.brightlightsfilm.com/73/73magno lia_sewell.php.

Sickels, Robert. "1970s Disco Daze: Paul Thomas Anderson and the Last Golden Age of Irresponsibility." *Journal of Popular Culture* (2002): 49–60.

Simmons, Tom. "*Boogie* Opera: Eddie, Douzi and Artistic Convention." *Journal of Popular Culture* 33.4 (Spring 2000): 101–121.

Stanley, Timothy. "Punch-Drunk Masculinity." *The Journal of Men's Studies* 14.2 (Spring 2006): 235–242.

Tait, R. Colin. "That 70s Sequence: Remembering the Bad Old Days in Summer of Sam." *Cinephile* 5.2 (Summer 2009): 17–23.

Thomson-Jones, Katherine. "The Literary Origins of the Cinematic Narrator." *British Society of Aesthetics* 47.1 (2007): 76–94.

Tincknell, Estella. "The Soundtrack Movie, Nostalgia and Consumption." *Film's Musical Moments*, ed. Ian Conrich and Estella Tincknell (Edinburgh: Edinburgh University Press, 2007): 132–145.

Udden, James. "Child of the Long Take: Alfonso Cuaron's Film Aesthetics in the Shadow of Globalization." *Style* 43.1 (Spring 2009): 26–44.

White, Rob. "Easy Words." *Film Quarterly* 61.3 (Spring 2008): 4–5.

Winter, Ben. "Corporeality, Musical Heartbeats, and Cinematic Emotion." *Music, Sound and the Moving Image* 2.1 (Spring 2008): 3–25.

Yacowar, Maurice. "Digging In." *Queen's Quarterly* 115 (2008): 94–103.

Zuromskis, Catherine. "Prurient Pictures and Popular Film: The Crisis of Pornographic Representation." *The Velvet Light Trap* 59 (2007): 4–14.

MAINSTREAM ARTICLES

Alleva, Richard. "Thicker Than Oil: *There Will Be Blood*." *Commonweal* (15 Feb. 2008): 19–20.

Anderson, Paul Thomas. "A Fantasy Fall Season; 'This, That and the Other.'" *New York Times Magazine* (14 Nov. 1999): 3.

———. "Holiday Films; A Valley Boy Who Found a Home Not Far from Home." *New York Times* (14 Nov. 1999): 3.

Ansen, David. "Porn in the USA." *Newsweek* (6 Oct. 1997): 74–75.

"Arts, Briefly: Museum Salutes Tom Cruise." *The New York Times* (10 July 2007): 2.

Ascher-Walsh, Rebecca, and Maggie Murphy. "The Naked and the Dread." *Entertainment Weekly* (25 April 1997): 26–27.

"As They Like It." *Hollywood Reporter—International Edition* (15 April 2003): 78.

"'Ballad' Reception Rosy." *Daily Variety* (10 March 2005): 11.

Bell, James. "Jonny Greenwood." *Sight & Sound* (Feb. 2008): 34.

"Berlin Recycling." *Sight & Sound* (April 2000): 4–5.

Bessman, Jim. "Mann Blossoms on Reprise Soundtrack." *Billboard* (13 Nov. 1999): 5–6.

"Boogie Nights." *Entertainment Weekly* (19 Jan. 2001): 25.

"'Boogie'-oogie-oogie." *Premiere* (Sept. 1997): 72–77.

Burr, Ty. "Flower Power." *Entertainment Weekly* (28 July 2000): 159.

Cagle, Jess, and Mark Harris. "Boogie Nights." *Entertainment Weekly* (16 May 1997): 80.

Chang, Justin. "LA Crix Draw 'Blood' for Top Film Honor." *Daily Variety* (10 Dec. 2007): 4, 43.

Coker, Cheo Hodari. "Magnolia." *Premiere* (Sept. 2000): 84–85.

Corliss, Richard. "Dirk Diggler: A Star Is Porn." *Time* (6 Oct. 1997): 88.

Dargis, Manohla. "An American Primitive, Forged in a Crucible of Blood and Oil." *New York Times* (26 Dec. 2007): 1.

Davies, Tanya. "Cruising to Success." *Maclean's* (7 Feb. 2000): 43.

Davis, Daniel. "Brush with Fame." *Movieline's Hollywood Life* (Jan. 2004): 40.

Denby, David. "San Fernando Aria." *New Yorker* (20 Dec. 1999): 102–103.

———. "Uppie Redux?" *New Yorker* (28 Aug. 2006): 70–77.

Eliscu, Jenny. "Fiona Apple." *Rolling Stone* (6 Oct. 2005): 64–66.

Ellis, Bob. "The Exhaustion of Endless Praise." *Encore* (April 2008): 12–13, 36.

"Fade Out." *Written By: The Magazine of the Writers Guild of America* 3.9 (Oct. 1999): 56.

Fernandez, Walter, Jr. "There Will Be Blood." *CinemaEditor* (2007): 48–50.

Fleming, Michael. "Anderson Has Faith in Hoffman." *Daily Variety* (3 Dec. 2009): 1, 25.

———. "Anderson Project Beckons Sandler." *Daily Variety* (10 Nov. 2000): 1, 25.

Fleming, Michael, and Ian Mohr. "Miramax, Par Draw 'Blood.'" *Daily Variety* (10 Nov. 2000): 1, 9.

"Follow the Leader." *Film Comment* 46.1 (Jan.–Feb. 2010): 8.

Friedman, Bonnie. "Reality Bites." *New York Times* (4 Feb. 2007): 9.

Galloway, Stephen. "Fresh Blood." *Hollywood Reporter—International Edition* (22 Nov. 2007): 22.

———. "The Mild Bunch." *Hollywood Reporter* (25 June 2002).

———. "The New Breed." *Hollywood Reporter—International Edition* (8 Feb. 2008): 1.

Garrett, Diane, and Dave McNary. "Freshman Class." *Daily Variety* (9 Jan. 2008): 1, 24.

Gilbey, Ryan. "Brave New Worlds." *New Statesman* (22 Dec. 2008): 78–79.

———. "Power, Corruption and Lies." *New Statesman* (11 Feb. 2008): 45.

Goldman, Michael. "Old-Fashioned Filmmaking." *Millimeter* (Nov.–Dec. 2007): 8–14.

Gopalan, Nisha, and Alex Lewin. "2020 Vision." *Premiere* (Feb. 1999): 66–75.

Grover, Ronald. "Oscar Night: Why *Juno* Might Win." *BusinessWeek Online* (21 Feb. 2008): 22.

Gunshanan, Jim. "*Boogie Nights*: Nocturnal Missions." *Creative Screenwriting* 5.6 (Nov.–Dec. 1998): 24–26.

Haskell, Molly. "Summer Films: Star Power; Tom Cruise, Team Player." *New York Times* (30 April 2000): 10.

Hayes, Dave. "Wider Release gets 'Blood' Pumping." *Daily Variety* (14 Jan. 2008): 12.

"Heeeere's Jonny! Greenwood, of Radiohead." *Film Score Monthly* (Jan. 2008): 1.

Hemblade, Christopher. "New Films." *Empire* (Nov. 1997): 50.

Hirschberg, Lynn. "His Way." *New York Times Magazine* (19 Dec. 1999): 52.

Hoey, Matt. "Blood Lines." *Written By: The Magazine of the Writers Guild of America* (Dec. 2007): 44–50.

Holfer, Robert. "Helmer Noms Relegated Star Power to Backseat." *Variety* (14 Feb. 2008): A13.

Holloway, Ron. "2nd Motovun Film Festival." *Kinema* (Spring 2001): 87–89.

"How to Put a Gloom on All the Doom." *Daily Variety* (4 Jan. 2008): A3.

"In Production." *Sight and Sound* 20.2 (Feb. 2010): 9.

James, Nick. "Black Gold." *Sight & Sound* (Feb. 2008): 30–34.

Jameson, Richard T. "Flying Dutchman." *Film Comment* (March–April 1997): 11–12.

Jensen, Jeff. "Paul Thomas Anderson." *Entertainment Weekly* (1 Feb. 2008): 41.

Jones, Kent. "P. T. Anderson's *Magnolia*." *Film Comment* (Jan.–Feb. 2000): 38–39.

Karger, Dave, and Jeffrey Wells. "Porn Again." *Entertainment Weekly* (20 Sept. 1996): 10–11.

Kauffman, Stanley. "The Rake's Progress." *New Republic* (10 Nov. 1997): 32–33.

Kaufman, Anthony. "Paul Thomas Anderson." *Daily Variety* (6 Feb. 2008): A2.

Keil, Beth Landman, and David Amsden. "Sushi Kingpins Hit a Raw Nerve." *New York* (6 March 2000): 11.

Kemp, Stuart. "In London, 'Blood' in the Thick of It." *Hollywood Reporter—International Edition* (14 Dec. 2007): 4, 66.

Kendricks, Neil. "Paul Thomas Anderson: Moviemaking Genius?" *MovieMaker* (April/May 2000): 44–45.

Kenny, Glenn. "Making It." *Premiere* (Sept. 1997): 78–79.

Kirshling, Gregory. "'Blood' Complex." *Entertainment Weekly* (11 April 2008): 62.

———. "Shake, Shake, Shake." *Entertainment Weekly* (15 Feb. 2008): 47.

Kit, Borys. "*Blood* Transition Not in Vain." *Hollywood Reporter—International Edition* (4 Jan. 2008): 18.

Klawans, Stuart. "Films." *Nation* (7 Feb. 2000): 34–36.

Korman, Ken. "Movies." *Sound & Vision* (Nov. 2000): 145–146.

Lim, Dennis. "If You Need a Past, He's the Guy to Build It." *New York Times* (6 Jan. 2008): 14.

Lyons, Charles. "Rebel Rousers." *Daily Variety* (19 June 2001): 1, 26.

Maslin, Janet. "Film Festival Review; An Actor Whose Talents Are the Sum of His Parts." *New York Times* (8 Oct. 1997): 1.

McCarthy, Libby. "Day-Lewis Palms Kudo." *Daily Variety* (5 Dec. 2007): 5.

McCarthy, Todd. "Paul Thomas Anderson." *Esquire* (March 2000): 221.

McKinley, Jesse. "A Night Out With/The Broadway Babies; That Rarity, a Sizzling Opening Night Party." *New York Times* (12 March 2000): 1.

McNary, Dave. "Anderson, Chan join WMA." *Daily Variety* (28 April 2008): 6.

Obst, Lynda. "The Two Hollywoods; Hollywood Squares and Hipsters." *New York Times Magazine* (16 Nov. 1997): 135.

Olsen, Mark. "Singing in the Rain." *Sight & Sound* (March 2000): 26–30.

"Paramount, Miramax Team for Anderson's 'Oil!' Take." *Hollywood Reporter—International Edition* (24 Jan. 2006): 47.

"Paul Thomas Anderson." *Esquire* (Oct. 2008): 92.

"Paul Thomas Anderson." *MovieMaker* (2009): 20.

"PEN Center USA West Award Winners Announced." *Written By: The Magazine of the Writers Guild of America* (July 1998): 44.

Pincus-Roth, Zachary. "Casting Directors Grope with Groups." *Daily Variety* (30 Nov. 2007): A1, A16.

Pizzello, Stephen. "Blood for Oil." *American Cinematographer* (Jan. 2008): 36–55.

———. "Setting an Oil Derrick Ablaze." *American Cinematographer* (Jan. 2008): 40–41.

"Punch-Drunk Love." *Premiere* (Sept. 2002): 58.

Quinn, Jason. "Blood on Her Hands." *Produced By: The Official Magazine of the Producers Guild of America* (Winter 2007): 75–80.

Rawe, Julie. "Live from New York: Bedbugs!" *Time* (13 Nov. 2006): 175.

Richardson, John H. "The Secret History of Paul Thomas Anderson." *Esquire* (Oct. 2008). http://www.esquire.com/features/75-most-influential /paul-thomas-anderson-1008.

Rochlin, Margy. "Film; The Innocent Approach to an Adult Opus." *New York Times* (12 Oct. 1997): 13.

Rhodes, S. Mark. "Brion of All Trades." *Film Score Monthly* (Sept. 2004): 11, 44.

Romney, Jonathan, and Frances Stonor Saunders. "Every Petal Tells a Story." *New Statesman* (20 March 2000): 76.

———. "Take 2000." *New Statesman* (25 Dec. 2000): 76.

Ryan, Tim. "For Hush-Hush Roth Plot, Proof in Pudding Coupon." *Daily Variety* (19 March 2001): 5.

Sarris, Andrew, et al. "The Next Scorsese." *Esquire* (March 2000): 217–225.

Schwarzbaum, Lisa. "Bloody Great." *Entertainment Weekly* (11 Jan. 2008): 56–57.

Scott, A. O. "It's Suddenly So Last Year, That Once Bold New Guard." *New York Times* (7 Sept. 2008): 35.

Seitz, Matt Zoller. "One Filmmaker's Vivid Tales of Fathers and Other Strangers." *New York Times* (4 Jan. 2008): 7.

Shattuck, Dianne Spoto. "Tracking Aimee Mann." *Independent Film and Video Monthly* (March 2005): 27–29.

Smith, Gavin. "Night Fever." *Sight & Sound* (Jan. 1998): 6–10.

Stephens, Chuck. "The Swollen Boy." *Film Comment* (Sept.–Oct. 1997): 10–13.

Tapley, Kristopher. "Paul Dano." *Daily Variety* (7 Dec. 2007): 20.

"There Will Be Blood." *Boxoffice* (Oct. 2007): 47.

"Twists of Fate in LA Lives." *New York Times* (17 Dec. 1999): 1.

Udovitch, Mim. "The Epic Obsessions of Paul Thomas Anderson." *Rolling Stone* (3 Feb. 2000): 46–49.

Vary, Adam B. "Paul Thomas Anderson, *Hard Eight*." *Daily Variety* (19 Jan. 2006): B3.

Weisman, Jon. "There Will Be Blood." *Daily Variety* (17 Dec. 2007): A6.

"Well Rider of the Week." *Entertainment Weekly* (3 Feb. 2006): 53.

Wexler, Barbara, and Laurence Lerman. "Look Who's Talking." *Video Business* (26 June 2000): 18.

Willman, Chris. "A Little 'Nights' Music." *Entertainment Weekly* (14 Nov. 1997): 90.

———. "The Music (*There Will Be Blood*)." *Entertainment Weekly* (9 Nov. 2007): 59.

Zeitchik, Steven. "'Rebels' without a Backlot." *Variety* (11 Sept. 2006): 7.

MOVIE REVIEWS

Ansen, David. "Making a Killing in Oil." *Newsweek* (17 Dec. 2007): 74.

Anwar, Brett. "Black Gold." *Film Review* (March 2008): 54–60.

Arthur, Anthony. "Blood and 'Oil.'" *New York Times Book Review* (24 Feb. 2008): 31.

Beale, Lewis. "There Will Be Blood." *Film Journal International* (Jan. 2008): 36.

Blake, Richard. "After Sunset." *America* (10 March 2008): 18–20.

Brennan, Simon, and Katherine Heintzelman. "Boogie Nights." *Premiere* (May 1998): 95.

Chagolian, Steve. "Lensers Fete *Blood*." *Daily Variety* (28 Jan. 2008): 8, 17.

Chang, Justin. "Directors Shoot Down Convention." *Daily Variety* (18 Dec. 2007): 7, 25.

Collins, Rachel. "Reinventing the Reel." *Library Journal* (1 March 2003): 91.

Denby, David. "Hard Life." *New Yorker* (17 Dec. 2007): 106–109.

———. "There Will Be Blood." *New Yorker* (28 Jan. 2008): 19.

Dick, Leslie. "Reviews." *Sight & Sound* (April 2000): 56.

Doherty, Thomas. "*Boogie Nights.*" *Cineaste* (April 1998): 40–41.

Douthat, Ross. "Well, Well, Well." *National Review* (28 Jan. 2008): 55.

Edelstein, David. "It's a Gusher!" *New York* (24 Dec. 2007): 95–100.

Edwards, Simon. "*There Will Be Blood.*" *Ultimate DVD* (June 2008): 86.

Falcon, Richard. "Reviews." *Sight & Sound* (Jan. 1998): 44.

"Fallen." *New York Times* (23 Feb. 1997): 26.

Freydkin, Donna. "Day-Lewis Has Recognition in His 'Blood.'" *USA Today* (11 Dec. 2007).

Grant, Tracey. "Crosscuts." *North American Review* (Sept.–Oct. 2009): 44–45.

Guzman, Dave. "*There Will Be Blood.*" *Inside Film* (Feb. 2008): 40.

Handy, Bruce. "Striking Oil, Striking *Blood.*" *Vanity Fair* (Jan. 2008): 42.

Hayes, Dade. "'Blood'-Thirsty Crix." *Daily Variety* (7 Jan. 2008): 7.

Hofler, Robert. "*There Will Be Blood.*" *Daily Variety* (16 Nov. 2007): 20.

Holden, Stephen. "Suspense-Filled Puzzle Draped in a Dark Mood." *New York Times* (28 Feb. 1997): 7.

Jones, Alan. "*There Will Be Blood.*" *Film Review* (March 2008): 102–103.

Kelly, Christopher. "Crude Truth." *Texas Monthly* (Dec. 2007): 68, 70.

Kerr, Philip. "Punch Drunk From Modern Life." *New Statesman* (10 Feb. 2003): 44.

Klawans, Stuart. "A Hard Man." *Nation* (28 Jan. 2008): 32–34.

Kuczynski, Alex. "A Hollywood Gift Says, 'I Love Literature.'" *New York Times* (7 Dec. 1997): 1.

Lane, Anthony. "Long Story." *New Yorker* (14 Jan. 2008): 19.

Leydon, Joe. "*Sydney.*" *Variety Movie Reviews* (24 Jan. 1996): 2.

Levy, Emanuel. "*Boogie Nights.*" *Variety Movie Reviews* (21 Sept. 1997): 1.

———. "Film Reviews." *Variety* (13 Dec. 1999): 105–16.

"*Magnolia* (film)." *Film Review* (July 2004): 127.

McCarthy, Todd. "'*Blood*' Runs Deep." *Variety* (5 Nov. 2007): 32, 41.

———. "*Punch-Drunk Love.*" *Variety* (27 May 2002): 23–24.

McClintock, Pamela, and Dave McNary. "B.O. a River of 'Blood.'" *Daily Variety* (28 Dec. 2007): 1, 11.

McGill, Hannah. "*There Will Be Blood.*" *Sight & Sound* (Feb. 2008): 82–83.

Mermelstein, David. "This Year's Models." *Daily Variety* (12 Dec. 2007): A4, A11.

Morgenstern, Joe. "For This Year's Movies, Small Was Beautiful." *Wall Street Journal* (28 Dec. 2007): W2.

———. "Notable New Movies." *Wall Street Journal* (1 Jan. 2000): A20.

———. "Oil Epic Should Strike Acting-Oscar Gold, Too." *Wall Street Journal* (28 Dec. 2007): W2.

Mottram, James. "Bloody Hell." *Film Review* (March 2008): 61–63.

"Museums, Societies, Etc." *New Yorker* (10 Dec. 2007): 110.

Petrakis, John. "*There Will Be Blood.*" *Christian Century* (29 Jan. 2008): 44.

"Pick of the Week." *New Statesman* (18 Feb. 2008): 45.

Pittman, Frank. "Blood and Guts." *Psychotherapy Networker Magazine* (March–April 2008): 79–81.

"*Punch-Drunk Love* (Film)." *Sight & Sound* (Sept. 2003): 69.

Rainnie, Ian. "*Punch-Drunk Love* (Film)." *Premiere* (July/Aug. 2003): 104.

Romney, Jonathan. "*Punch-Drunk Love.*" *Sight & Sound* (July 2002): 17.

Rozen, Leah. "*There Will Be Blood.*" *People* (14 Jan. 2008): 35.

Schwarzman, Lisa. "A Second Opinion." *Entertainment Weekly* (28 Dec. 2007): 110–112.

Stackpole, John. "Paul Thomas Anderson, the Writer/Director of 'Boogie Nights.'" *Audience* (Dec. 1997–Jan. 1998): 30–31.

Travers, Peter. "The Polarizer." *Rolling Stone* (24 Jan. 2008): 70.

———. "*Punch-Drunk Love* (Film)." *Rolling Stone* (10 July 2003): 79.

Williams, Linda Ruth. "Reviews." *Sight & Sound* (Jan. 1998): 36–37.

Willyard, Cassandra. "*There Will Be Blood.*" *Geotimes* (April 2008): 44.

index

MacDowell, James, 28, 157
"Machine Gun" (song), 83
Mackey, Frank "T. J." (character), 2,
    3, 4, 6, 7, 8, 9, 10, 29, 113, 120, 121,
    123, 127, 136, 139, 140, 141, 142,
    143, 178, 181, 192, 197, 204, 231,
    238
Macy, William H., 8, 97, 107, 113, 122,
    124, 139, 172
Madsen, Virginia, 200, 203
Magnolia (1999), 2, 3, 5, 6, 7, 9, 10, 12,
    16, 17, 18, 19, 20, 21, 24, 25, 27, 29,
    36, 37, 38, 40, 44, 50, 54, 56, 57, 63,
    64, 69, 71, 88, 101, 102, 107, 111,
    112–47, 150, 151, 152, 153, 154, 155,
    156, 158, 160, 161, 162, 163, 164,
    165, 169, 170, 172, 173, 176, 178,
    179, 181, 182, 185, 186, 188, 189,
    192, 197, 198, 204, 206, 208, 214,
    223, 226, 228, 231, 234, 237, 238,
    242
Magnum, P.I. (television program), 39
Malick, Terrence, 112
Mamet, David, 20, 38
"Mama Told Me Not to Come" (song),
    80, 109
Mann, Aimee, 27, 114, 124, 125, 126,
    127, 135, 137, 145, 169, 170, 226
Mann, Michael, 112
Marcie (character, *Magnolia*), 136, 138
Marky Mark and the Funky Bunch,
    95
Martha the salesgirl (character, *The
    Master*), 241–42
M*A*S*H (1970), 203
Master, The (2012), 3, 13, 25, 29, 40, 54,
    105, 178, 179, 196, 198, 206, 207,
    236, 237, 238, 239, 240, 241, 242,
    243, 244, 245
Matrix, The (1999), 112
McCarthy, Todd, 112, 186, 225
McCarthyism, 236
McGill, Hannah, 213

McGillis, Kelly, 6, 140
McLaren, Angus, 222
McQuillan, Deanna Boyd, 215
McQuillan, Matthew, 215
Melville, Jean-Pierre, 48
Melvin and Howard (1980), 52
Memento (2000), 49
Mendes, Sam, 113
Messiaen, Olivier, 227
Miami Herald (newspaper), 175
Midnight Cowboy (1969), 39
Midnight Run (1988), 37
Miller, Rebecca, 220
Minghella, Anthony, 113
Miramax Studios, 15, 16, 40, 72, 75,
    76, 119, 223
Mission Impossible (1996), 120, 156
Mission Impossible II (2000), 121
Mitchell, Elvis, 112
Mitchum, Robert, 161
modernity, 238
Molina, Alfred, 9, 80, 142, 172
Mon Oncle (1958), 160
Moore, Julianne, 7, 80, 108, 113, 120,
    172
Mottram, James, 42, 43, 47, 74, 161,
    169, 171
Mr. Deeds (2002), 172
MTV, 163
Mulholland, William, 218
Mulvey, Laura, 91
Murphet, Julian, 4, 28, 177, 178, 181,
    206, 211, 213, 214
My Left Foot (1989), 216

Nashville (1975), 83, 94, 100, 115, 129,
    203
National Broadcasting Company
    (NBC), 114
Nazis, 48
NC-17 rating, 77, 88, 89
Nena, 80
Network (1976), 33

"99 Luftballons" (song), 80, 82
New Kids on the Block, 95
New Line Studios, 10, 16, 27, 40, 69, 72, 75, 76, 77, 78, 79, 89, 102, 107, 108, 109, 116, 118, 119, 122, 128, 130, 144, 145, 146, 152, 163, 164, 165, 219
Newman, Michael, 11, 32, 33, 34, 41, 42
New Republic (magazine), 75
Newsweek (magazine), 78, 108, 130, 225
New Yorker, The (magazine), 199
New York Film Festival, 107, 108, 233
New York Times (newspaper), 124, 217, 223
New York University Film School, 19, 20, 36, 38
Nicholson, Jack, 174, 218
Night of the Hunter (1955), 161
Night Ranger, 80
Nilsson, Harry, 160
9/11 attacks, 130, 131, 132, 211
Nixon, Richard, 37
No Country for Old Men (2007), 224, 235
noir (genre), 10, 13, 26, 32, 34, 41, 47, 48, 49, 50, 64, 76, 128, 152, 201, 206, 217
Noir, Guy (character), 202
Nolan, Christopher, 11, 49
Norton, Edward, 123, 131
nostalgia, 70, 71, 72, 78, 79, 82, 84, 85, 86, 87, 114, 131, 155

O'Connor, Kevin J., 196
Office Space (1999), 130
Oil!, 195, 205, 207, 208, 209, 210, 211, 213
ondes Martenot, 227
"One [Is the Loneliest Number]," 160
O'Neill, Kel, 194, 220, 223

Only Entertainment (book), 165
On the Lookout (video series in *Boogie Nights*), 16, 83
On the Prowl (video series), 83
Opening of Misty Beethoven, The (1976), 72
Orange County Register (newspaper), 175
"organizational man," 236
Oscars (Academy Awards), 108, 145, 203, 216, 221, 224, 226, 234
Oswalt, Patton, 135
Out of Sight (1998), 39, 49
Out of the Past (1947), 48
Outlaw Queen, The (1957), 53
Oz, Frank, 39

Pacino, Al, 94, 95
Painted Fire (2002), 185
Paltrow, Gwyneth, 7, 32, 243
"Paper Bag" (song), 162
Paramount Studios, 76
Paramount Vantage/Paramount Classics, 190, 222, 223, 229
Parker, Alan, 36
Parker, Nicole Ari, 93, 141
Parker, Todd, 82, 106
Parma, Phil, 113, 136, 137, 140
Partridge, Earl (character), 113, 114, 121, 123, 126, 127, 135, 136, 140, 178, 214, 231
Partridge, Jack (character), 4, 135, 139
Partridge, Linda (character), 113, 117, 127, 136, 139
Partridge Family, The (television program), 114, 139
Pathé camera (1910), 24, 226
Paths of Glory (1958), 207
Patterson, John, 164
Payne, Alexander, 112
Peberdy, Donna, 138, 139
Peirce, Kimberly, 113
Penderecki, Krzysztof, 205

Udovitch, Mim, 124, 164
Underneath, The (1995), 49
USA Today (newspaper), 174, 186
Usual Suspects, The (1995), 49

Vance, Courtney B., 39
Vanishing, The (1993), 39
Vanity Fair (magazine), 211
Variety (magazine), 163, 186, 198, 199,
    217, 220, 225
Verhoven, Paul, 89
VHS videotape, 38, 68, 70, 71, 72, 73,
    83, 84, 85, 89, 108, 156
Videodrome (1983), 90
Virgin Suicides, The (1999), 112
voice-over narration, 134, 135, 151

Wadd, Johnny (character), 103
Wahlberg, Mark, 4, 70, 72, 95, 96,
    106, 120, 178
Walters, Melora, 7, 26, 63, 113, 120,
    127, 172
"war on terror," 130, 132, 211, 214
Waterboy, The (1998), 173
Watson, Emily, 153, 165, 172, 173, 216
Waves, Amber (character), 7, 80, 83,
    91, 92, 93, 96, 97, 104, 106
Waxman, Sharon, 5, 42, 43, 44, 73,
    76, 90, 95, 96, 108, 130, 162, 172,
    198, 199
Wedding Singer, The (1998), 79, 156
Weinstein, Harvey, 15

Welcome to the Dollhouse (1995), 41
Welles, Orson, 72, 119
West Kern Oil Museum, 220
What about Bob? (1991), 39
What Do Kids Know? (television pro-
    gram in *Magnolia*), 113, 114, 133,
    134, 143
What's Your Name? (sound record-
    ing), 174
What the Hell Happened to Me?
    (sound recording), 174
When the Pawn (sound recording),
    162
Wild Bunch, The (1969), 33
Wilder, Billy, 48
Wild Wild West, The (television pro-
    gram), 36
Willis, Bruce, 89, 163
Winfrey, Oprah, 139
"Wise Up" (song), 27, 125, 126, 127
Wong Kar-wai, 108
Wood, Matthew, 234
World War II, 11, 24, 29, 48, 236, 237,
    238, 239, 240, 241, 242, 243, 245
Worm (character, *Magnolia*), 141

Yankee Doodle Dandy (1942), 202
"You've Got the Touch," 73

Zeitchik, Steven, 199
Zuromskis, Catherine, 90, 91, 93

Lightning Source UK Ltd.
Milton Keynes UK
UKOW01f1952290616

277366UK00001B/45/P